THE HORROR

Investigator Gary Bell came into the office, sat down, and attempted to ask Bissell a few questions, to no avail. The big, blood-covered man slouched in his chair and stared at the walls in front of him, ignoring Bell. He refused to respond to Bell in any way and didn't look around the room or make a sound.

Another officer began to take photographs that he knew would be needed in the course of the investigation. He asked his deputy to remove the material from Bissell's pocket while he took pictures. The deputy carefully put on a pair of exam gloves. The first item he pulled from the pocket was a bloody $5 bill, the only money that would be found on Bissell and apparently the only cash he had left. The other item in the pocket, the mass of bloody tissue that the officers had discovered earlier and thought might have been a finger, now appeared to be a human esophagus, approximately six inches long.

BLOOD HIGHWAY

SHEILA JOHNSON

PINNACLE BOOKS
Kensington Publishing Corp.
http://www.kensingtonbooks.com

Some names have been changed to protect the privacy of individuals connected to this story.

PINNACLE BOOKS are published by

Kensington Publishing Corp.
850 Third Avenue
New York, NY 10022

All Kensington Titles, Imprints, and Distributed Lines are available at special quantity discounts for bulk purchases for sales promotions, premiums, fund-raising, and educational or institutional use. Special book excerpts or customized printings can also be created to fit specific needs. For details, write or phone the office of the Kensington special sales manager: Kensington Publishing Corp., 850 Third Avenue, New York, NY 10022, attn: Special Sales Department, Phone: 1-800-221-2647.

Pinnacle and the P logo Reg. U.S. Pat. & TM Off.

First printing: July 2004
10 9 8 7 6 5 4 3 2

Printed in the United States of America

For James, Sue, Don and Rhea,
but most of all, for Patty.

ACKNOWLEDGMENTS

Without the help, cooperation and trust of District Attorney Mike O'Dell, Sheriff Cecil Reed, Lead Investigator Mike James and all the rest of the personnel in the DeKalb County, Alabama, District Attorney's Office and Sheriff's Department, this book would not have been possible. As in countless other situations, they have all given me their encouragement and support and, as always, they have my wholehearted gratitude.

Investigator Johnny Bass of the Lookout Mountain Judicial Circuit in Summerville, Georgia, and Detective Eddie Colbert of the Chattooga County Sheriff's Department generously opened their files and provided a great deal of information on the case against Hayward Bissell in their state, as well as countless highly entertaining anecdotes about their experiences while gathering information in Ohio.

My friends and former colleagues, photographers extraordinaire Scott Turner and Steven Stiefel, generously provided many of the photos that helped document Hayward Bissell's dramatic change in appearance during the time he was incarcerated.

Thanks also to Don and Rhea Pirch and James and Sue Pumphrey. I hope that having your stories told will help provide closure and bring you peace.

Todd Graves spent a great deal of time listening to

Hayward Bissell's own accounts of his crimes, and I thank him for coming forward and providing the investigators with that information and also for telling me many other stories of his conversations with Bissell.

Charlene Booher and Linda Rogers provided much valuable information and insight, along with their favorite photo of Patty, and I hope they and the rest of Patty's family and friends will consider this book a tribute to the memory of the little girl they loved so much.

Special thanks to my mother, Olena Beasley, who has always believed that I'd amount to something sooner or later.

Prologue

When winter storms strike the rural South, a part of the nation that is usually unprepared for severe winter weather, communities pull together and neighbors begin helping neighbors. The ice storm that gripped Northeast Alabama on January 23, 2000, proved to be no exception to that rule. The storm had brought sleet and freezing rain as it moved into the area at the start of the weekend, and as the temperature dropped that Sunday, many families were thankful for the extra emergency preparations they had made earlier in the winter. Quite a few people living in the suburban areas believed it was better to be safe than sorry and had stocked their pantries with nonperishable foods and batteries and laid in extra supplies of water, wood and kerosene just in case the threat of Y2K turned out to be a reality. The new year came and went and computers across the land still functioned, so the extra food and other necessities weren't needed after all. But judging by the predictions of local weather forecasters, those unused Y2K supplies were about to come in very handy, both for the families who had stockpiled them and the friends and neighbors they would share them with.

By midafternoon, a light freezing rain had begun to deposit a second layer of ice on the already-damaged timber in the northernmost towns of DeKalb County, Alabama. Fallen trees lay across streets and driveways, and power lines sagged and collapsed from the weight of an ever-lengthening fringe of icicles. Many people who lived on the county's hundreds of miles of rural mountain roads were preparing to head for the homes of family members or friends in the valleys, where conditions weren't usually quite as severe as at the higher elevations and the electricity might stay on at least a little while longer.

Residents of the little mountain resort town of Mentone, a quaint village situated at the highest point in the county, expected to have some major problems with the coming winter storm. Life in Mentone was relatively quiet and slow paced in the winter season. Any severe weather event became a major issue, with people often left stranded in their homes for days with no electricity.

Mentone first began attracting summer visitors in the mid-1800s, when a fifty-seven-room Victorian-style resort hotel was built on the brow of the mountain overlooking the town of Valley Head. The "summer people" from around the world came to Valley Head by train and rode up to the top of the mountain in horse-drawn carriages. Its scenic beauty and mineral springs made Mentone a popular summer retreat, and wealthy visitors began to build luxurious vacation homes and cottages in the area.

As time passed, the number of year-round residents increased and Mentone became a small, close-knit community. From May through August, the rustic shops and stores are filled with vacationing families and hundreds of campers attending the many summer camps and resorts located on the mountain. But in fall and winter, the visitors return to their homes and the little town once again belongs to the "locals," who look forward to a quiet, peaceful off-season. And to the people of Mentone, an ice storm like the one moving into the area was a serious matter. Accumulation of ice and sleet on streets and power lines could easily leave them stuck for several days on top of their beautiful mountain with no phones, no electricity and no way to travel on the icy roads.

Shelves of convenience stores in the area and clustered along the nearby Georgia state line had been emptied of milk and bread by early Sunday morning, and four-wheelers buzzed along the slippery highways all day in search of stranded drivers in need of help.

By that evening, over twenty-five thousand homes in the county would be without electricity. For a few, that would be the very least of their problems.

Don and Rhea Pirch were slowly driving north on Sunday afternoon, trying to reach their home in Mentone before the ice storm made roads impassable. They had been on a trip to Atlanta, taking in the Norman Rockwell exhibit at the High Museum of Art, then stopping to visit relatives in central Alabama when the storm began. News of the swiftly forming ice in the northern part of the state cut their trip short and sent them heading for home.

The trip to Atlanta had been a much-needed diversion for the couple; Don had broken three ribs in an accident just forty-five minutes into his first day of work in the new year and was still recuperating. A weekend spent riding in the pickup truck had been painful at times, but seeing the exhibit had been well worth the discomfort to Don. He and his wife were great Rockwell fans, and the exhibit was a once-in-a-lifetime treat for both of them.

Rhea drove the truck as they inched their way along

the slippery highways, the ice accumulation increasing as they headed toward home. Unnerved by the downed power lines and damage to trees along the sides of the road, the couple began to wonder if they would be able to make it all the way home before the highway department began closing some of the roads in the Northeast section of the state. They began to talk about what their options might be if fallen timber completely blocked the highway before they reached Mentone. A motel room might be very hard to find, with so many people seeking shelter in town.

James and Sue Pumphrey had a snug, comfortable mobile home located near the end of County Road 641 on the outskirts of Mentone. It was heated with gas, and their gas range enabled them to cook hot food without being completely dependent on electricity. They always had plenty of food stored in their large chest freezer in case of emergencies, and their long-standing habit was to cook for their neighbors who were left without electricity during winter storms. They also cooked for the rescue squad workers and road crews who might be working in their neighborhood when winter weather brought down power lines and left highways slick with ice. On that Sunday, James and Sue prepared hot meals for the neighboring family, who had been left with no means of cooking when their electricity went off. James and Sue had no children of their own, and they doted on the several small children who lived in the house next door. Even if the neighbors decided to head elsewhere for shelter later that afternoon, the Pumphreys would see to it that the children had a hot meal before they left home.

Down the mountain from Mentone, in the neighboring town of Valley Head, Walter Pullen readied his tractor for an afternoon he planned to spend up on the mountain helping his Mentone friends clear their driveways and streets of fallen timber. It was a family custom for the Pullens to pitch in and help the local rescue squads and volunteer fire departments whenever they were needed. Walter knew that although his tractor might be slow, it could easily handle roads that some of the smaller rescue vehicles might not be able to travel.

DeKalb County sheriff Cecil Reed was taking advantage of a rare opportunity to rest for a few hours at his home on the brow of the mountain at Fort Payne, the county seat located a few miles south of Mentone and Valley Head. It had been a miserable weekend so far, and the weather was continuing to worsen. The chance for a good meal and a short nap might not come again for quite a while, because if this storm turned out to be as bad as local weather forecasters were predicting, he'd probably get called back out into the freezing rain before nightfall. At least it was unlikely there would be any major crimes taking place in this sort of weather; with so much ice on the roads, Reed expected that the main problems his deputies would encounter that evening were likely to be stranded motorists and house fires.

Valley Head chief of police Ken Busby wasn't officially on duty, but he was out making the rounds in his patrol car nonetheless, watching for drivers in trouble and keeping a close eye on the weather. As he scouted the area for motorists in need of help, he talked on the car radio with his assistant chief and Mentone police chief Johnny Ferguson as they also patrolled, comparing notes on road conditions and storm damage in their adjoining jurisdictions.

Whether traveling, working or sitting safely at home, everyone had the weather uppermost in their minds. Even though ice storms were a fairly common winter event in the Northeast Alabama mountains and valleys, they were nothing to take lightly. And this storm, adding to the accumulation of ice already on the ground from the previous days, promised to be a bad one. As the people readied themselves for the emergency conditions they knew might lie ahead, a deadly threat of an entirely different nature was approaching the county on the highway leading from the Georgia state line.

No amount of advance preparation could protect Mentone's residents from the living, breathing evil bearing down on them from the East, faster and far more dangerous than the cold black ice.

It wasn't even 4:00 P.M. yet, but it was shaping up to be a long, miserable evening for Chief Busby. Winter storms always made for long, cold hours of extra work for law enforcement, and the town of Valley Head was definitely going to be hard hit. Careless motorists would have to be pulled out of ditches, blocked roads would need to be barricaded, and both state and county road department crews had to have constantly updated information on highway conditions.

Atop the mountain overlooking Valley Head, Mentone was already losing power as falling trees and accumulating ice brought down electric lines, and now the chief's patrol car radio was blaring a "be on the lookout" (BOLO). According to the county 911 dispatcher, an older-model Lincoln Town Car had just been involved in a hit-and-run incident in Mentone and was believed to be on its way down Highway 117 toward Valley Head.

Busby turned his car toward the mountain and headed up Highway 117, but before he reached the top of the steep, winding road to Mentone, he met the Lincoln speeding downhill. He spun the patrol car around and followed the vehicle, shouting into his radio for backup. Busby wasn't in uniform, and he wished he had his gun. He had left it behind, thinking he wouldn't need it; the worst problems he had expected to encounter that evening were falling trees and slippery streets.

Mentone police chief Johnny Ferguson and Valley Head assistant chief Wayne Wooten made it to the intersection of U.S. Highway 11 and Alabama 117 just in time to throw a roadblock into place as the Lincoln came barreling down the mountain and through the town of Valley Head into Hammondville. When the car reached Hammondville Crossroads, the intersection of Highway 117 and U.S. 11, Ferguson cut in front of the car and Busby swerved into place behind it. Wooten blocked the intersection, jumping out of his car and approaching the Lincoln with his gun drawn. The driver responded by racing his engine ominously, answering the officer's action with a threat of his own, but Wooten stood firm and refused to move. He aimed his gun above the headlights at the unseen driver, shaking his head and shouting, "Don't do it"; meanwhile, Ferguson approached the driver's side of the car with his weapon drawn.

The sight of two officers with firearms pointed in his direction must have convinced the driver he wasn't going to get away. He offered no resistance when Ferguson jerked open the car door and dragged him out by his shirt, but he left the car in gear. It began to move forward, running over the driver's ankle, but the man never made a sound and gave no indication he felt a thing.

As Ferguson and Busby wrestled the huge man onto the ground, they realized his shirt was wet. They almost recoiled with shock when they realized it was soaked with blood. The officers attempted to handcuff their prisoner, but their regulation cuffs wouldn't fit his enormous wrists. Instead, they grabbed a pair of leg irons out of one of the patrol cars and used them for handcuffs.

While the two men dealt with the Lincoln's driver, Wooten jumped into the rolling Lincoln to bring it to a stop and park it. To his shock, he nearly landed on top of a large bloody knife lying on the seat. Then he smelled the overwhelming coppery stench of fresh blood, glanced over at the passenger's seat and realized, to his horror, that he wasn't alone in the car.

Hayward Bissell had driven into DeKalb County, Alabama, bringing the corpse of his murdered, horribly mutilated girlfriend along for the ride.

his fingers. Don said a silent prayer of thanks that the car had such a big, flat hood; at least he was able to hang on to it with the car traveling, fully accelerated, down the highway. Don felt his boots strike against the bumper, and he got a foothold and used the extra leverage to push himself up farther onto the hood.

Then he raised his head, looked up and found himself face-to-face with a nightmare looking back at him from the other side of the Lincoln's windshield.

Don was staring directly at the car's driver, but all he could see was the man's eyes. Everything else around the two men suddenly seemed to go black, as though they were the only two people inside a long, dark tunnel. Don couldn't see anything else inside the car; he couldn't see the pavement rushing beneath the Lincoln's wheels or the blur of ice-coated underbrush on the sides of the road as they sped by. All he could see were those cold, deadly eyes filled with contempt and hatred.

"At first, I thought it was road rage," Don said. "Then I looked into his eyes and I saw he was a madman."

Rhea watched, paralyzed with fear, as her husband was carried away down the road clinging onto the hood of the speeding Lincoln. She could hear Don yelling for the driver to stop as the car continued to accelerate, but the horrifying ride was far from over.

Don knew the car was going much too fast for him to risk trying to jump off, and he kept hoping that maybe the driver would stop or at least slow down. All he could do was attempt to keep holding on as the car sped down the highway.

"I kept yelling for him to stop, asking him why was he doing it, why, why . . . but he just kept going; he kept it floored," Don said. "The look in his eyes brings chills to me now. I'll never forget that; those eyes looking right at me."

Then the driver glared furiously at Don. He held his middle finger up to the windshield in an obscene gesture, and Don knew that, one way or another, his ride was about to be over. The look of hatred on the man's face told his unwilling passenger something was about to happen, and Don tried to prepare himself for whatever was coming. He prayed the driver wouldn't slam on the brakes and throw him forward off the hood, then drive over him.

Without warning, the Lincoln suddenly swerved hard toward the left. Don went flying off the hood and was thrown head over heels, landing hard in the icy ditch beside the road. As he hit the frozen ground and rolled into the ice and mud in the bottom of the ditch, Don felt a sharp, tearing pain in his knees and feared that his legs had been broken.

The Lincoln didn't stop, or even slow down. It kept on speeding down the road until it disappeared out of sight over a hill. Rhea sprinted down the highway to her husband's side, terrified that he was seriously injured. Don was afraid the driver might turn around and come back to attempt to run down his wife. As he lay helplessly in the ditch, he knew he had to send her away to safety. If the madman returned and she was still standing there beside the road, Rhea would be an easy target.

"Go back and get help," he gasped as Rhea reached his side. "Go back down to the main road and flag somebody down. Hurry!"

Rhea turned and ran back toward Highway 117 as fast as she could, frantic with fear. She knew she was running for her husband's life.

Chapter 2

"It was like he didn't have a soul."

James Pumphrey had been busy cooking all day on Sunday, helping his neighbors who might find themselves without electricity for several days during the ice storm. Earlier in the day, James and Sue loaded their truck with several large plastic tanks and bottles, which they had filled with spring water, hauling enough water from a nearby stream for everyone in the neighborhood whose electric water pumps were inoperative. Then at midafternoon, the middle-aged couple sat down to an early supper. It had been a quiet, peaceful day, the silence broken only by the loud, cracking sounds of breaking trees as the accumulating ice weighed their branches down. It had also been a very busy day, and the Pumphreys were tired. They were glad to have a chance finally to sit down and rest for a while.

After supper, as James stood at the sink washing dishes and looking out the kitchen window at the ice glistening on fallen pine limbs in his front yard, he realized a car was sitting across the road inside the gate to his neighbor's pasture. The trunk lid was raised and had been left up, and a big man was walking up the road toward the house. James and Sue's chocolate

Labrador retrievers, Reese and Cocoa, barked a warning at the man who was now starting up the driveway. The dogs had never in their lives shown any aggression toward a stranger, but James watched in surprise as they began growling and ran down the drive to meet this man with their teeth bared. The hair on their backs stood up and they sniffed the air as they challenged him, barking furiously.

James assumed the man's car must have hit a patch of ice and slid off the road; he didn't notice that the locked pasture gate was standing open because it had been rammed. As he stepped out onto the porch to see if the stranger needed any help, he saw his two dogs charge toward the man. He watched, shocked, as the female dog jumped up and snapped at the intruder's hand. The man struck back at the dog, and she turned and ran up the steps and onto the porch.

Things began to happen so quickly, James thought perhaps the dogs had bitten the big man. Then he saw that Cocoa was bleeding, and noticed for the first time that the man now approaching the porch steps was covered in blood. James knew instinctively that something was terribly wrong, and he asked the man, "Did my dogs bite you?"

James turned around and looked on the porch behind him, trying to see what had happened to Cocoa. When he turned back around, the stranger was in front of him, standing on the bottom step. With no warning, without saying a word, the big man reached up and struck deep into James's abdomen with the large, sharp knife he was carrying.

Confused and unsuspecting, James never saw the knife hidden in the intruder's huge hand. Even if he had seen the man was carrying a weapon and was preparing to use it, the attack was so sudden that there was no way to defend against it. James didn't even realize he had been stabbed in the stomach until he noticed the blood gushing from the deep wound, and he had no idea how seriously he had been injured. James managed to stagger back inside the door as the attacker followed him up onto the porch, his knife slashing furiously at the dogs who tried to protect their master from the deadly intruder.

"Whatever you do, don't open that door, I've been stabbed!" James yelled to his wife. But before they could close and lock the door, the stranger reached inside and grabbed Sue by the collar, trying to pull her outside onto the porch to continue his murderous attack. As he held on to her with one hand, he kept stabbing at the dogs with his long knife as they snapped and bit at him.

Sue screamed at the man, crying and begging him, "Please don't do that to my dogs," but he kept pulling her from the doorway, staring at her with eyes that showed no sign of human feeling. Sue knew she should expect no mercy if her attacker succeeded in dragging her out onto the porch.

"I'll never forget his face," she said, "and I'll never forget his eyes. That's what caught my attention, with everything going on so quickly. His eyes were just unreal. It was like he didn't have a soul."

Sue was almost in shock and unable to fight her way free of the madman's grip, but the dog she dearly loved, who was almost like a child to her, was ready and willing to sacrifice himself to save her. The male Lab, Reese, continued to attack the intruder after his mother, Cocoa, lay on the ice in the front yard, dying from her wounds. When Reese saw his mistress in danger, he quickly worked his way between her and the stranger. The dog fought with all his might, and when the man let go of Sue to fight back, the heroic Lab gave his life to buy Sue enough time to get inside the house and lock the door.

"If it weren't for our dogs, we wouldn't be here," Sue said. "They were just like our babies. We never had any kids, and we loved them dearly. They saved our lives. They were our angels. A lot of people might not understand that, but they did what they did to give us enough time to get back in the house. They saved us. They knew what they were doing."

While the crazed attacker turned his attention to Reese, stabbing the brave dog to death and cutting his throat, all but decapitating him, James and Sue managed to get to the bedroom, where a rifle and shotgun hung on the wall over their bed. In their struggle to get the .22 rifle down from the gun rack, one of the rounds fired accidentally, striking their freezer, which sat in the next room.

Through the kitchen window, the couple saw the man had finished mutilating the bodies of the two dogs and was heading around the trailer to the back of the house, looking for a way to get inside and finish them off. Sue tried to help James stand and hold up the rifle, and they both held the stab wound in his abdomen, where his internal organs were threatening to spill loose. Their only chance to save themselves was to get to the back door before the man could break in, and try to confront him with the rifle. They struggled to the door and onto the back porch, and as the attacker came around the corner of the trailer, James and Sue raised the rifle and pointed it in his direction.

"It took him and me both to hold that gun up," Sue said. "He went down on his knees and I had to help him."

James told the intruder, "You take another step and I'll kill you." The man ignored the warning and kept coming. James tried to fire the rifle, but for the first time since he'd owned the gun, it jammed. The Pumphreys thought they were doomed, but luckily, the intruder didn't realize the rifle had misfired. He saw the weapon, clearly realizing the threat that a firearm presented to him, and spoke to his victims for the first time, saying, "Don't shoot me, I'm leaving!"

The big man turned around and ran back down the driveway and across the road toward the car he'd left parked by the pond in the pasture. Moments later, the Pumphreys heard the car's engine roar to life and saw the Lincoln speeding back down the road toward Mentone.

"If I had got the shotgun down out of the gun rack, I would have killed him," James said. "But I got the .22 instead. It had never jammed before; not one time since I'd had it had that gun jammed, and I've shot it hundreds of times. The way I look at it, the Lord God did it because He didn't want that man's blood on my hands."

James was quickly beginning to go into shock from his critical wound, and later said that he couldn't remember crossing the yard and getting into his truck with Sue's help. He didn't realize that he blacked out momentarily as he sat in his driveway trying to start the truck's engine, and barely knew he was driving the truck slowly down the road toward Highway 117 to look for help.

Sue tried frantically to keep James awake as he drifted in and out of consciousness on his way down the icy highway, and she was terrified that the truck would slide off the road at any time. When she saw a group of people and several vehicles pulled over along the side of the road, a wave of relief washed over her. With her help, James managed to get the truck stopped just seconds before he slumped over the steering wheel.

"Somebody help me; James has been stabbed; please, I need help!" she screamed, jumping out of the truck and stumbling toward the crowd.

Sue had no way of knowing the crazed, knife-wielding stranger had gotten there first, and the people were gathered there on the roadside to give emergency care to someone who had already looked into those same cold, merciless eyes.

Chapter 3

"There's a body in the car!"

Walter Pullen kept an eye out for stranded drivers as he steered his tractor up Highway 117's steep curves from Valley Head. He drove through Mentone toward the Georgia state line to help other volunteers and utility workers who were busily clearing the roads on top of the mountain. Along the highway that Sunday afternoon were the usual number of cars that had slid into ditches and trees that were lying across driveways—the typical problems that went along with episodes of freezing rain in the wooded mountain areas of North DeKalb County. Walter knew he'd see the usual amount of winter-weather emergencies, but the last thing he expected to see that day was Rhea Pirch running frantically down the highway toward him, waving her arms and screaming for help.

Rhea couldn't believe her luck when she realized the man on the tractor was going to come to her rescue. Her lungs were burning as she gasped for air and tried to tell him what had happened to Don.

Walter Pullen was astounded to hear that Rhea's husband had been intentionally run down on the road, and as she ran back to stay with Don, Walter hurried to one of the nearby homes where he knew the residents had a rescue squad radio that could summon help even though the phone lines were down. Within a matter of minutes, volunteers from the Lookout Mountain Rescue Squad began receiving reports of a hit-and-run victim in need of immediate medical attention on County Road 641. With help on the way, Walter started back to do whatever he could for Don and Rhea.

James McCray had driven into Mentone to pick up a generator and was returning home when Rhea flagged him down. Don still lay shivering in the ditch, where his attacker had thrown him, and he was getting dangerously chilled and was on the verge of going into shock. James began to work with Don, trying to do whatever he could to help Rhea keep him warm until a DeKalb Ambulance Service vehicle could make it up to the top of the icy mountain.

A young couple from Fort Payne had driven up to Mentone to check on a friend who lived at the end of County Road 641, but when they arrived, they found no one home. As they turned around to leave, they noticed what appeared to be a silver-colored car with its trunk lid raised, backed in beside the pond in a pasture across from their friend's driveway. The pasture gate was open and a large, dark-haired man was walking toward the road.

As the couple drove their Jeep back toward the main highway, they saw Rhea and James McCray at the side of the road, kneeling over Don as he lay in the ditch. They stopped to see what had happened, and gave McCray a blanket they had in the Jeep. Rhea told them about the bizarre hit-and-run attack, and said that Don had been run down by a big, light-colored car.

"Can you go somewhere and call 911?" McCray asked as he covered Don with the blanket.

While the couple went for help, they realized the car they had just seen parked at the pond near their friend's home fit the description Rhea had given them and that it might have been the hit-and-run vehicle. After they found a phone and made the call to 911, they went back to tell James McCray and Rhea what they had seen. The young man stopped and got out, joining the group of people who had started to gather on the side of the road to help Don, and his girlfriend waited for him in the Jeep. Walter Pullen's call to the rescue squad was beginning to bring several responders, and Walter had returned to the scene and parked his tractor on the roadside to wait with Don and Rhea for an ambulance to arrive.

Rhea was growing more anxious by the moment. She wondered how much longer it was going to take to get her husband to the hospital, and she looked up hopefully when she heard the growl of a motor in the distance. Her heart began to pound wildly as she suddenly realized something wasn't right; the sound was coming from the wrong direction, and she began to scream a warning to those around her.

The Lincoln came roaring back out of the mist like a runaway train, headed straight for the group of people standing at the side of the road.

This can't be happening! Rhea thought.

The car sped up as it approached, and the driver rammed his car full-force into Walter Pullen's tractor. The horrified bystanders scattered into the ditch. They could see the driver duck down behind the dashboard and Rhea panicked, thinking the man was going for a gun. Instead, he popped back up behind the steering wheel, backed the Lincoln up several yards, and aimed the car toward the terrified group of people who surrounded Don, trying to shield him as he lay helpless in the ditch.

The driver seemed to be determined to try one more time to crush Don under his wheels, but at the last minute he swerved back onto the roadway without striking any of the bystanders. Then the Lincoln raced off out of sight down Highway 117, headed toward Mentone.

Rescue workers who had already reported the first hit-and-run incident began shouting new warnings into their radios. Police cars from Mentone and Valley Head who were on their way to the scene of the first accident began, instead, to head toward the car's most likely route of travel, through Mentone and down the icy mountain road into Valley Head and Hammondville.

Mentone assistant police chief Jeff Bain had been notified of the initial hit-and-run incident by 911 and was en route to the location on County Road 641 when he met the Lincoln headed toward town. He reported its direction of travel to the dispatcher and decided to continue on to the stretch of roadside where the group of people waited for DeKalb Ambulance Service to arrive and take Don to the hospital. While bystanders gave Bain the Town Car's tag number and told him about the driver's intentional attempt to run them down, a small tan Ford Ranger pulled up.

When Sue Pumphrey saw the crowd of people and rescue vehicles gathered beside the road, she helped James to stop their truck, then jumped out, screaming that James had been stabbed and she needed help. In the midst of all the panic and confusion around her as people stabilized Don and rushed to the aid of the Pumphreys, Rhea Pirch was sure of one thing.

She knew James Pumphrey surely must have been attacked by the same madman who, less than half an hour earlier, had carried her husband, Don, for a wild, terrifying ride on the hood of his car.

* * *

Scores of patrol cars were headed toward Mentone from other towns in all directions around the county, but the three officers closest to the action that Sunday afternoon were Police Chief Johnny Ferguson (Mentone), Police Chief Ken Busby (Valley Head) and his assistant chief, Wayne Wooten. The three men had been working long hours over the weekend, dealing with problems caused by the ice storm, and so far, the worst storm-related incident had occurred when one of Valley Head's parked patrol cars was totaled by a tree when it fell on the car, crushing it beyond repair. Police cruisers were a major expense for small towns, and Valley Head's city budget would be hit hard by having to replace the car, even with insurance.

Now they had a hit-and-run driver barreling down the highway toward the mountain, and at the same time calls were coming in about a stabbing incident that had evidently just occurred somewhere up on the same road, County Road 641. Officer Bain was on the radio reporting the two incidents and advising them to use caution; a man had been assaulted with a knife, he said, and his dogs had been killed.

Chief Busby wasn't officially on duty, but he'd been out all day anyway, keeping an eye on the worsening weather conditions. Instead of wearing his uniform, he had dressed in the warmest clothes he could find. He hadn't brought his gun because he expected to spend most of his time with a chain saw, cutting fallen trees out of the way on back roads so emergency vehicles could get through if needed.

Busby had stopped for gas at a convenience store in Valley Head when he heard the BOLO repeated on a light blue older-model Lincoln Town Car that had been involved in a hit and run on a county road on the other side of town, out in the direction of the Georgia line. The car evidently had just returned to the scene, rammed into a tractor, and tried to run down a group of people.

Busby quickly finished fueling his car and hurried toward Mentone to assist. The going was maddeningly slow on the ice-slicked road, but Busby drove as fast as he dared through Valley Head and out to the intersection leading to the road up the mountain to Mentone. He started up, but before he made it to the top of the mountain, he saw a pair of headlights coming downhill toward him at a dangerously high rate of speed.

When the chief slowed to get a look at the oncoming car, he realized it was the Lincoln. As it sped past him, he turned around to follow it, calling its Ohio tag number in to the sheriff's department dispatcher and asking for backup from Chief Ferguson.

Ferguson was at his home taking a break when Busby's call came, and he had also heard Officer Jeff Bain say on the radio that there had been a stabbing at another location. Ferguson rushed to grab his gear and head toward the intersection of Highway 17 and U.S. 11, just past Valley Head in Hammondville. That was the most likely route the suspect would take; the Interstate was only about a mile from the intersection, and the Lincoln needed to be stopped before its driver had a chance to reach I-59.

Wooten was also at home, listening to his handheld radio as he sat down to eat supper. When he heard Busby had an emergency situation and needed assistance, he left his food untouched on the table and rushed to his patrol car, letting the other officers know he was on his way to back them up.

As they headed toward a confrontation with the suspect's vehicle, the three men talked back and forth by radio to determine the best way to proceed. They decided that they would attempt to take down the hit-and-run driver by conducting a felony stop at the intersection at the foot of the mountain.

Wooten reached the crossroads first, stopping his patrol car and turning on his flashers. He could see headlights of the three vehicles coming down the mountain with Ferguson in the lead, the Town Car following him, and Busby behind the Town Car. Ferguson turned on his blue lights as he neared the intersection where Wooten waited.

As the big car approached the crossroads, Ferguson blocked the road ahead of the Lincoln and Wooten blocked the intersection while Busby pulled up close behind the car. They had the suspect effectively stopped and boxed in, but that was only half the battle. They had no way of knowing if the driver was armed with anything more than the knife he was believed to have used already to commit the assault; a hail of bullets could fly from the stopped car at any moment, and the policemen had no cover.

As the officers approached the Lincoln, its driver made an effort to get away by making a move to go around Ferguson's vehicle, and Wooten stepped in front of the car in a brave attempt to stop it. He and Ferguson approached the car with their guns drawn, and Wooten stood directly in front of the car in the glare of the headlights with his weapon pointed above the lights at the unseen driver, shaking his head back and forth.

"Don't do it. Don't do it," Wooten shouted as the driver hesitated for a few seconds, then raced the motor threateningly, inching the big car toward Wooten. The officer stood his ground and kept his gun trained on the driver until the Lincoln finally stopped moving forward. Ferguson shouted to the suspect to raise his hands into the air and ordered him out of the vehicle. When there was no response, Ferguson jerked open the car door and grabbed the driver, attempting to pull the man out by his shirt.

The job proved to be a great deal harder than he expected. The man was enormous, and his shirt was completely soaked with blood. Wooten noticed the windshield was broken and bloodied on the passenger's side. The driver had left the Lincoln in gear when the officers dragged him out, and as they attempted to get a secure hold on him, the car began to roll forward.

The rear wheel rolled over the big man's ankle, but he showed no reaction; the man didn't make a sound or indicate in any way that he even felt the tire run over his foot. Busby and Ferguson pulled the suspect back away from the car, wrestled him facedown onto the pavement, and hoped they'd be able to keep him there if he decided to get back up again. He was offering no resistance at the moment, but they knew that could change at any time.

As the Lincoln began to speed up its forward roll, Wooten chased after the car and jumped inside. He shoved the gearshift into park, shut off the engine, and was shocked to discover that he had nearly landed on top of a large, bloody knife lying on the seat beside him. As he hurriedly slid away from the knife, he noticed for the first time that someone else was in the car, sitting in the passenger's seat. He started to say, "Step out of the car," but the words stuck in his throat.

The stench of blood was suddenly overpowering, and Wooten saw that the passenger's left arm, which lay close to him on the front seat, was missing its hand. The hand had been severed neatly at the wrist and was lying on the floorboard, along with what appeared to be several internal organs.

Wooten steadied himself and took a closer look at the small figure in the seat next to him. It was a young girl, or perhaps a very small woman, and her seat belt had been carefully fastened and her clothing rearranged over the gaping hole in her chest, where her heart and liver had been cut out. Her throat was cut from ear to ear, and her eyes looked as if they had been gouged out. Her right leg had been cut off at the knee and tossed onto the backseat floorboard.

Wooten stared at the awful carnage for a moment, unable to believe what he saw. The small form, so terribly mutilated, momentarily shocked him into silence; then he scrambled out of the car and began to shout to Ferguson and Busby. "There's a body in the car!" he yelled, fighting against the panic rising inside him.

Busby and Ferguson rushed over to stand with Wooten outside the car. They looked inside at the evidence of a terrible, violent death, barely able to comprehend the horror of what had been done to the tiny, doll-like woman.

"When I saw her, I felt cold chills all over my body," Busby later told a reporter for the Fort Payne *Times-Journal*. "You can be in law enforcement for years and then you run across something very unusual, especially for such a small town."

"I thought it was a mannequin at first, because the cuts were so precise and it was such an unreal thing to see," Ferguson said.

The woman sat there, belted into the passenger's seat, still and silent, unable to tell her story and beyond calling for help. No one would ever be able to help Patricia Ann Booher again, not her family or friends, and especially not Hayward Bissell, her boyfriend and the father of her unborn child.

Hayward Bissell couldn't help her because he was lying facedown on the nearby pavement, covered with her blood, his oversize hands cuffed with a pair of leg irons.

Chapter 4

"My foot is broke."

Law enforcement officers go to work every day without knowing what they may encounter during their shifts, or what situations they may find themselves in before they once again go off duty. Ider patrolman Randall Smith had no idea what was in store for him when he left home to go to work that Sunday afternoon. He expected a great deal of problems with the weather, since Ider was situated high on Sand Mountain in the northern section of the county, and he planned to keep a close eye out for falling temperatures and worsening conditions. He expected it would be a long, cold evening with very little traffic and nothing much to do except watch the thickening layer of ice as it coated the roads and trees.

Smith was sitting in his police car at his favorite vantage point in town, the crossroads that marked the center of Ider's tiny business district, when he heard Mentone police receive their first call about the hit-and-run incident. A few minutes later, Smith heard Chief Busby say he had spotted a vehicle matching the description of the suspect's car traveling down the mountain from Mentone. Busby said he planned to try and keep the vehicle in sight and not attempt to stop it until he had some backup.

This situation sounded far more urgent—and much more interesting—than sitting and watching icicles lengthen on the power lines. Smith started toward Valley Head to assist, and he and other officers from Ider and the nearby town of Henagar were some of the first to arrive as backup. They found the Town Car already stopped and Hayward Bissell lying unmoving on the pavement. He remained still, silent and bloody, with his hands cuffed behind his back with leg shackles.

"Is everything all right?" Smith asked Wooten.

"There's a dead girl in the car," a still-shaken Wooten replied.

Smith walked over and looked into the vehicle and saw the small body sitting in the front passenger's side, slumped over toward the driver's seat. Her seat belt was still fastened, and Smith saw her right leg had been severed at the knee and was lying on the back passenger's-side floorboard. Her left hand, he noticed, was severed at the wrist and was lying on the front passenger's-side floorboard. Smith stood there staring, shocked at the violence that had been done to the girl. He had never seen such a brutal murder.

Ider officer Thomas Hubbard and Smith began roping off the area with crime scene tape, and Hubbard drew his revolver and covered Bissell while paramedics arrived and checked the body for a pulse. Smith could see that the victim's throat had been cut and it appeared that her eyes were missing from her head. A bloody lock-blade knife lay open on the front seat where Wayne Wooten had been sitting when he jumped in the car to stop the Lincoln's forward roll.

Smith walked over to Bissell, still lying on the ground, and Hubbard covered him with his revolver until DeKalb deputy Jim Mayes pulled his county squad car up to the crossroads. Mayes told Hubbard, Smith and Henagar officers Sergeant Kent Gilley and Patrolman Randy Garrison to get the suspect up and load him into the back of the Ider patrol car.

Bissell had remained completely silent from the moment he was pulled from the Lincoln at gunpoint. But as the officers attempted to get him up off the pavement and onto his feet, he spoke to them for the first time.

"I can't," he said. "My foot is broke."

Hubbard told him once again to get up, and told him the officers would help him to his feet. Bissell decided to cooperate, and he turned over and the men managed to get him up and walked him over to the waiting patrol car.

"Has anyone searched him yet?" Randall Smith asked Busby.

When Busby said Bissell had not been searched, Smith started patting him down, checking for weapons. Then Bissell spoke for the second time.

"There's a rock in my pocket," he said slyly, as if inviting someone to look into his pocket and verify his comment. Smith searched his pants pockets and didn't find anything.

Lieutenant Jimmy Harris of the sheriff's department had set out for Hammondville as soon as he heard the radio traffic. Harris, who usually served as the officer in charge of night shifts, told Smith and Deputy Lamar Hackworth to put Bissell into the patrol car and take him to the sheriff's office.

"His arms were totally covered with blood, as well as his shirt and pants," Hackworth said. "He kept his hand on his shirt pocket, like he was trying to hide something."

One of the officers pulled the pocket open and looked inside, unsure of what he was seeing.

"I think it's a finger or something," he told the other men.

"Leave it in there and carry him on to the sheriff's office," Harris said.

Later, as Bissell was being transported to the sheriff's department, he sat like a statue in the back of the patrol car, remaining silent and staring blankly ahead. Other than stating, "My foot is broke," he had not spoken except for his other comment to Patrolman Smith about having a rock in his pocket. No one paid any attention to his seemingly nonsensical remark at the time, but after the object was discovered in his shirt pocket, the officers wondered what they would find when they reached the sheriff's office and searched their prisoner more thoroughly. The contents of Bissell's shirt pocket would soon become an issue of major interest.

The intersection quickly became crowded with more patrol cars and emergency vehicles as law enforcement units from several agencies around the county kept arriving and the painstaking work of processing the crime scene began.

Jimmy Phillips, one of the county sheriff's longtime detectives and one of the old hands in area law enforcement, was accustomed to being called out to crime scenes at all hours of the day and night, and in every kind of weather. On this particular Sunday evening, he happened to be closest to the location and got there a few minutes ahead of his fellow county investigators. He had received a call from 911 advising him to be en route to the scene of a murder at Hammondville Crossroads, and he arrived to find the area already secured and the Lincoln cordoned off with crime scene tape.

Phillips began processing the Lincoln, taking careful note of all the possible evidence both inside and on the exterior of the car. He took countless photographs of the small body sitting in the front seat, noting the terrible details of the victim's injuries. Patricia Booher's blue cloth jacket, he noticed, was buttoned up and her seat belt was fastened. She wore a black shirt, black-and-white pants and sneakers. A hand and what appeared to be a heart were lying on the passenger's-side floorboard, and a bloody knife lay on the driver's seat. Phillips saw that the victim's throat had been cut and she appeared to have suffered massive chest wounds, but her clothing had been carefully rearranged over the worst of the injuries. A pair of small, metal-framed glasses lay on the front seat, crumpled and blood spattered.

Investigator Clay Simpson had also been dispatched by 911 to the murder scene, and he, too, walked around the Lincoln, taking an additional series of pictures of the victim and the car from every angle. Then he began the careful process of collecting and recording items of physical evidence.

The items recovered from inside the Town Car included a Kissing Crane lock-blade knife, a Smith & Wesson lock-blade SWAT knife and the box it came in, a man's brown leather jacket, a black leather purse and a pair of women's glasses. Inside the purse was a checkout slip from the Norwalk, Ohio, Public Library. Patricia Booher had gone to the library on Thursday, January 20, and checked out several books dealing with relationships, depression and babies. The titles included *Is Your Child Depressed?*, *When Feeling Bad Is Good*, *After the Baby Is Born*, and *Good Women Get Angry*. The books were due to be returned in early February; ironically, at the top of the checkout slip was printed, HAPPY NEW YEAR!

Other items in the purse included grocery lists, a budget tallying monthly expenses and bills, coupons, grocery cash-club cards, and reminder cards for doctor appointments. The purse also contained a $20 bill, tucked away out of sight, probably the only money Patricia had that Hayward Bissell had not taken from her.

A receipt for a 1300 Winchester twelve-gauge shotgun was also found in the car; Bissell sold the shotgun on January 19 to a store called The Outdoorsman in Norwalk, which paid him $150 for the gun.

Each item of potential evidence found in the Lincoln was carefully bagged and labeled for location, time and date of recovery. When Simpson finished bagging and tagging the loose items inside the car, he drove on to the Pumphrey home on County Road 641, where he had also been dispatched to photograph and process the scene of an assault that had taken place there earlier in the afternoon.

At that time, authorities had no idea that the assault, the hit-and-run incident and the murder of the tiny woman sitting in the Town Car had all been committed by the same person, but they were beginning to suspect the crimes were likely to be connected. They knew the Lincoln was the same car that had been used in the hit-and-run assault, and the other pieces of the puzzle were quickly beginning to fall into place.

Simpson arrived at the Pumphrey home to find the scene secured by officers who had arrived earlier. The bodies of the two chocolate Labs lay where they had died in the yard, overturned furniture and large amounts of blood were on the front porch, and a blood trail led from the porch around to the end of the trailer and on toward the back porch. Once again, Simpson carefully photographed the scene and bagged the physical evidence, then left for the sheriff's office to lock the materials from both crimes in the evidence room.

Two mountain ranges run parallel to each other on opposite sides of Interstate 59 for the length of DeKalb County. Mentone is one of several small communities that lie on the brow of Lookout Mountain, to the east of the interstate. On the west side is Sand Mountain, one of the most thickly populated rural areas in the nation. Many of DeKalb County's nine municipalities are situated on Sand Mountain's broad plateau of farmland, and most of those small towns were faring somewhat better than their neighbors to the east during the winter storm of January 23, 2000.

The accumulation of ice around the town of Crossville was not nearly as heavy as in Mentone; Crossville lay around thirty miles to the southwest of Mentone, at the southern end of the county and at a much lower elevation. The roads were less icy there, but Brad Hood was keeping a close watch on the weather around his Crossville home and throughout the rest of the county. As a cameraman for WHNT-TV, Channel 19, in Huntsville, Alabama, Brad was responsible for film coverage for the station's busy Sand Mountain Bureau. His territory included DeKalb County, and the ice storm was of major interest to the station. Storm coverage had led all the news broadcasts for the past couple of days, and area farmers and commuters were watching Channel 19, depending on the station as always for the latest updates on conditions in their communities. Brad had been filming storm damage for the past couple of days as the layer of ice grew thicker, the number of fallen trees and power lines continued to increase and more homes lost their electric service.

It was beginning to get dark, and Brad would have loved nothing better than spending a quiet, cozy evening at home with his family. When his police scanner began to crackle with the static of radio traffic from the north end of the county, he heard the report of a hit-and-run incident at Mentone and knew his quiet family time was over for that particular evening. Brad grabbed a warm jacket, loaded his equipment into the station's bright red Jeep Cherokee emblazoned in yellow with Channel 19's logo, and started the drive down Sand Mountain to the interstate.

The scanner traffic was confusing, Brad thought, continuing to follow the radio activity as he drove down a steep mountain gap and reached the town of Collinsville, where he turned onto the entrance ramp of I-59 at the 205-mile marker, going north toward Fort Payne and Mentone. Much of what he was hearing was unintelligible, as though the officers were excited. Transmissions overlapped, and dispatchers seemed hesitant to broadcast many details of the situation over the radio. It sounded as if the suspect had returned to the scene of the hit-and-run incident, then had been stopped shortly afterward at the intersection at the foot of the mountain. There was also mention of a stabbing incident that had apparently taken place somewhere in the same area.

This must be something more than just an ordinary hit and run, Brad thought. *They sure don't want to put out much information about it over the air.*

As Brad listened to the scanner and carefully watched the pavement on the interstate for patches of black ice that formed on bridges and overpasses, he heard familiar voices joining in on the radio traffic. It sounded as though almost all the county investigators, the sheriff and many of his deputies were coming out for this one. In addition, they were being joined by several local departments, rescue squads, fire departments, Fort Payne city police units and state troopers, who were already patrolling the city streets, county roads and highways in the area. Something major must be going on for so many units to be responding.

Then Brad caught fragments of a radio conversation between Investigator Mike James and another officer at the scene where the hit-and-run vehicle had been stopped. As Brad listened, his heart began to pound and his knuckles turned white as he gripped the steering wheel tighter.

"I can't call you on my cell phone; it's not working," James said to the officer. "Just go ahead and tell me how many body parts you found in the car."

Brad knew he was onto something big this time; something much, much bigger than an ice storm. Stories like this one didn't come along very often in his coverage area, and certainly not right here in his home county.

"Oooooh, shit!" he yelled out loud as he gritted his teeth, hoping he wouldn't go into an uncontrollable slide on the black ice dotting the interstate. He prayed the Jeep would hold the road as he gunned it up the slick highway toward Mentone.

When Brad reached the 218-mile marker exit at the southern end of Fort Payne, he decided to detour into town and stop by the sheriff's department for better directions before he continued on to Mentone. From the garbled radio transmissions, he couldn't determine the exact location of the crime scene. Several different places had been mentioned in the scanner traffic; some units seemed to be talking about a couple of different locations on County Road 641, and others were giving their site as the intersection of Highway 117 and U.S. 11.

When the WHNT-TV Jeep pulled into the parking

lot closest to the back entrance of the county jail, Brad saw an Ider patrol car parked near the door with someone seated in the back. As Brad hurried past the car on his way to the door, he glanced at the man inside. He was an enormous fellow with wild, bushy hair and dark smears on his face, sitting shackled in the backseat and staring blankly out the windshield. He turned his head toward Brad as the cameraman hustled past the car on his way inside, intent on finding out where the action was taking place.

Brad Hood didn't realize it at the time, but he was much closer to the action than he knew. He'd just had his first look at Hayward Bissell.

Mike James, who would be named the lead investigator on the Bissell case, arrived at Hammondville Crossroads ready to go to work. He drove up to the crowd surrounding the taped-off vehicles and immediately began organizing the processing of the scene, quickly turning chaos into order while conferring with Deputy District Attorney (DDA) Ben Baxley, the first representative of the district attorney's office to arrive at the site. James could see that the small woman sitting in the Town Car with Ohio license plates appeared to have been dead for only a short period of time, and when he touched her, he found the body was still warm. After DeKalb Ambulance Service paramedic Gregory Jay Harris checked Patricia Booher's body for a pulse and failed to find one, James checked to make sure the necessary photographs had been taken; then he okayed the removal of the body from the Town Car by the coroner. He also asked Officer Hubbard to get the names of everyone who was present, then get them moved back away from the crime scene.

Investigators Phillips and Simpson finished their documentation and evidence-collecting duties at the scene; then Simpson left for the Pumphrey residence and Phillips headed for DeKalb Baptist Medical Center in Fort Payne to interview the assault and hit-and-run victims, who had been taken there for treatment.

The large group of law enforcement and emergency personnel who converged on the scene had been engaged in a frenzy of activity at the intersection since backup began to arrive, but when the time came to remove Patricia Booher's body from the car, a hush fell over the crowd. The officers fell silent and stood by respectfully as Hubbard helped Deputy Coroner Billy Weldon place Patricia Booher's corpse into a body bag and carry it to a waiting hearse from Corner Stone Chapel in Ider. The two men gently collected her hand and heart from where they lay on the floorboard and retrieved her severed right leg from the backseat—the leg that still wore a small tennis shoe and a Mickey Mouse sock.

After Mentone assistant chief Bain learned what had happened to James and Sue Pumphrey, he decided to go back and check the Pumphrey home and the neighboring houses to see if there were any more assault victims in need of help. When he pulled up into the Pumphreys' driveway, he noticed a dog lying in the yard to the right of the driveway with blood covering the ground around it. The icy blades of grass on the ground, and the thick coating of ice covering each twig on the branches that hung down over the dog's body, looked like a canopy bed of sparkling crystal. Another dog lay dead under the sagging boughs of a pine tree on the opposite side of the driveway, also surrounded by sparkling fringes of hanging, red-spattered icicles. Bain walked up the drive to the back of the trailer and noticed a blood trail leading from the back door and continuing around the end of the trailer. He didn't want to risk disturbing any evidence, so he decided to pull his patrol car back to up the road and block the driveway until Investigator Clay Simpson arrived.

When Simpson got to the Pumphrey residence, he walked into yet another scene reminiscent of a bloody horror film. The front porch of James and Sue Pumphrey's home, which only hours earlier had been spotless and welcoming, now looked like a slaughterhouse. A set of white lawn chairs had been overturned and were heavily splattered with blood, and blood soaked the welcome mat and the porch floor that led into the house. Blood dripped down the steps and onto the ground, and the two chocolate Labs, Reese and Cocoa, lay in the front yard, where they had died after fighting to the last breath—doing everything they could possibly do to protect their owners.

Simpson was accustomed to dealing with the aftermath of violence, but for two such gruesome events to happen almost simultaneously was all but unbelievable. For the second time that evening, the investigator photographed a grisly crime scene in careful detail and collected and bagged evidence that he would later log into the evidence room at the sheriff's office.

Chapter 5

"He's eating the evidence!"

Investigator Danny Smith, an officer of the Ninth Judicial Circuit of Alabama, which includes adjoining DeKalb and Cherokee Counties in the northeastern corner of the state, primarily worked in Cherokee County, but was always on hand whenever his DeKalb County colleagues needed assistance with a major crime. On that Sunday evening, Smith came to the crime scene at Hammondville Crossroads and took temporary custody of Hayward Bissell while the other investigators finished their on-site work. Smith was searching the suspect for weapons prior to loading him into the Ider patrol car for transport when he discovered the mass of bloody tissue in Bissell's shirt pocket. Bissell became noticeably nervous and apprehensive when Smith discovered the material in his pocket, so Smith and Lieutenant Harris decided to leave it where it was until they got the prisoner to Mike James's office in the sheriff's department for processing and interrogation.

Danny Smith, county deputy Lamar Hackworth and Ider officer Randall Smith rode along with Bissell in the Ider patrol car for the trip into Fort Payne. When they got to the back entrance of the jail, they took the prisoner up the stairs of the sheriff's department to James's second-floor office. Hackworth later observed that Bissell kept his hand on his shirt pocket most of the time as though he were trying to hide something, despite his earlier comment about having a "rock" in his pocket.

The men took Bissell upstairs to Mike James's office, pulled a chair around in front of the desk and told Bissell to sit down. The prisoner apparently decided he preferred to sit behind the desk in James's own chair and started walking around the desk to take a seat.

"Stop and come back around here and sit down where we told you to," the officers told Bissell, but he ignored them and kept trying to park himself in James's chair behind the desk.

Deputy Hackworth decided he'd had enough of Bissell's continuing refusal to do as he was told, so he used his foot to scoot the chair away from the prisoner as he once again tried to sit down. Bissell almost fell down; then he finally decided it was time to cooperate. He walked back around the desk and seated himself in the chair he had originally been directed to take.

Investigator Gary Bell came into the office, sat down, and attempted to ask Bissell a few questions, to no avail. The big, blood-covered man slouched in his chair and stared at the walls in front of him, ignoring Bell. He refused to respond to Bell in any way and didn't look around the room or make a sound.

Danny Smith began to take photographs that he knew would be needed in the course of the investigation. He asked Deputy Hackworth to remove the material from Bissell's pocket while he took pictures, and Hackworth carefully put on a pair of exam gloves. The first item he pulled from the pocket was a bloody $5 bill, the only money that would be found on Bissell and apparently the only cash he had left. The other item in the pocket, the mass of bloody tissue that the officers had discovered earlier and thought might have been a finger, appeared instead to be a human esophagus, approximately six inches long. Hackworth pulled it partially out of the pocket so Danny Smith could photograph it, then left it in Bissell's pocket while the men waited for Mike James to arrive.

When James got to his office, Danny Smith, Lamar Hackworth and Randall Smith stepped out of the office into the hallway and shut the door so that James and Bell could begin their questioning. A few minutes later, the two men left the office and went downstairs to begin some of the paperwork on the case, leaving Danny Smith and Randall Smith to keep an eye on the prisoner. Randall Smith went inside the office to stand behind Bissell, and Danny Smith remained sitting just outside the door in the hallway.

"I noticed Bissell slump to the left, pull his left hand up to his shirt pocket and take out the esophagus," Randall Smith said.

Bissell sat still for a couple of seconds, then slumped to the left once again, pulling his left hand up to his mouth, and Smith saw to his shock that the prisoner was attempting to eat the esophagus.

"No, don't do that!" Randall Smith shouted at Bissell as he pushed the prisoner's hand down away from his mouth.

"Hey, he's eating the evidence!" the horrified officer yelled to Danny Smith as the other officer, hearing the commotion, ran into the room. As soon as he saw what was happening, Danny Smith turned and ran downstairs to tell Mike James what was taking place upstairs in his office, and he returned with another deputy, Johnny Brown.

The two officers told Randall Smith to take the esophagus away from Bissell and bag it as evidence.

Officer Randall Smith never before had been called on for such bizarre duty during the course of his work with the Ider Police Department, but he stepped right up to the plate that evening with a queasy stomach but without hesitation. He held his hand under Bissell's hand that gripped the esophagus, and told him, "Give it to me."

Bissell hesitated a few seconds, then dropped the esophagus into Officer Smith's hand. Investigator Danny Smith took more photographs of the suspect as the organ was bagged as evidence. Bissell made no attempt to stop the officers from taking away his prize; while the severed organ was being removed from his grip, he sat motionless in the chair, continuing to stare blankly ahead, his head drooping and blood streaking his face and the corners of his mouth.

Bissell was then taken downstairs by the group of officers to be strip-searched, and Mike James took blood samples from his face, hands, body and clothing. Danny Smith photographed the scratches, bruises, abrasions and bloodstains that were scattered over his entire body.

Shortly after 5:00 P.M., James began to prepare for his first attempt to question Hayward Bissell. Since the other investigators were on duty around the county, busily working three separate crime scenes and interviewing the Pirches and Pumphreys at DeKalb Baptist Medical Center, James enlisted Gary Bell's aid. The two officers had worked together on many occasions, but this would prove to be the most bizarre interrogation they had ever tried to conduct.

At 5:10 P.M., Bell advised Bissell once again of his rights, but there was no indication the man paid any more attention to what Bell was saying to him than he had paid the first time, or that he even heard what he was being told. He remained unresponsive, sagging in the chair, with his head lolled forward. James made still another attempt to advise Bissell of his rights against incriminating himself and, this time, Bissell surprised the officers by replying in a normal tone of voice that he understood his rights and was willing to answer their questions.

That unexpected statement marked the beginning of forty-five minutes of confusing, rambling, sometimes contradictory, remarks, with Bissell appearing rational one minute, then making bizarre comments the next. He claimed to understand where he was and why he was being questioned, but it soon became apparent that the suspect was, by turns, either highly delusional or pretending to be.

"I am a secret agent with the Secret Service," he announced pompously, adding that James and Bell were not "cleared" to receive the answers to the questions he was being asked. He didn't request the presence of an attorney, but he claimed that he was being questioned under duress because the investigators were asking questions of him "without the proper security clearance."

Bissell told the detectives he was a friend of Patricia Ann Booher's, and that he was on a top-secret mission, the major part of which was "terminating" her. He claimed his supervisor at the Secret Service was a man named David Wilbur Light, and even gave James and Bell a telephone number for "Agent Light." Bissell said his Secret Service badge number was 666, and stated that he worked out of an office in Cleveland, Ohio.

When Bissell was asked if he killed Patricia Ann Booher, he answered matter-of-factly, "I killed no one else."

He told James and Bell he killed Patricia in the parking lot of a service station in Georgia, and said that he committed the murder and the awful mutilation of her body using a knife.

"She was killed in the prescribed method used for killing black witches," he said.

Bissell said the pair had come south from their hometown of Norwalk, Ohio, because bringing the young woman from Ohio to Georgia to kill her "was part of the assignment." He continued to complain that he was being questioned under duress because the investigators were not "cleared" to hear the answers he gave.

When the eerie questioning session ended, Bissell was booked into the jail and his clothing was taken as evidence. At the time of his arrest, he wore a blue short-sleeved pocket T-shirt, dark blue Dockers pants and size-12 white Reeboks. He only had $5 in his pocket, the same bloody $5 bill that shared pocket space with the severed esophagus. Following his booking, Bissell was dressed in a jail uniform, loaded back into a patrol car and taken to nearby DeKalb Baptist Medical Center for treatment of the dog bites on his hands. He had received several defensive wounds on his left hand while fighting and stabbing the Pumphreys' two dogs, and the jail staff felt they needed to be treated at the hospital in case of infection.

By the time the patient arrived, the hospital grapevine had already started buzzing with rumors about what the ambulance crew had encountered when they arrived on the emergency call to Hammondville Crossroads. An extremely skittish emergency room staff was waiting for the patrol car, and they were grateful for the presence of the officers who stood close by as they treated Bissell for lacerations to his left hand and left index finger. His hands were swabbed with Betadine, some of the deeper wounds were stitched up, and he was bandaged and returned to the jail with aftercare instructions sent to the jailers.

Later that evening, Bissell was questioned again. This time, James was joined by Detective Tim McDonald of the Dade County, Georgia, Sheriff's Department and Agent James L. Harris of the Georgia Bureau of Investigation (GBI). Dade County sheriff Phil Street had been contacted by DeKalb County authorities and notified that a possible homicide might have occurred in his county. Street contacted Agent Harris and asked him to go along with McDonald to Alabama to assist in questioning the suspect. The officers hoped to determine exactly where the crime had taken place in order to determine jurisdiction.

Lieutenant Jimmy Harris had returned to the sheriff's department from the crime scene at Hammondville Crossroads, and he went downstairs into the jail to bring Bissell up for the interview. As they started back up the steps, Bissell apparently decided Harris was not of high-enough rank or status to escort him to the second floor.

"Your clearance is not high enough for you to either talk to me or to take me anywhere," Bissell informed the officer.

"What is your name and badge number? My name is Hayward William Bissell and my badge number is 666."

Harris gave Bissell his badge number and told him that his name was Jimmy Harris. About that time, GBI agent James Harris started down the stairs in their direction, and Bissell noticed the two men wore almost identical name tags.

"What's your name?" he asked Agent Harris.

"I'm Agent James Harris with the Georgia Bureau of Investigation," the agent answered.

"What's *your* name?" he asked Lieutenant Harris.

"Jimmy Harris, with the sheriff's department."

Bissell looked back and forth between the two men. "You're trying to kill me," he announced to the two Harrises.

Agent Harris quickly retreated back upstairs out of sight, and after a few moments of reassurance that the men were not trying to kill him, Lieutenant Harris took Bissell to the second floor with no further incidents.

Bissell came to the interview only partially dressed; the jail had no full sets of clothing on hand that were large enough to fit him. He was brought into the interrogation room looking somewhat less gruesome than during his earlier interview, no longer covered with splashes and smears of blood. James read him his Miranda rights once again and Bissell agreed to talk to Agent Harris and the other detectives.

This questioning session proved to be far more informative than the first, but no less confusing. Bissell alternated freely back and forth between possible fact and obvious fiction as he willingly answered questions.

"I am a secret agent for the Secret Service," he announced proudly, "and I have successfully completed my mission." He went on to confirm that he had terminated Patricia Ann Booher, to whom he said he had been engaged three times, by cutting her throat, gouging her eyes out, cutting her heart out, removing her right leg and then removing her left hand.

"I had been sent on missions involving her three times before," he said, "but I had never before been ordered to terminate her. At first, I was ordered to put her out on the side of the road, but I didn't want to do that because I cared for her."

Bissell told the officers he and Booher had been traveling from Ohio to visit his parents, who lived in

Florida. He said they left the Chattanooga area that morning and drove toward Atlanta on I-75. Somewhere in North Georgia, he said, he exited the interstate and drove west until he came to a small town in a rural area.

"I don't remember the name of the town," he said, "but it had a Dollar General store and another store that started with the letters *A B.* We parked at that store a few minutes and then drove another fifteen or twenty minutes until we came to a service station."

The station, he said, had a yellow sign with red letters on the outside and a milk advertisement. The gas pumps were red and blue.

"I went in to use the bathroom," he said. "When you went into the store, the counter was on the left side and the rest room was in the back of the store on the left."

When he left the store, he told the officers that he walked back to the Lincoln and got in.

"At that time, I received orders to terminate her and I did so in the manner in which I had been directed," he said. The orders he received, he claimed, were coming from inside his head. Bissell told the officers he terminated Booher with two knives that could be found inside the Lincoln, a Smith & Wesson knife and another knife known as a Kissing Crane. Investigator Simpson had bagged both knives at the scene, and they were already logged into the evidence room downstairs.

When the officers asked him if it had hurt to carry out his orders, killing the woman he claimed to love and, by his own account, had been engaged to, he calmly replied, "No, it did not hurt me at all."

After he had killed Patricia, Bissell said, he seatbelted her back into place in the front passenger's seat of the Town Car and continued on, still receiving orders to make "lefts" and "rights" from inside his head. He claimed he didn't know his destination, but the route the "voices" inside his head told him to take was conveniently bringing him on a direct route to Interstate 59, with an interchange only a couple of miles west of Mentone.

Bissell then told the investigators the murder and dismemberment of Patricia Booher took place only ten to fifteen minutes before he attempted to run down Don Pirch in Mentone. He claimed he had been directed to ram into Pirch's truck and then run over the driver.

"I shot the driver a bird," he said, referring to the obscene gesture he made at Don Pirch, "while he was hanging on to the hood of my car."

Then, Bissell said, he received additional orders.

"After that, I was directed to drive down a road and terminate another man," he said. "I attempted to terminate this man by stabbing him with my Smith and Wesson knife, and then I used it to kill two dogs."

Bissell said the man he had stabbed ran into his home and returned with a silver .22 rifle. The man had said, "If you don't leave, I will kill you."

After leaving there, Bissell claimed he was directed by the voices in his head to ram into a "bucket tractor" and then was ordered to drive into a crowd of people standing on the side of the road. He told the officers the esophagus found in his shirt pocket before the first interview was from one of the dogs he had been ordered to terminate and he had been directed by the voices to take it with him so he could eat it at a later time.

According to Investigator James, Bissell once again claimed to be aware of where he was and why he was being questioned. This time, however, he appeared to be more paranoid than before and would not agree for the interview to be tape-recorded by the investigators. He was also unwilling to sign any statements. Bissell continued to claim repeatedly he was making his statements under duress because the officers were not Secret Service agents and were not authorized to conduct the investigation or to interrogate him without the proper clearance.

"This was an approved mission," he repeated, over and over, during the session. "It was an approved mission, and you don't have the proper clearance to question me."

While Hayward Bissell was at the DeKalb County Sheriff's Department being booked into jail and questioned by officers from several agencies, his Mentone victims were being stabilized by paramedics and rushed to DeKalb Baptist Medical Center. Sheriff Cecil Reed had headed for the hospital when he was notified by his dispatcher of the hit and run, the stabbing incidents and the body that had been found in the car of the suspected assailant. When the ambulance pulled up to the emergency room entrance, Reed wanted to be waiting there to talk to the two men who had been attacked.

Reed, a lifelong civil servant and a veteran of law enforcement in DeKalb County, was highly regarded by the citizens in his jurisdiction. During his many years of public service, as a deputy sheriff and police officer, circuit court clerk, then as chief deputy for sixteen years before being elected sheriff, he had always made a special effort to help the victims of violent crimes. This case, however, was shaping up to be unlike anything Reed had dealt with in his long career. In addition to checking on the welfare of the assault victims and their family members, the sheriff also hoped to help his investigators piece together the details of the bizarre string of crimes they now realized had all been committed by the big man in their custody.

When the ambulances carrying James Pumphrey and Don Pirch arrived at the emergency room, hospital personnel hurriedly prepped James for emergency surgery and rushed him to the operating room. Don was wheeled in and immediately taken for X rays to check for broken bones.

"I met Sheriff Reed at the door of the emergency room," Rhea Pirch said, "and he introduced himself and told me they caught the guy, and there was a body in his car, and that it was still warm. If I wasn't in shock yet, that put me there."

In the operating room, Dr. Jeffrey Thompson readied his team to perform exploratory surgery on James Pumphrey. The preliminary examination showed an almost five-inch cut extending from his navel downward and to the left. Some of his abdominal contents were protruding through the wound, and James had suffered a significant loss of blood.

James was dazed and weak, but he was fully conscious when he arrived at the hospital. He was a deeply religious man, and before he was anesthetized, James asked the doctor to wait for just a moment.

"I asked Dr. Thompson if he would mind saying a prayer with me," James said, "and I asked the Lord God to guide his hands and be with us during the surgery."

The doctor gladly paused, and he and his patient said their prayer together, joined by several of the nurses and technicians in the operating room. Then the surgery to save James Pumphrey's life began.

Dr. Thompson found that James's small intestine had been completely severed, and he performed a tricky bowel resection, an exploratory laparotomy, and repaired the abdominal wall. The injuries were serious, and the possibility of infection was great. James would be a very lucky man if he made it through the operation and recovery without developing some major complications.

Following the surgery, James went to the recovery room for several hours, then was taken on to the intensive care unit (ICU) for the remainder of the night. His wife sat patiently in the ICU waiting room, visiting James for a few allotted minutes at a time, even though she herself was traumatized from the horrifying assault. Later, Sue would need counseling to recover from the lingering effects of the incident, but caring for James was first and foremost in her thoughts. Her concern for her husband was the glue that held her together during the aftermath of Bissell's attack.

While Don Pirch was being examined and treated, his wife, Rhea, sat alone in the emergency room wondering what she should do. There was no one she could call; all of their friends and family members lived in the Mentone area, and their phones were out because of the ice storm. She couldn't call them for help, or even notify them of what had happened. Rhea was finally able to see Don after he was returned from the X-ray unit and it was confirmed he had no broken bones. She was quite surprised, however, to learn that the hospital was preparing to release him. He had a contusion on the left hip, abrasions to both legs and was in a great deal of pain, but he was being discharged nonetheless. He had nowhere to go and no way to get there, but he was still being sent home.

"Don's clothes had been cut off of him and held for evidence, and he wasn't able to walk without assistance," Rhea said. "A nurse gave him a scrub suit two sizes too big, and he was left without shoes or socks. He didn't even have crutches."

After leaving the crime scene at Hammondville Crossroads, Investigator Jimmy Phillips came to the hospital with the intention of interviewing the victims and any other witnesses who might be waiting there. He found Don and Rhea sitting alone in the emergency room lobby, with no way to get home and nowhere else to stay. Their truck was still up in Mentone, its driver's-side door nearly torn off. Don was ill prepared to venture out into the freezing rain, barefoot and with only a thin set of scrubs to protect him against the cold.

"Mr. Phillips filled us in on the grisly details of what had happened. He tried his best to help us find a motel to stay in, but he had no luck," Rhea said.

"All the motel rooms in Fort Payne were booked due to the ice storm. We were finally given a ride back to our house in Mentone by a patrolman."

When the Pirches reached their home, they could see, even in the darkness, that their yard was a total disaster area.

"It looked like a tornado had hit it," Rhea said. "Trees and limbs were down everywhere, and our power was out."

The electricity would remain out for four more days, and during that time the couple had nothing but gas heat, candles and some camping gear to cook with. Don couldn't walk at all the next day, and his problems were compounded by the lack of electricity or telephone service.

"I had to leave my husband alone during those days so I could go to work," Rhea said. "I knew we were in for the long haul, that Don wouldn't be able to work, possibly for months, and I knew I couldn't afford to miss more than one day."

Rhea agonized over leaving Don at home by himself while she went to work, knowing he could hardly get around and had no way to phone for help if he should need it. Having to fend for himself while he was injured was hard to do, and it was even harder to sit home alone, in pain, with nothing to do but think about the hit-and-run incident. But as hard as it was, there were many times during those four tough days when Don and Rhea Pirch told themselves it could have been far worse. They remembered what Jimmy Phillips said to them while he was filling them in on the story of Bissell's other victims that Sunday evening.

"You're so lucky," he told them, "because this guy was out to kill."

Around 7:00 P.M. on Sunday, while investigators coaxed information from Hayward Bissell and doctors treated the injuries of his victims, the police department in Norwalk, Ohio, received a call from DeKalb County chief deputy Eddie Wright informing them that Bissell was in custody in Alabama and under investigation for the murder of Patricia Booher. Wright related the gruesome details of the afternoon's events to the Norwalk authorities, and upon hearing what had happened, officers were soon on their way to the Firelands Village complex on Norwalk's Spring Street to check the apartments of both Bissell and Booher. They wanted to insure that the crime had not occurred or begun in their jurisdiction and to check the two apartments for possible evidence or signs of a struggle.

After contacting Jim Conway, Norwalk's assistant city law director, for instructions on how to proceed in handling the situation, the officers obtained permission to search Bissell's apartment from his legal guardian, Kathleen P. Carnahan, his aunt. Kathleen was more than willing to cooperate, and Detective

Sergeant David Light and Officer David Ditz drove to her home in North Fairfield, Ohio, where she signed a waiver of consent to search the apartment of her nephew.

The Firelands Village apartment complex was part of North Coast Properties and was managed by Linda Rogers. She was contacted by Norwalk police and was very shocked and upset to hear of Patricia Booher's death. She had been Patricia's friend and confidante since the young woman first rented an apartment in the complex, and was able to provide the officers with a great deal of useful personal information about Patricia, enabling them to contact Patricia's family, friends and other Firelands Village residents who might be able to help in the investigation. Rogers sent her maintenance supervisor, Steve Grose, to open the two apartments for the officers with a master key, and Sergeant Marty Horvatich and Detective Jim Fulton had Grose unlock Patricia's apartment first.

When they went inside, the officers found the apartment was neat and clean, with nothing that seemed to be out of order, and nothing appeared to be obviously missing. There were no signs of a struggle, and nothing to indicate that Patricia might have been forcibly taken. A phone bill with long-distance charges was taken by the officers in order to gain contact phone numbers for Patricia's family, and an eight-inch by ten-inch color portrait was also taken to send to Alabama to be used for identification purposes if necessary. Four messages had been left in her voice mail and were retrieved by the officers as possible evidence.

When they were finished checking the apartment and were satisfied that nothing was obviously out of order, the officers asked Grose to relock the door; then they went to Bissell's apartment in another building of the complex. When they got there, they noticed the door was slightly ajar, and Sergeant Horvatich reported back to police headquarters that he could hear loud music and the sound of running water. He decided to wait about entering the apartment, even though the door was open, until he heard from Light, and as soon as Light radioed that permission to search had been secured from Kathleen Carnahan, Horvatich and Fulton entered Hayward Bissell's apartment.

A steady stream of water was running from the kitchen faucet, and a radio had been left playing loudly in the living room; otherwise, they found nothing else to be unusual. Everything in the apartment was extremely clean and well organized, and items on the shelves and in the dresser and cabinet drawers were lined up and stacked precisely by color, size and category. Nothing was out of place, and the officers found nothing that gave any indication the homicide might have occurred there. Except for the fact that the apartment's occupant had walked out and left for an out-of-state trip without even closing the door, leaving the kitchen faucet turned on and the radio blaring, there was nothing out of the ordinary.

Very little was found in the apartment that provided investigators with any clues to Bissell's daily life. A copy of *U.S. Cavalry* magazine and a Smokey Mountain Knife Works catalog lay on an end table in the living room, and a few prescription receipts and insurance papers were in the bedroom dresser drawers, along with copies of Bissell's birth certificate, child support court records and marriage license. Officers noted that Bissell had a sizable collection of model cars and Hot Wheels, but few other personal items.

Once again, Grose secured the apartment for the officers.

Norwalk police chief Mike Ruggles later told a reporter from the *Norwalk Reflector* that his officers were a little bit apprehensive about venturing into Bissell's apartment after hearing from Alabama police about what had been done to Patricia Booher. Images of Jeffrey Dahmer's horrendous crimes flashed into the policemen's minds as they went into the apartment, not knowing what grisly surprises might be waiting for them inside.

"When we entered, we were afraid we would find that the murder happened here," Ruggles said, adding that the officers cautiously opened Bissell's freezer to check its contents and were extremely relieved that it contained none of the horrifying items they had imagined.

"He led a pretty mundane lifestyle, kept to himself," Ruggles told reporters about Bissell.

Ruggles said that one of his officers had called him at home on Sunday night and told him what had happened, and at first he was doubtful.

"It's almost beyond belief," he said. "Once in a while, they fall through the cracks, but how on earth could you predict something like that? We knew he was off at times, but nothing violent like this. We were all skeptical until we talked to the detectives in Fort Payne."

After hearing the appalling details of Bissell's Alabama arrest from those DeKalb County detectives, Ruggles and his officers were convinced. The man they realized was "off at times" had indeed fallen through the cracks, and he was far more disturbed than they could have ever suspected.

Chapter 6

"This is all a mistake."

By Monday morning, word of Hayward Bissell's gruesome crime spree had spread like wildfire among the news media in Alabama, Georgia and Tennessee. Satellite trucks from TV stations in the closest large cities of Huntsville, Birmingham and Chattanooga filled several parking lots around the DeKalb County Jail, and the lobby of the sheriff's office was packed with reporters and cameramen waiting for a press conference scheduled for 10:00 A.M. Rumors of mutilation, cannibalism and missing body parts circulated wildly among the reporters, and there was much speculation about one particular story that claimed Patricia Booher's eyes were missing and might have been eaten by Bissell.

Earlier that morning, Mike James had asked the deputies to bring Bissell up from the basement jail to his second-floor office for another round of questions, this time to try and determine the exact location where Patricia Booher was killed. James explained to Bissell that this might require him to travel with the investigators to Georgia, and once again carefully explained his rights against self-incrimination.

This time, the big man had no intention of cooperating.

"I don't understand what's happening here," Bissell said. "I'm an agent of the Secret Service. This is all a mistake."

Bissell told James he would make no further statements, and said for the first time that he wanted to speak with an attorney.

"I'm not authorized to travel to Georgia," he said, refusing to go there with the investigators.

Since the prisoner had requested an attorney and would say no more, James knew the interview was over.

The roads between my home in South DeKalb County and my office in Fort Payne were still slick in places that Monday morning, and the trip to work was going much slower than usual. I was running late, so I went straight to the sheriff's office without stopping by my desk at the Fort Payne *Times-Journal*, where I covered crime and law enforcement in DeKalb County.

I had heard some early details of Sunday afternoon's incidents on my home police scanner. When falling power lines blew a transformer and cut off the electricity to my house, I kept listening until the scanner's backup batteries went dead. This was by far the biggest story I'd ever had a chance to cover, and I was frustrated by my inability to get up to the scene or even to continue following the action by radio. Unlike my friend Brad Hood, I didn't have a four-wheel-drive work vehicle equipped with radios and scanners. All I could do was walk the floor and wonder what was happening up in Mentone. I could hardly wait for morning to come, and I hoped the weather conditions would improve enough overnight to enable me to get to work the following day.

When I pulled into the courthouse parking lot and saw all the satellite trucks, I knew the competition was going to be fierce, and if I wanted to get on the inside track, I'd better hurry. I grabbed my notebook and ran up the steps of the sheriff's department, making it inside the front door and into the lobby just in time to see Sheriff Reed ushering everyone into his small office for the press conference. As the TV cameramen jostled for positions inside the room, the sheriff stopped me outside the door and pulled me aside.

"Where's your camera?" he asked.

In my haste to get into the building, I'd left it in the car.

"Run and get it; they're about to bring Bissell downstairs," he said. "He'll be coming down from Mike's office any minute. Wait over there out of sight in the stairwell and get a picture, and I'll fill you in on everything later."

As I ran back outside to my car to retrieve the camera, I gave thanks for the good relationship I had with Sheriff Reed and his officers and jail personnel. While the rest of the reporters were inside the sheriff's office for the press conference, I was going to get the best break of my career.

I ran back inside with my lungs burning, and caught my breath while I waited on the first-floor landing, checking and double-checking my camera and flash. Then I heard voices coming from up above, and footsteps coming down the stairs. The first person to come into view was Deputy Van McAlpin, one of the tallest, huskiest officers in the county. Behind him, in white jail pants and a white T-shirt that barely stretched over his huge chest, was the prisoner.

Hayward Bissell looked even larger than McAlpin, and my first thought was that Van, despite his size and strength, might have a hard time controlling the man if he decided to become unruly. Bissell was moving slowly down the stairs, and came to a sudden stop when my flash went off for the first time. As I lowered the camera, he raised his head and stared directly at me.

"Who's that?" he asked.

Mike James was coming down the steps behind Bissell.

"She's just a reporter," he said. "Go on, keep moving."

As Hayward Bissell came down the stairs toward me, he kept his eyes locked with mine. It was a good thing I got that first shot, because I didn't hang around for another one. My instinct for self-preservation won out over my desire to get more exclusive photos, and I took off downstairs ahead of the prisoner and his escorts, ducking out the back door of the jail. Those deadly eyes boring into mine had me thoroughly spooked, and I decided the best place for me was well out of his reach. I watched from outside through the plate glass doors, and Bissell watched me as he was walked down the steps into the jail.

After Bissell was safely back downstairs behind the thick red steel door of the jail, I slunk back inside in disgrace with Mike James's laughter ringing in my ears.

"What did you take off in such a hurry for?" he teased.

I may have turned chicken when I came face-to-face with a killer, but at least I got the first shot of the man who was making headlines throughout the Southeast and in his home state of Ohio. My photo of Bissell, the first taken of him after his arrest, was picked up by the Associated Press and ran nationwide in newspapers and on the Internet. It would be the first of many times I'd be there, waiting with my camera when he was brought up from his jail cell. And those eyes, staring so intently at me every time, would always leave me unnerved.

After the press conference, Reed held another meeting in his office for me and a couple of latecomers who didn't make it in time for the first briefing session. As I walked into the room, the sheriff handed me a photo of Bissell's Ohio driver's license and Patricia Booher's ID card.

The photo on Bissell's license showed a man who looked very different from the bushy-haired inmate I had just encountered on the stairs. The man on the driver's license was neatly groomed but unsmiling, with an aloof, haughty expression on his face. He was listed as being six feet four inches tall and weighing four hundred pounds. His address was an apartment on Spring Street, in Norwalk, Ohio.

Patricia Booher also lived at that 26 Spring Street address, but in a different apartment. She was only four feet ten inches tall and weighed 105 pounds. She looked like a pleasant young woman with an open, hopeful smile. The physical differences in the two people were extreme, to say the least, but the biggest difference was in their facial expressions. If the eyes were truly the windows of the soul, Patricia Booher's eyes showed that she was a friendly person who wanted to be happy and well liked. Hayward Bissell, on the other hand, looked almost threatening, as though he were challenging the camera to capture his image. The windows of his soul appeared to be tightly closed.

Sheriff Reed began going over the details of the previous afternoon's events. He had carefully prepared a lengthy set of notes on the series of crimes and disclosed, as usual, as much information as possible.

"We received a call Sunday at three forty-three P.M. on a hit-and-run incident on Highway 117 in Mentone," he said. "A 'be on the lookout' bulletin was released on the light blue Lincoln Town Car bearing Ohio license plates involved in the incident."

Reed said the vehicle was stopped by Valley Head, Mentone and Hammondville units around 4:00 P.M. at the intersection of U.S. 11 and Highway 117.

"Upon approaching the car and taking the driver, Hayward William Bissell, thirty-seven, of Norwalk, Ohio, into custody, the officers discovered the horribly mutilated body of a twenty-five-year-old white female in the car," Reed said.

"The victim has been identified as Patricia Ann Booher, also of Norwalk, Ohio. She had received numerous severe wounds and injuries, and some parts of the body had been severed."

Reed said his investigators were working with Georgia authorities to determine the jurisdiction of the murder case.

"It is unknown at this time if the murder occurred in the car or elsewhere, or whether it occurred in Georgia or Alabama. The woman appeared to have been dead only a very short time when a stabbing and a hit-and-run incident were committed by the same subject, and the body has been taken to the Alabama Department of Forensic Science for autopsy."

The sheriff went on to describe the incidents involving the Pirches and the Pumphreys and gave an update on their conditions as of that morning. Don Pirch, he said, had been released from the hospital following treatment of his injuries, and James Pumphrey remained hospitalized in stable condition following his Sunday-evening surgery.

Rumors of drug dealing, witchcraft and Devil worship had spread, as they always seem to do in parts of the rural South, as a possible cause behind the gruesome murder and the vicious assaults on Pirch and Pumphrey. Reed, though, put those rumors to rest in short order when the opportunity arose.

In response to a question about the possibility of

Bissell being acquainted in some way with either of the assault victims, Reed said, "Absolutely not, no way. They were complete strangers. These people were all solid citizens, real salt-of-the-earth folks, good people, and they were attacked by a total stranger without any provocation whatsoever."

Authorities in Norwalk, Ohio, had been contacted, Reed said, and had not yet provided information on whether or not Bissell had any previous police record, but did say they "knew him well." They were expected to send copies of materials in their files very soon.

DeKalb County and Georgia authorities were in the process of trying to determine jurisdiction in the murder charge, he repeated, and Bissell was expected to be charged in DeKalb County with assault and attempted murder in the stabbing and hit-and-run incidents. The Town Car, he said, was currently impounded at the county maintenance barn's fenced lot and would be taken to Huntsville for complete forensic testing.

After finishing his lengthy statement and answering several additional questions, Reed settled back in his chair and spoke informally with those of us left in the room.

"This is one of the most unusual cases I've dealt with during all my years here in the county," he said, shuffling the sheaf of papers that related the details of Sunday's events.

"We have no idea how or why Bissell came to be in the Mentone area. We've had some pretty bad episodes here, but not one that tops this."

Reed leaned back in his chair and shook his head, baffled by the events of the past twenty-four hours. The sheriff was a family man, with a wonderful wife, two children and four grandchildren, a "people person." He had clearly been deeply disturbed by the mindless, unexplained violence that had taken the life of such a small, defenseless young woman.

One of the reporters speculated that Bissell might have been traveling through the area either on or headed for the interstate, since I-59 runs the entire length of DeKalb County.

"We have a lot of travelers coming through the county," Reed answered, "but not many that stop by with a body in the car."

Chapter 7

"If I never see another naked four-hundred-pound man, it'll be too soon for me."

Jail overcrowding has been a serious problem for years in DeKalb County, as well as in all of Alabama's other counties. Sheriff Reed and his staff have struggled to maintain the best possible conditions for inmates under such poor circumstances, but there was only so much they could do with the limited space available.

Jail conditions were somewhat relieved when the county commission approved the building of two temporary dome housing units, to be used until a new jail facility could be constructed. But during Hayward Bissell's tenure in the jail, the domes were not yet completed and ready for use, and he occupied a cell downstairs in the basement of the sheriff's department, where all the rest of the county's male inmates were housed.

Tuesdays and Saturdays are visiting days at the jail, and visitation is one of the things that helps make the overcrowded conditions more bearable. It gives inmates as well as their loved ones something to look forward to, and a large amount of family members always crowd the lobby in the mornings to sign in for appointments to visit with the inmates in the afternoon. On the morning of Tuesday, January 25, the would-be visitors arrived to find a large sign posted on the front door: VISITATION CANCELED.

Since Hayward Bissell returned to his cell on Monday morning after refusing to talk any further with the investigators, his behavior had become more and more out of control. By that night, he had demolished everything in his cell, ripping pipes and plumbing out of the wall and discarding what little clothing he had that would fit him. Puddles of water stood in the floors throughout the jail, and Bissell's constant ranting and screaming was grating on the nerves of everyone within hearing distance. Rumors quickly spread among the inmates as they began to swap stories of Bissell's nakedness and his alleged cannibalism and mutilation, and he was said to have been caught, facedown in the toilet, eating his own feces, by one of the deputies.

When Chief Jailer Bill Lands arrived for work on Tuesday morning, the already-bad situation caused by Bissell had gotten even worse. His jailers told Lands their new resident had gotten up on the wrong side of the bed again that morning, and his fellow prisoners were paying the price. His outrageous behavior continued as jailers tried to cope with a flooded jail full of nervous, edgy inmates, and Lands decided to suspend visitation that day because of the added security risk. In order to visit with the inmates, their family members had to go to visiting rooms that were located downstairs inside the jail. Under the present circumstances, there was no way Lands was going to allow anyone, neither the prisoners nor their visitors, to be put into a dangerous situation.

If the other prisoners hadn't been so leery of the maniacal giant, they would probably have given the jailers a hard time about losing the visiting privileges that helped make their time in lockup more tolerable. Under the circumstances, however, losing visitation was the last thing on their minds.

"Get that crazy mother out of here, man," one inmate begged the jailers. "He's creeping everybody out with all that carrying on, and the toilets are all shot to hell."

"I can't stand much more of his hollering and banging around," griped another prisoner. "He's making everybody sick to their stomachs just thinking about all that mess he's up to over there in that cell."

Few people outside the department realized the seriousness of the situation inside the jail. Damaged plumbing, water standing in the floor and Bissell's unnerving, continuous raving was more than enough to spur the other inmates of the overcrowded jail to rioting, but so far the men were remaining strangely quiet and almost fearful. Those few who complained out loud to the jailers were being very careful to do so in a low tone of voice that they were sure would not carry along the corridor to the cell where Bissell yowled constantly as he banged his head against the bunk.

Upstairs in the sheriff's department, Bill Lands wasn't any better satisfied with the situation than the prisoners were. The uproar over the new inmate had caused a lengthy list of problems, and that list was growing by the minute. Visitors, some of whom had traveled long distances to see prisoners, were angry when they learned they were going to be turned away, not understanding the decision had been made with their own safety in mind. They were resentful, and most were standing around in the crowded lobby and outside in front of the building, voicing their dissatisfaction loudly and in no uncertain terms. Lands tried to explain his decision to a few disgruntled visitors and met with little agreement; then he finally gave up.

"Aw, let 'em fuss," Lands said to his jailers. "I'd rather they'd be mad than to be in danger."

While the inmates' families were busy complaining to Lands and his staff, Sheriff Reed was on the phone with District Attorney (DA) Mike O'Dell discussing Bissell's upcoming bond hearing, set for a short time later that morning.

"There's no way we can bring him up to the courtroom," Reed told O'Dell. "He's entirely too dangerous to be taken out of his cell at this time. We just can't take that kind of security risk, especially with all these people milling around."

Reed and O'Dell decided their best option would be to hold the bond hearing downstairs in the jail so that Bissell would not need to be removed from his cell, and district judge Lee Clyde Traylor and his court personnel were informed of the situation. A short time later, Traylor and his staff, along with an entourage that included O'Dell's representatives, Reed, Lands, other jail personnel and a number of reporters, began to descend the stairway into the basement.

Under normal circumstances, the DeKalb County Jail is not a particularly unpleasant place despite its overcrowded state. That morning, however, it was eerily reminiscent of a medieval dungeon. The air was dank and damp due to the puddles of standing water throughout most of the jail, and the lights were dim in the hallways because of electrical problems caused by the flooding. The group of press and court officials were careful of their footing as they made their way through security doors and down a maze of passageways to Bissell's cell.

As the group rounded the corner and approached

the cell, they were met with a shocking sight. Hayward Bissell sat on the bunk with his back toward them, stark naked. His waterlogged cell was strewn with his discarded clothing, and feces from his broken toilet floated out through the bars and drifted gently down the hallway.

When Bissell realized he had visitors, he slowly began to turn his head toward them.

"It was the scariest thing I ever saw; it was just like Marlon Brando in that scene in *Apocalypse Now,*" said Monia Smith, a reporter with the *DeKalb Advertiser.* "His eyes—I just can't describe the look in them."

Smith's reporting work was a part-time job; during the school year, she was a teacher at Adamsburg Elementary School. On that Tuesday morning, classes were dismissed due to the continuing power outages on the mountain in the Adamsburg community near Fort Payne, so Smith came to the jail to check on Bissell's status. She arrived in time for the hearing, and found herself downstairs with the rest of the group outside the cell, watching as the prisoner slowly rotated his head in their direction, then kept staring at them as he began rhythmically banging his head on the framework of his bunk.

As Judge Traylor stood in front of the cell in his robes and began to read the charges against Bissell, the naked man turned to face the group and began shouting obscenities. Several of the onlookers edged back reflexively when Bissell approached the bars, but Traylor ignored the prisoner and calmly continued to read. He had been a judge for many years, an attorney for years before that, and he was completely and totally unflappable. During his long career he had seen almost everything imaginable in the legal system, and what he hadn't seen for himself, he'd heard about. It would take far more than a four-hundred-pound naked cannibal to rattle Judge Lee Clyde Traylor.

Monia Smith had ducked back out of sight around a corner when she saw Bissell was naked, and was grateful to be spared the spectacle of Bissell glaring furiously at his visitors as he cursed and screamed and began to masturbate. Judge Traylor continued to conduct the bond hearing as though he were upstairs in his chambers, while Bissell flogged himself with increasing enthusiasm.

"I didn't want to see any more," Smith later told a colleague. "If I never see another naked four-hundred-pound man, it'll be too soon for me."

As Judge Traylor finished the legal requirements of the bond hearing from hell, he appointed Hoyt L. Baugh, a Rainsville attorney, as Bissell's legal counsel. Traylor denied bond in the case, the hearing was swiftly concluded, and the shaken witnesses wasted no time standing around outside the cell. They fled the jail and rushed up the stairs, breathing in great gulps of fresh air, thankful for their safe return to the relative calm of the crowded lobby of the sheriff's department.

Later that day, circuit judge Randall L. Cole issued a court order calling for Bissell's mental evaluation.

"The defendant who is housed in the DeKalb County Jail is presently engaging in conduct that appears to be irrational and a need exists for him to be immediately evaluated by mental health professionals," the order stated.

It was the first of many orders Judge Cole would issue in the case of the *State of Alabama* v. *Hayward W. Bissell.*

Chapter 8

"I probably need to start reading."

Early on Tuesday morning, before Bissell's performance in the jail basement, Mike James placed a call to Johnny Bass, his colleague and longtime friend, an investigator with the Lookout Mountain Judicial Circuit in Georgia. From what James had been able to gather, he believed it was likely that Bissell had murdered Patricia Booher in Bass's jurisdiction, which included Chattooga and Walker Counties in Georgia.

Bass had been away from the office on Monday due to the ice storm, but when he arrived for work at the Chattooga County Courthouse on Tuesday morning, the gruesome crime discovered just over the state line in Alabama was the primary topic of conversation. When Bass received James's call, his first question was "Hey, buddy, what in the hell have y'all got going on over there?"

James filled Bass in on the details of Sunday's events, then told him Bissell was giving information that might indicate the murder occurred somewhere across the state line into Georgia, possibly in one of the adjoining Chattooga County towns of Summerville, Trion or Lyerly.

"Just see if any of this stuff he's told us makes any sense to you," James asked Bass. "See if any of these places he's told us about sound familiar; if anything he said to us rings a bell with you."

James began to read from Bissell's account of passing by a Dollar General store, then a seeing a sign for a business with the letters *A B*, and then driving by another store that was yellow and red with a milk advertisement. Bass immediately knew exactly what areas of town Bissell was talking about.

"Just past the Dollar General store, there's a business called A & B Concrete," Bass told James, "then over on the other side of town, about fifteen minutes away, there's a Discount Food Mart store that's yellow and red, and they have some big signs out front that advertise milk."

It appeared that Bissell had quite accurately described the buildings on a section of the highway leading from Summerville into Trion and continuing on in the direction of Menlo and Cloudland, Georgia, and Mentone, Alabama. Bass and his friend Eddie Colbert, a Chattooga County sheriff's investigator, were about to be drawn into one of the strangest cases of their careers.

Later that morning, after Bissell had plenty of time to rest up from his strenuous performance during the bizarre bond hearing, he had an interesting conversation with an inmate in a nearby cell. Jailer Michael Toombs overheard some of what was said, and immediately reported the information to the investigators.

Bissell was talking to his neighboring inmate about the murder.

"I heard voices in my head, and they told me that I owned all the stores," he said of the neighborhood where he claimed the murder took place.

"We've done this before," Bissell said to the man,

without indicating who "we" were or what it was they had allegedly done.

He told the inmate there were a lot of trees and wooded areas and a great many streets in the neighborhood around the gas station where he claimed that he had killed Patricia.

When Toombs told the sheriff what he had heard and the sheriff called the investigators, James asked Toombs to approach the inmate Bissell had spoken to and ask the man if he would try to find out more about the murder site. The inmate was willing to cooperate, and a short while later, he tried to initiate another conversation with his neighbor. Bissell, however, had said all he intended to say on the subject for the time being. He spoke no further, and spent the next couple of hours lying silent and naked on the bunk in his cell.

Shortly after 1:00 P.M. on Tuesday afternoon, two agents of the U.S. Secret Service arrived at the DeKalb County Jail to conduct an interview with Hayward Bissell. They had been notified by Mike James that Bissell had repeatedly claimed to be a Secret Service agent, and they had come to question him in the hope they might be able to help investigators gain more information in the case.

"He probably won't talk to you," Bill Lands told the two agents, shaking his head. "He's not cooperating today, and he really had himself a time this morning, showing off for the judge."

Lands went on to describe Bissell's outrageous behavior and his refusal to wear clothes, and told the agents about some of the disgusting acts his officers had witnessed the prisoner committing in his cell. Lands then introduced them to Hoyt Baugh, who agreed for the two agents to talk to Bissell. Baugh warned them, however, that his client was being extremely uncooperative and would probably not respond to their questions with anything but more of his head banging and obscenities.

"I tried to speak to him earlier this morning," he said, "but he told me that he wouldn't talk to anyone but his power of attorney from Ohio, and I couldn't get him to come out from under his bunk."

"Would it be all right with you if we spoke to Mr. Bissell privately?" the agents asked, thinking Bissell might be more cooperative if his new court-appointed attorney was not in sight during the interrogation.

Baugh agreed, and the group went downstairs into the jail to attempt to interview the prisoner in his cell, hoping they would fare better than the judge and the unfortunate court officials and reporters who had preceded them earlier that day.

Bissell was lying motionless on the bed in his cell with his eyes closed, still naked, when his visitors approached. Baugh stood out of sight around the corner of the cell while the two agents spoke to the prisoner and identified themselves as Secret Service personnel.

"I don't have anything to say until after I speak to my power of attorney from Ohio," Bissell said angrily. "I won't speak to anyone else."

"We are agents of the Secret Service," they repeated, "and we have received information that you are an agent also."

Bissell opened his eyes.

"Get me some clothes," he said.

After he got dressed, Bissell became somewhat more talkative, but remained doubtful of the status of the two agents' security clearance. The agents explained that he could talk to them without jeopardizing his own security.

"It's okay to talk to your fellow agents," they assured

him. "All three of us have the same top-secret clearance."

"My clearance is higher than top secret," Bissell replied, "and I shouldn't talk to you about my secret mission."

"Tell me about your secret classification," one agent said. "Are you a Class Q or Class L?"

"I have a top-secret clearance of Q," Bissell said proudly.

Satisfied that the two agents had security clearances on the same level as his, Bissell finally began to answer their questions.

"Have you ever been in the military?" they asked.

"I was in the 102nd Quartermaster Unit, 101st ABN Division at Fort Campbell, Kentucky, from 1981 to 1983," Bissell answered. He went on to tell them about his next duty station, which he said was in Schweinfurt, Germany, with the 4th BN, 34th Armor, 3rd Armor Division, where he claimed that he helped design and field the M1 tank in 1984. His MOS, or specialty, in the army was as a fuel handler. He said he received an honorable discharge in 1984 and left the army at Fort Dix, New Jersey. He also claimed to have received his basic training in Fort Jackson, South Carolina.

One of the agents, who spent a twelve-year career in the military before joining the Secret Service, carefully questioned Bissell about his army career in an attempt to judge his thought patterns, truthfulness and knowledge. He was surprised when Bissell was able to answer his questions in detail, giving answers he could have known only if he had indeed been in the army and had been stationed in the locations he described. His answers concerning military matters were accurate and articulate, and at times he seemed to the two agents to be of above average intelligence.

After leaving the army, Bissell said, he returned

home to Norwalk, Ohio, where he told the two Secret Service agents he had functioned as the "eyes and ears" for the local police department. He later moved for a time to the adjoining town of Greenwich, Ohio, where he said he was also the "eyes and ears" for the Greenwich police.

"Tell us how you became involved with the Secret Service," the agents asked.

"It started back in the 1980s, while I was in the military," Bissell said, "and has continued since that time. It has to do with a special secret program I designed."

The program, according to Bissell, sent messages through a satellite to an implant in his head, which he said was located behind his left ear. The messages, he said, gave him instructions on what his missions were to be and when he was to have them completed.

"The program is classified," he kept repeating throughout the interview. "I can't release the details of any of my secret missions."

Bissell then claimed he had received some orders during the 1980s and had been late completing the assignment. He had been forced to go on his latest mission because he had put off finishing his earlier orders, and said that he was being disciplined. When the agents asked what his orders were, he replied, "It had to do with the assassination of a double agent."

"What has been your toughest assignment?" the agents asked.

"This last mission was pretty tough," Bissell said, "but I've been on worse assignments. This one was hard because of the personal feelings involved. I have a heart of steel, but tender insides."

Bissell said his last mission had brought him to the DeKalb County Jail and claimed that he had been to the jail previously, but he would not say what he believed had brought him to the jail in the past. He would only say that it had to do with his mission, the ordered assassination of a "double agent."

Although he referred to her repeatedly as his girlfriend, never once during the interview did Hayward Bissell speak the name of the double agent he believed he was ordered to assassinate, Patricia Ann Booher.

The two agents had no trouble encouraging Hayward Bissell to talk about his girlfriend, their engagement and the trip they had supposedly been making to Winter Haven, Florida, to visit his parents. According to Bissell, he and Patricia had discussed possibly ending their engagement on several occasions before the trip, and she told him that if they broke off their engagement, she did not want to keep the ring he had given her. He told the agents about a conversation he and Patricia had regarding her engagement ring:

"What would you do with the ring if I gave it back?" she had asked him. "You'd probably buy a gun, wouldn't you?"

"Yeah, maybe I will," he told her.

Bissell then told the agents he had suspicions at that time about his girlfriend being a double agent, but it was not until they set out from Ohio on the way to Florida that he received two different signals through his secret program, satellite and implant about the assassination of the double agent. He said he finally realized who the double agent was, and he knew from that point that he had no choice but to kill her.

"I confirmed the identity of the double agent based on a single question I asked her," Bissell said. "After I received the final signal, I didn't know which direction to take. I drove about a mile away from a gas station in Georgia and stopped in the middle of the road. At that point, I had to make a decision about which block to choose." Bissell motioned with his hands, indicating left or right.

"I asked my girlfriend which block she thought, and she picked the wrong block," he said. "I knew from that point she was indeed the double agent and my mission was to assassinate her. I knew it had to be done immediately, because I had put off a mission from a long time ago, and this mission was my disciplinary punishment for failure to complete the earlier one."

Bissell continued to claim this particular assignment had not been his toughest mission, although this one was sensitive and his personal involvement made it tough for him.

"I've conducted harder missions," he said.

The interview with the two Secret Service agents lasted around forty-five minutes, and produced far more information than the previous attempts to question Bissell, most likely because of the rapport he developed with his "fellow Secret Service agents." But a great deal of the interrogation consisted of Bissell's rambling tales of secret missions and satellites. In her official report concerning the interview, one of the agents described him as being "very inconsistent with his thought pattern, jumping from one topic of discussion to another. He repeatedly went off on tangents throughout the entire interview, and continuously referred to 'implants' and receiving 'signals' in reference to his missions. Bissell would always point to his head, directly behind his left ear, when he spoke of 'implants' and 'signals.'"

At the conclusion of the interview, one of the agents asked Bissell if he owned or used a computer.

"No, I don't have access to one," he answered.

"How about movies; have you seen any that interested you lately?"

"Not really."

"Do you do much reading? Are there any books you're interested in?" the agent asked.

"No," Bissell said. "I don't read very much." He shifted position on the narrow bunk in his cell and looked around at the flooded floors and the wreckage of broken pipes and plumbing fixtures surrounding him.

"I guess I probably need to start reading," he said.

Chapter 9

"He is absolutely, certifiably crazy as hell."

Hayward Bissell's court-appointed attorney was as relieved as Sheriff Reed and the county jail's staff when Judge Randall Cole ordered Bissell transferred to the Taylor Hardin Secure Medical Facility in Tuscaloosa, Alabama, for mental evaluation. At the request of the sheriff, Cole ordered the transfer because of Bissell's extremely disruptive behavior in the jail and his destruction of the pipes, plumbing and other fixtures in his cell. It was determined to be in everyone's best interest to get Bissell into the institution as quickly as possible. A court order was hurriedly prepared on Tuesday afternoon, and preparations were begun to transfer Bissell from the county jail to Tuscaloosa.

"He is absolutely, certifiably crazy as hell," said Hoyt Baugh. During his years as a defense attorney, Baugh had worked a number of capital cases before, but none of them had been even remotely similar to the one he had been handed this time.

Baugh spoke to local newspapers about his newest client, who waited to be transferred for evaluation.

"This will be an easy case to prove," Baugh said.

"Somebody dropped the ball not to keep him locked up. He's been in mental hospitals before, and the doctors knew he was mentally ill. In talking to family members, he's had these problems for some time. He is absolutely crazy, and his activity in jail is so bizarre."

Baugh said that since he had been appointed to represent Bissell, he'd had four visits with his client, and most of them hadn't been very productive.

"He was very reluctant to speak with me until he got 'clearance' from those who could do so. He said he couldn't talk to the officers because they didn't have high-enough clearance for them to talk to him."

Bissell's Lincoln Town Car had been loaded onto a trailer and hauled to the state forensic science laboratory in Huntsville, Alabama, on Wednesday. A complete processing of the vehicle for evidence would take place there, since the car was believed to be the actual crime scene where the murder of Patricia Booher had been committed. Investigators also believed the car might bear some additional physical evidence of the assaults on Donald Pirch and James Pumphrey.

The car had been stored inside a locked storage lot at the county road department headquarters since its Sunday impoundment, and the workers there were glad to see it taken away, even if for a short time.

"That thing gave us the heebie-jeebies sitting out there in the lot," one road department worker said. "Every time I drove past it and looked at it, I thought about what they say happened in it."

By Thursday, January 27, 2000, all preparations were in place, and the carefully planned transfer of Hayward Bissell to Tuscaloosa for mental evaluation was ready to begin.

Sheriff Reed held an early meeting with waiting reporters and told them that Bissell had calmed down some since his arrest. He had stopped banging his head on the wall of his cell, but he still refused to wear clothing. The plumbing had long since been completely torn out of his cell, but he continued screaming a lot and refused to carry on a conversation with jailers.

"He never talks to us; he talks to himself," Reed said.

Plans had been made for the transfer to take place under heavy guard because of Bissell's unpredictable behavior, and Sheriff James Hayes of neighboring Etowah County loaned Reed a heavily reinforced transport van, two of his specially trained officers and a large Plexiglas shock shield, used in riot control and in dealing with out-of-control inmates. If that was not enough to handle the prisoner, Reed told the reporters, his deputies planned to wrestle physically with Bissell if necessary to get him from his jail cell into the transport van.

When everything was in place for the transfer to begin, deputies went to Bissell's cell and told him he was going to the doctor, and said that he needed to get up and get dressed. When he acted as if he didn't understand, one of the officers explained to him in detail exactly what the consequences were going to be if he attempted to assault any of them during the process of transporting him.

The shock shield proved to be sufficient incentive for Bissell to control his behavior after he was given a demonstration of its function, according to the sheriff.

"The shield kept him under control," Reed said. "It is held against the body and has electric current if needed to keep the subject under control. The shield can handle anybody. Mr. Bissell was in pretty good condition this morning. He wasn't dressed, but he put his pants on. We had to put on his shirt."

Once again, Bissell had to wear leg irons as handcuffs on his huge wrists, and the deputies fashioned a set of leg restraints out of several pairs of plastic flex-cuffs, since standard leg irons were far too small to fit.

Reed said Bissell had been told he was being taken to the doctor, and said he was being fairly cooperative compared to his previous behavior in the jail.

"I asked him how he was doing, and got a few answers," Reed said. "He has made several statements to our investigators concerning his crimes, but nothing that I'd call a solid confession. He doesn't appear to have any remorse."

A large crowd of cameramen and reporters were waiting in the parking lot outside the back entrance of the county jail when Hayward Bissell was escorted out of the building by Mike James and the Etowah County officers. Dozens of other deputies and jailers stood close by as the group left the building and headed toward the transport van. Bissell wore a pair of white jail-issue pants and a white T-shirt, the largest one deputies could find at the local Wal-Mart. It still wouldn't stretch to cover his massive stomach.

James steered Bissell across the parking lot toward the van, keeping a tight hold on the prisoner's right arm, with one of the Etowah County deputies gripping his left arm and another deputy following close behind holding the shock shield at the ready.

Bissell remained silent, offering no resistance but staring at the crowd of reporters gathered to get a photo of the man who was making headlines nationwide. He only spoke once when officers were loading him into the van. He was attempting to step up into the van and was in an awkward position and unable to duck his head low enough to clear the van door.

"Wait a minute. . . . Wait a minute," he said, trying to pull his head inside the vehicle.

Once inside the van, the prisoner lay down in the seat with his eyes closed and ignored the dozens of flashes from the cameras of photographers gathered outside the van. Reporters, who had hesitated to come close enough to get within Bissell's reach while he was being escorted out of the jail, now crowded up against the van windows, peering through the thick glass and heavy steel bars to get a better look at the huge man.

Taylor Hardin Secure Medical Facility, which only takes mentally disturbed patients who have been involved in felonies, would have custody of Hayward Bissell until such time as he was determined to be ready to be returned to the jail and able to stand trial, Reed said, then he would be transferred back to DeKalb County.

His return, however, would be something that jail personnel would not be looking forward to.

"He needs to be transferred to a facility for people in his condition," Reed told reporters. "I have dealt with people with some of the same problems he has, but never one who was charged with that kind of crime. We have had some pretty bad crimes here, but never one with body parts cut off, chopped away from the body. It was terrible."

Reed said the results of a preliminary autopsy indicated any one of Booher's many severe wounds could have caused her death. The coroner had found that her eyes, previously believed to be missing, had been, instead, forced back into her skull but were still present. She was believed to have been murdered inside the car, but the sheriff said jurisdiction in the case could not be determined and murder charges could not be filed against Bissell until authorities determined whether the car was located in Alabama or Georgia at the time the murder was committed.

Even as Bissell was being loaded into the transport

van, work was beginning downstairs to clean up the jail and restore it to normal operating conditions. Several inmates volunteered to work on the plumbing fixtures and pipes while others continued to mop floors and hallways. The men were anxious to clean up their cells and dry out their damp bedding. And visitation, suspended during Bissell's stay, would return to its normal schedule on Saturday afternoon.

As the reinforced van pulled out of the parking lot at the rear of the jail, a county officer watched as the van drove uphill beside the courthouse and out of sight, carrying Hayward Bissell to Tuscaloosa and out of the county for an undetermined period of time. Then the deputy summed up the feelings of the entire sheriff's department.

"Good riddance," the officer said.

Shortly after Bissell left on his way to Taylor Hardin, Sheriff Reed and Investigators Mike James and Clay Simpson headed for a meeting they had scheduled with Chattooga County, Georgia, authorities to try and determine the jurisdiction of the homicide case. Bissell had been charged in DeKalb County with two counts of attempted murder and one count of first-degree attempted burglary, and Reed said "good progress" was being made in Georgia with investigation into the case there.

"We have contacted people in Georgia we needed to interview," Reed said, adding that the media coverage had proved to be very helpful by causing several individuals with useful information to come forward.

The meeting in Georgia proved to be a disappointment to DeKalb County authorities, however, since no decision of jurisdiction was announced at its conclusion. A great deal of wrangling back and forth was taking place between the two district attorneys' offices about the legal technicalities of determining jurisdiction, and while the meeting on that subject was taking place, the investigators from both counties stepped down the hallway for a meeting of their own.

"We all took a walk down the hall, and we decided that working this case couldn't wait until it was determined whose jurisdiction it would eventually be," Johnny Bass said.

"We all decided to go ahead and get on it before any valuable evidence might be lost, like any blood evidence that might be in the parking lot or in other locations. If anyone waited around to see whose case it might turn out to be, we'd be sure to lose a lot of important evidence. We decided we weren't going to let that happen."

After spending the day with Chattooga County officials, Sheriff Reed declined to make very many comments about the status of the case, saying that any statements concerning jurisdiction would have to be issued by Chattooga County sheriff Ralph Kellett or Chattooga County district attorney Herbert "Buzz" Franklin.

This prompted speculation that Bissell would be charged in Georgia with murder, but Sheriff Kellett also declined to make a statement to that effect.

"We're still investigating the case and following reports and leads," Kellett told the press, "and Sheriff Reed and his staff are being a great help. I don't want to speak for Mr. Franklin, but I feel he'll be very open with information when the time comes for an announcement. He's very concerned with this case."

Kellett did confirm, however, that Georgia State crime scene technicians spent most of the day in Chattooga County on Thursday, working on an area at a graveled convenience store parking lot in Trion, Georgia, in search of evidence. Bass had asked them to come, even though they seemed reluctant at first.

"What type of evidence is it we're supposed to be looking for?" Bass was asked.

"We aren't sure, but can you please just come and look?" he replied.

The technicians came to the Discount Food Mart parking lot on what was without a doubt one of the coldest days of the year, Bass said, and searched the area without being sure of what they were looking for or where it might be found. The scene, Kellett told the press, had been contaminated by weather conditions and by vehicles driving through the lot. However, several rust-colored spots were found on the ground where the Lincoln was believed to have been parked, and preliminary tests run at the scene determined the spots were human blood. Samples were taken to the state crime laboratory to compare them with Booher's blood.

"No findings from that search are available yet, but once something starts developing, we'll make an announcement from my office or from the district attorney's office."

Kellett also said Bissell's car was seen stopped on a county road near Summerville, Georgia, on Sunday morning, and a witness who came forward after seeing press coverage of the murder claimed she saw both Bissell and Booher inside.

"The car was stopped in the street in front of her home," Kellett said. "She noticed the road was blocked with fallen trees; then she noticed the car had Ohio tags. The woman in the car was alive at that time."

Authorities would soon find out that quite a few other people in Northwest Georgia noticed the Lincoln Town Car with Ohio tags that Sunday. As word spread about the murder, more and more witnesses contacted the investigators to come forward and say that they, too, had seen the car in their neighborhoods. Those people later learned they were among the last to see Patricia Booher alive on the final day of her life.

Chapter 10

"Dispel the ugliness and restore it with honor."

Despite the fact that Hayward Bissell had been transferred out of the county jail to a state secure mental facility for evaluation, his terrible crimes continued to be one of the primary topics of conversation in the Southeast and much of Ohio.

In DeKalb County, Patricia Booher's murder made continuing headlines, overshadowing the ice storm that knocked out electrical service to fifty thousand people for several days. The Fort Payne *Times-Journal*'s newspaper racks sold completely out day after day, due to titillating headlines such as VICTIM'S EYES FOUND, and the paper's managing editor, Patrick Graham, published a continuous update of the case from day to day. Graham, a young family man devoted to his wife and little daughters, was as horrified as his readers by Hayward Bissell's crimes, but he was also an astute businessman with a keen sense of what makes newspapers sell. He knew that those readers could hardly wait to get their hands on the paper each day to find out the latest gruesome developments in the story.

The paper's on-line edition featured the Bissell coverage and photos on its Web site; it saw its average hits jump from 63,000 per month to 92,500 hits during the month of January 2000.

E-mail poured into the newspaper from around the nation, with inquiries about the case coming from California, North Carolina and Texas, plus Bissell and Booher's home state of Ohio. True crime Web rings and Internet chat rooms with members around the world carried updates on the case daily.

Five days following Bissell's arrest, one true crime fan posted his version of the information he had learned on-line, passing along a colorful but somewhat inaccurate account of the case. Referring to Bissell as a "400-pound nutcase," who had gone on a killing rampage in Alabama, the fan told of Patricia Booher's murder and the subsequent assaults on Don Pirch and James Pumphrey. "He dragged some guy with his truck," the fan claimed, "then down the road he stabbed another man to death, along with his two Labradors." Thankfully, this was not the case, for James Pumphrey had not died of his injuries.

The true crime fan went on to describe Booher's mutilation in graphic detail and told of Bissell's claim to be a member of the Secret Service and his belief that his girlfriend was a double agent. In closing, the fan added that Bissell was said to be severely paranoid and was hearing voices. Although the posting was not entirely accurate with all of its information, the message garnered quite a few responses and comments on the case from on-line readers.

Others who learned of the Bissell case via the Internet were not at all hesitant to voice their opinions when they contacted the *Times-Journal* to comment on the story.

"You guys fry 'em down in Alabama, right? Send me a plane ticket; I'll pull the switch on that scum," said one man from Bissell's home state of Ohio.

Several Ohio newspapers relied on the *Times-Journal* for background information on the crime, since the case was big news for many northern Ohio communities. They called Graham with requests for stories and photos, contact names and numbers, and countless other pieces of information it would have been hard for them to obtain at such a distance. Graham reciprocated by exchanging stories with the newspapers about the developments on the case in Ohio, receiving a steady stream of articles from the Ohio papers with valuable background information on both Bissell and Booher. The *National Enquirer* also covered the story, calling the Fort Payne newspaper several times for information and photos. The *Enquirer* ran a full-page article on the case in its "Crime Story" section titled CORPSE TAKES A RIDE IN MADMAN'S TRAIL OF TERROR in its April 4, 2000, edition.

Hayward Bissell's crime spree was big news, but the real heart of the story was the tragedy of Patricia Booher's violent and untimely death. As more and more details began to emerge about the couple, their relationship and their backgrounds, the loss of the innocent and trusting young woman described so often as a "real sweetheart" was felt by countless people, many of whom mourned her death even though they never knew her in life.

On Friday, January 28, funeral services were held for Patricia at the Kubach-Smith Funeral Home in Norwalk, Ohio. The open casket served as a testimony to the remarkable mortuary skills of the Kubach-Smith staff, and had been suggested by the Reverend Paul Lamb, pastor of Patricia's church, the First Baptist Church of Norwalk. Reverend Lamb felt that an open casket might help to dispel some of the gruesome images left in the minds of friends and family by the detailed press coverage of Patricia's mutilation, and his intuition proved to be right. Kubach-Smith had worked miracles.

"Our purpose today is to dispel the ugliness and restore it with honor," Lamb told the large crowd assembled in the funeral home's chapel for the funeral.

"Patty is experiencing no grief. She is not scared. I don't think that Patty had to suffer for long because God took her right away."

Patricia had joined the church a year earlier, and Lamb said she "immediately became a part of that group of people who love her," enthusiastically attending potluck dinners and other church activities.

Countless other close friends, such as Linda Rogers, attended Patricia's funeral and mourned her loss along with family and church members. At the funeral service, Rogers read a poem she had written as a touching tribute to Patricia. It was titled "You're Welcome," because of Patricia's habit of always responding with those words when anyone said "Thank you" to her.

In her poem, Rogers described Patricia as always having a smile on her face, a peaceful, gentle nature and a friendly hello for everyone each day. She never forgot her manners, Rogers said, and was always very sincere.

"If you asked me today what I remember most about Patty," she said, "it would be the way she always said, 'You're welcome.'"

Rogers told those at the funeral that if Patty were still here today and she could thank her for touching her life, she was sure she would hear her say, "You're welcome."

Rogers said she knew now why those words seemed to stand out, because she knew that Patty was welcome to enter into Heaven and to share a home with the angels. And when God said to Patty, "Thank you, Patty, for coming home," Rogers said she was sure Patty said, "You're welcome."

The large crowd of mourners at the funeral were very touched by the poem, for they all remembered Patty's courtesy and consideration. On many occasions, they, too, had been told "You're welcome" by the young woman who was being laid to rest that day.

Rogers also recounted to those in attendance at the funeral just how much the young woman was liked by the other residents in the apartment complex where she lived.

"She was a real sweetheart," Rogers said. "She made many friends, and many people cared about her very much."

During the service, Reverend Lamb urged those in attendance to make a Christian effort to rise above their hatred for the man who had taken Patricia Booher's life in such a horrific manner.

"Folks, we're going to have to learn to forgive," Lamb said. "Many have come here and we're angry, and we wish things that aren't that good for the person who did this to her. We have to put those things aside."

As the mourners filed out of the funeral home into the bright sunshine on Friday afternoon at the end of the forty-minute service, they remembered the girl whose greatest wish was to be happy and to have friends. There were not many people in Patricia's immediate family; her obituary listed her survivors as her sister, Charlene Booher of Norwalk, Ohio, her father, Vernon Booher of London, Ohio, her mother, Jan Ewers of Springfield, Ohio, and a special aunt, Betty Booher of Clarksfield, Ohio.

But countless other people had fond memories of Patricia, and they spoke of her to the press in the days following her murder.

Charla McAbier was Patricia's tutor at EHOVE (Erie, Huron, Ottowa Vocational Education) Career Center, where Patricia studied general merchandising and was involved in the Distributive Education Clubs of America.

"It really upsets me," McAbier said. "I just envision this sweet girl in my mind, and I keep remembering how she was when she was here—a sweet, petite, likable, happy girl. She always seemed to have a smile on her face, and her eyes seemed to dance when she walked into a room. It's just devastating to think of what she had to go through."

McAbier described Patricia as being somewhat shy, trusting and a little naive, but said that once she became comfortable in EHOVE's general-merchandising program, she gained a great deal of self-confidence and became more outgoing.

"You could just tell it was for her," McAbier told reporters from the *Norwalk Reflector.* "We really saw changes in her. We felt really confident she was going to be successful. She loved to please people. If you gave her any positives, she would just gleam. Everyone just really liked Patty."

Her teachers at Western Reserve High School, where Patricia graduated in 1994, also remembered her as being well liked.

"She was a very sweet girl, a very hard worker who never gave up," Elizabeth Kolenko, her former English teacher, told the *Reflector.*

"Everyone was shocked, especially since she was such a pleasant child. This is very hard for everyone."

Janice Timman was Patricia's friend, and Timman's mother lived in the same apartment complex as Patricia and Hayward Bissell. Timman said Patty was a person who was very easy to get along with, someone who got a great deal of pleasure from even the smallest things in life.

"If you didn't like Patty, you didn't like yourself," Timman said.

Charlene Booher, Patricia's sister and closest relative, had talked to Patricia on Thursday, when Patricia broke the news that she was five weeks pregnant with Hayward Bissell's child. According to her sister, Patricia was thrilled about the pregnancy, and she told Charlene that Bissell was "happy about it," but did not mention that she had any plans to go on a trip to Florida with him that weekend.

"That wasn't like her, not to tell me if she had plans," Charlene said. "I don't think she went with him of her own free will."

Charlene said her sister was really fond of Bissell, "but no one knew he was a psycho and had problems. Unfortunately, she found out a little late. She was a good person. She was really trusting. I hope other people can learn something from this. Be careful and not so trusting."

"It's a shame this happened to Patty," Hayward Bissell's ex-brother-in-law, Leonard Brown, told the *Sandusky Register.* "She was a very nice girl. She was shy. I don't know what the hell ever gave him that idea. I just wish this wouldn't have happened, that's all."

After Patricia Ann Booher's funeral, her mourners left the Kubach-Smith Funeral Home parking lot and the nearby Norwalk Masonic Temple parking area in a twenty-seven-car procession. They drove twelve miles to the Clarksfield Cemetery in Clarksfield Township, and following a ten-minute graveside service, Patricia was laid to rest.

At the same time his victim's funeral was taking place in Ohio, Hayward Bissell was being processed into Taylor Hardin Secure Medical Facility in

Tuscaloosa, Alabama, and authorities were searching through a graveled parking lot in Trion, Georgia, for evidence. Investigators reviewed the security tapes made on the previous Sunday at the Discount Food Mart adjoining the parking lot, and the films showed that both Bissell and Patricia were inside the store at 2:30 P.M. on the afternoon of January 23.

Only moments after the convenience store's cameras captured the final images of Patricia, her life ended horribly inside Hayward Bissell's Lincoln Town Car as it sat parked in the graveled lot. The people in attendance at her funeral less than a week later would be left to question how such a terrible thing could have happened to the sweet, trusting young woman they loved. But their questions could only be answered by a man with no answers to give; a man who sat, mute and motionless, locked inside a security cell under a twenty-four-hour watch.

Chapter 11

"He griped as a child, and he griped as an adult."

Hayward William Bissell was born on March 28, 1962, the second son of Howard L. and Magdalina Bissell. He had a brother one year older, another brother who was four years younger, and a half brother who was Magdalina's son from a previous marriage.

Howard L. Bissell served in the U.S. Army for nineteen years before settling in Ohio. He went to work at the Sandusky, Ohio, Ford plant and the family lived in nearby New London.

According to relatives, young Hayward was a constant complainer, a child who could never be satisfied.

"He was always griping," a family member told authorities after his arrest for murder. "He griped as a child, and he griped as an adult."

Bissell resented authority when he was growing up, the relative said, and never agreed with anything his father said. He always had behavioral problems at home and at school because he never wanted to obey. He did not want to do things that did not interest him, and he did not like to work.

"He abhors work and avoids working," a family member said.

Another relative said the boy had a couple of minor accidents as a child that might have resulted in concussions, and on one occasion Hayward told family members he had gotten down on his knees and saw a bright light. The relative later speculated to investigators about whether that incident might have been an early indication of the young boy's mental problems to come.

Hayward Bissell attended New London Elementary School and Fairfield High School, where he was an A, B and C student. Bissell later told mental-health counselors that he had fought frequently when he was in school but said that he was never expelled or suspended. He dropped out of school after the tenth grade, and psychiatric-treatment records from his later years speculated that his leaving school might have been partly due to his use of illegal drugs and alcohol, which allegedly began at age fifteen.

Howard L. Bissell retired in the late 1980s, and a decade later he and Magdalina moved to Winter Haven, Florida, along with their youngest son. They bought a home near the ballpark where the Cleveland Indians held their spring training, and Howard enjoyed going to the park to watch the team's workouts.

The Bissells' oldest son spent several years in the army and settled in Hawaii, and family members said he and Hayward seemed not to be particularly close and seldom kept in touch.

When his parents moved to Florida, Hayward remained in Ohio. He lived in Greenwich, a small town fifteen miles south of Norwalk, for several years. During that time, he was in and out of quite a few clinics and veterans hospitals, where he was treated for depression, suicidal thoughts and other psychological problems. His aunt, Kathleen "Kitty" Carnahan, of North Fairfield, Ohio, served as his power of attorney.

As his closest relative who still lived in the area, she had the unpleasant chore of having to deal with most of his episodes of aberrant behavior.

These episodes, however, did not start while Hayward was in the U.S. Army. By all accounts, his military career was quite successful and remained a lasting source of pride to him after he was discharged from service.

Hayward enlisted in the army in Cleveland, Ohio, on August 29, 1979. He was trained as a motor transport operator and qualified as expert on the M-16 rifle. He spent most of his enlistment stationed in Germany and received two Army Achievement Medals (AAM), the first in August of 1982 for outstanding performance in the support of M1 tanks during the Marne Team Battle exercise held in Germany:

"Specialist Four Bissell's ability to perform operator maintenance, operate the fueling system on his vehicle and drive his vehicle under strenuous and adverse conditions were instrumental in the accomplishment of this unit's mission," the commendation certificate reads. "His actions reflect distinct credit upon himself, his unit, and the Marne Division."

Bissell's other Army Achievement Medal, awarded in December 1982, was given for exceptionally meritorious service while assigned as a driver supporting the 3rd Battalion, 64th Armor:

"Specialist Four Bissell provided effective fuel support for the Battalion during numerous training exercises. He maintained his vehicle exceptionally well. It could always be relied upon whenever a support requirement developed. Specialist Four Bissell maintained an unblemished driving record with 2500 accident-free miles of operation. His knowledge, enthusiasm and desire to excel serve as an example for others to follow. Specialist Four Bissell's actions reflect distinct credit upon himself, his unit and the United States Army."

Earlier, Hayward had been cited by the commander of his battalion for meritorious performance of duty from December 1979 through August 1981:

"During this period, while assigned to the 102nd Quartermaster Company, he excelled in his performance of duties as a Heavy Vehicle Operator and was responsible for the timely delivery of aviation fuels to the 101st Airborne Division (Air Assault) and supported units. His devotion to duty reflects great credit upon himself, the 102nd Quartermaster Company and the United States Army."

Clearly, Hayward Bissell had found a comfortable niche in life, at least for the time he spent in military service. He found the regimented lifestyle satisfying, and he enjoyed his duties. It was after his honorable discharge in August 1985 that things began to fall apart.

Following his successful enlistment in the military, Hayward Bissell worked as a security guard in Toledo, Ohio, and in Norwalk at the Fanny Farmer candy factory and at McDonald's on Milan Avenue. He later lived on Social Security disability due to his continuing problems with depression and a bad back.

On October 11, 1985, Hayward Bissell married his first wife, Sherry Jane Brown. They had a little girl named Crystal. Their marriage was relatively uneventful at first, but things between them began to go downhill when Hayward became more and more threatening toward his wife during their increasingly frequent arguments. He began getting treatment for psychiatric illnesses during the first year of the marriage.

On January 29, 1989, when the couple lived on Chestnut Street in Norwalk, Sherry Bissell was assaulted by her husband and filed domestic violence charges against him. In the affidavit she gave to the Norwalk Police Department later that same day, she claimed an argument had started in the early afternoon in the kitchen of their home. Hayward slapped her, she said, knocking her into the refrigerator, and then told her to go into the bedroom. He followed her, yelling at her and threatening to drive her crazy so he could have her put away. He then pressed his fist against her face, Sherry claimed, and said he would put it through her head.

"He slapped me and I started to scream," Sherry said in the affidavit, "then he pushed me up against the wall and hit both sides of my head. I got in the shower and told him to leave me alone, and he slapped me again on the side of the head and banged my head against the shower and knocked me down."

Bissell walked away but stopped, turned around and asked his wife if she was okay. He told their daughter, Crystal, then four years old, that her mother had fallen in the shower.

"He threatened to take Crystal away and have me put away," Sherry told the police. She also said Bissell told her if he was put in jail, he would get out and make her life miserable. Sherry waited until Bissell left the house to visit a friend; then she called the police to report the incident. Officers went to investigate, and Sherry asked them to follow her to her mother's home, where she dropped off Crystal and came to the police station to press charges against her husband.

Sherry Bissell began divorce proceedings against Hayward following the assault, but the situation remained volatile. On March 20, Sherry was at the police station again after Hayward had an encounter with her brother, Leonard Brown.

According to Sherry's statement, Hayward told

Leonard, "I can't understand, after so many years of loving her, why she wants to divorce me."

Sherry told police that her brother asked Hayward not to talk to him about the couple's problems anymore, but Hayward was on a roll and he intended to have his say, whether Leonard wanted to hear it or not.

"He told Leonard that he thinks I'm having relations with my girlfriend and that if I keep fucking with him, paybacks are a bitch," Sherry's affidavit said. "He said he'd have that kid one way or another taken away, and if not, he will live on welfare and I can ram the twenty-dollars-a-month support check up my ass."

Sherry said Bissell had not otherwise bothered her in any way since her last court hearing, and had not threatened her to anyone other than her brother.

"I just want this reported in case something happens," she told the police.

At the request of the officers, Leonard Brown came to the station later that same day to file his statement.

"I don't want Hayward bothering me no more about the divorce," he told them.

Brown's affidavit recounted the threats Bissell had made to him regarding Sherry, his sister, adding that Bissell said he could have the court take custody of Crystal.

"Also Hayward is telling people in front of me and to me that Sherry is gay and she left him for another woman, which I can say she's not," Brown's statement read.

"I tried to tell him a couple of weeks ago that I didn't want to hear it anymore and that he shouldn't be running my sister down in front of me. Hayward also told me at that time that if I didn't shut up, he will beat my brains out and there will be nothing left in my head."

When officers asked Brown if he thought Bissell would try to do anything to Sherry, he said he didn't think he would hurt her, but he believed that Bissell would try to get even with her in some way. Leonard later would tell police that while Hayward was married to Sherry, he threatened to "cut her up into little pieces and feed her to her own mother."

After this incident, the divorce proceeded uneventfully and was granted on March 29, 1989. Sherry retained custody of the couple's young daughter, with visitation rights granted to Bissell. On April 12, the couple filed an agreement allowing Hayward visitation with the little girl on alternate weekends and holidays. Matters between the two seemed, at least temporarily, to be settled.

There were indications of plenty of other problems on the horizon, however. Hayward Bissell evidently had a lot of pent-up rage to vent, and he began to be involved in a series of bizarre incidents of assault, harassment and aberrant behavior that would steadily increase over the next several years.

These incidents would result in Bissell's numerous hospital and clinic admissions in at least nine different institutions throughout the region, but very few of the dozens of medical and psychological professionals who treated him would ever compare notes and realize the extent of Bissell's behavior problems. He usually came to the facilities, checked himself in voluntarily, then checked himself back out within a day or two. Since his admission had been voluntary, the staff could not prevent his leaving—whether or not they thought he should do so.

"There's nothing we can do to keep him here, since he came in of his own free will," one doctor told Bissell's worried relatives.

On July 5, 1989, a Norwalk woman came to the police station to report that her 1985 Ford pickup truck had been damaged while it was parked downtown. There had been a fight involving Hayward Bissell and another unidentified man, she said, which was witnessed by a friend of hers who saw the right front fender and hood of her truck damaged during the fight. Bissell, she said, had told her he would be responsible for taking care of the damage.

Bissell also had problems with one of his landlords, who reported to police in December 1991 that he had received some frightening threats from his unruly tenant.

The landlord said Bissell came into his office at the Dreamland Motel and threatened to cut the man's mail into small pieces because Bissell believed his own mail was being returned to the post office. The man then called his wife into the office in order to have a witness to his angry tenant's threats.

Bissell told the couple, "I don't like people from foreign countries. I'm going to kill one of them when it gets dark. I'm going to hurt somebody, them or their children."

This statement naturally alarmed the landlord, a man of Eastern European extraction.

Bissell then said he wasn't going to pay the rent so the landlord "could see how it feels."

"Me and my family, we're afraid of him," the worried man told the police. "He is a big fellow."

In June 1991, Bissell married Teresa Goble. They, too, had a daughter, Brittany. They separated after a few years, but had not gotten divorced by the time he began seeing Patricia Booher. Bissell's relatives told investigators there was also a history of domestic violence in his second marriage, but there was no documentation of any such charges because no incidents of abuse were ever reported to the police.

Teresa Bissell denied she had ever been afraid of Hayward during their time together; they had arguments, she said, and he made threats, but she said she wasn't scared of him. They broke up, she said, because Bissell got to where he never wanted to go out. While they were together, she said, he didn't keep guns or knives. He was very particular about putting things where they belonged, and she said he did a lot of the housecleaning because he wanted it done his way. He did smoke pot a few times while they were living together, Teresa said.

Hayward Bissell came to the Norwalk Police Station in February 1992 after he noticed a mark on his daughter Crystal's neck when he picked her up for their regular visit. When he asked her about it, Crystal told him her brother pinched her; however, she later said her mother grabbed her, causing the mark. Bissell reported the incident to the police, telling them he believed Crystal was living in a poor environment, with his ex-wife and her boyfriend fighting and arguing in front of the child. Crystal had told him, he said, that her mother's boyfriend had hit her mother in the face several times in the past, and Bissell said he feared that Crystal might have been struck by her mother.

Crystal told her father that Sherry did not hit her often, but had struck her one time on the bottom after grabbing her by the neck and leaving the red mark Bissell had noticed. Bissell asked the police to make a report of his complaint to Children's Services so that they would be aware of his concern about his ex-wife and her boyfriend fighting in front of Crystal. However, he also told the officers he believed that Crystal was otherwise well taken care of.

Hayward Bissell was hospitalized frequently in several different facilities over the following years, with the diagnosis usually listed as paranoid schizophrenia.

During a clinic visit in 1997, he reported to the counselor that he believed his apartment was bugged and had cameras hidden inside. He told doctors he had been given truth serum in a shot and in candy, claimed that he was hearing voices inside his head, and said that various people in the community were out to get him.

In February 1998, during a hospital stay after he reported that he was having problems with depression and suicidal thoughts, he told his doctors that the people in town "spilled blood all over the roads." He claimed that his alarm clock and his mind were being controlled by satellites, and said that certain people in town were trying to bite off his penis.

Greenwich, Ohio, is a small village located a short distance from Norwalk, and with only around fifteen hundred residents within its corporation area, many of those people become acquainted with one another. During the time that Hayward Bissell lived in Greenwich, the other residents could hardly keep from noticing the huge man who so often behaved in a strange manner.

Greenwich police chief Randall Kilgore was in a grocery store near his office on November 17, 1998, when Hayward Bissell came into the store and began staring at him. The chief, who had previously dealt with the big man during some of his episodes of bizarre behavior, nodded at him, but Bissell didn't respond except to keep on staring at him in a rather challenging manner. Kilgore decided that he would force the issue, so he walked up to Bissell and spoke.

"Good morning, Hayward, how you doing?"

Bissell didn't respond, except to keep staring at the chief. Kilgore decided his best move would be to go on to his office without trying for any further reaction.

Around ten minutes after Kilgore settled in behind his desk, Bissell came into his office and sat down.

"What can I do for you, Hayward?" a surprised Kilgore asked.

"Something evil has ahold of me," Bissell answered.

Kilgore asked his visitor just what kind of evil thing it was that he believed had hold of him, but Bissell stood up and said, "It's confidential."

Just as the big man started to leave Kilgore's office, the mayor of Greenwich burst into the room and confronted him.

"What were you doing sitting in my car?" the mayor asked Bissell angrily.

It seemed that the mayor had just bought a fine new Lincoln Town Car and had parked it near the grocery store. When Bissell came out of the store and saw the shiny new car sitting there, he walked over, got in and sat down, and started checking out the vehicle's plush interior. He had always had a preference for big cars, and the temptation to get into this one, brand-spanking-new, with all the available options, was just too great to overcome.

The mayor was furious.

"What do you want me to do, apologize?" Bissell asked. "Okay, then, I apologize. I'm sorry I got in the car; I shouldn't have done that."

Kilgore said that Bissell's apology seemed to be sincere, and it apparently pacified the disgruntled mayor. Satisfied that his new car wouldn't get invaded again, he left the police chief's office.

Kilgore then asked Bissell once again to tell him how he could help him, but Bissell still wouldn't elaborate about whatever "evil" thing he believed had hold of him.

"I can't help you unless you'll talk to me about it, Hayward," the chief said.

"I can't tell you; it's confidential," Bissell said once again; then he got up and walked out of the office without another word.

Kilgore later found out that soon after the incident in his office, Bissell had voluntarily checked himself into a mental institution, then checked himself back out a short time later. He sent out an Officer Safety Alert memo to all the men in the Greenwich Police Department, which read:

"On Tuesday, November 17, I talked with Mr. Hayward Bissell. He stated that something evil had gotten ahold of him. He was very incoherent at the time of my conversation with him. I have since learned that he checked himself into a mental facility and checked himself out the next day.

"I understand that he may be under the influence of nonprescription drugs. Approach him with caution if you have to deal with him."

In December, Bissell told psychiatrists, "A banshee is beaming thoughts into my head." This might have been the evil something that he believed "had ahold" of him when he visited Kilgore, but Investigator Bass speculated that Bissell's real reason for going to see Kilgore was because he knew he was about to get in trouble for getting into the mayor's new car.

"He went on to Kilgore's office and started talking like he did about something evil possessing him, and he did it before the mayor had time to get there and complain to Kilgore about him getting into the car," Bass said. "This follows his pattern of using his supposed mental problems to get himself out of trouble."

An incident occurred on Christmas Day, 1998, that bore some eerie similarities to the events surrounding Patricia Booher's murder. That evening, around 11:30 P.M., police in the town of Newark, Ohio, received a "man with a gun" call at Nick's Saloon on Second Street

South. While several officers were at the scene in response to that call, a man drove up in a blue Chevy Blazer and asked them for help. The driver of the vehicle behind him, he said, had been following him, riding his bumper all the way from Utica, Ohio, back to Newark.

When an officer approached the driver and asked why he was following the Blazer, the man said, "It's confidential."

The officer repeated the question, and the driver replied, "It's top secret. What's your clearance?"

On further questioning, the man's answers made it obvious there was a definite problem of some kind, and the driver, Hayward Bissell, was asked to step out of the car. He kept repeating, "It's top secret," and claiming he was a government agent.

Bissell told the officer he was on medication for depression, and he was handcuffed and taken to the Newark Police Station, where it was decided he should be taken to a local hospital for psychological evaluation. Newark police contacted one of Bissell's relatives, who told them that their prisoner had a history of mental illness, and he was taken to the hospital and released into their custody.

Still in treatment the following March, Bissell told a doctor he thought he had lice, and voices in his head had told him to urinate in his milk and drink it to get rid of the lice. He evidently decided later, before he drank any of the milk with added ingredients, that it would not be in his best interest to follow this particular set of instructions from the voices.

When Hayward was released from the hospital on May 2, 1999 his aunt, Kathleen Carnahan, was made his general power of attorney and guardian.

In the spring of 1999, while Bissell was still living in Greenwich, Ohio, he told a relative he'd recently had a "mental breakdown" and said that he had been using marijuana along with his prescription drugs. He was cooking a meal in his apartment one evening, he said, and believed he must have fallen asleep and left a pot on the stove. When he woke up, his apartment was on fire, and the next thing he knew, he said, he was standing outside in the snow with firemen all around him.

Bissell was taken to the hospital for treatment of a burn he received on his arm and, after evaluating his condition, the emergency room staff decided he should be transferred to a mental facility.

"He told me he had tried to escape twice," the relative told investigators, "but he said that he got caught both times before getting off the property."

At that point, Bissell began to describe some of his bizarre episodes at the institution, incidents which would be mirrored later by his behavior in the DeKalb County Jail.

"He said that at one point, he had a bowel movement and was looking into the toilet when a voice told him he needed to rub the feces all over himself in order to get better," the relative said.

"The voice also told him that if he ate it, it would get into his system quicker and he would get better quicker. He told me he realized, 'What am I thinking?' and flushed the toilet.

"He also told me he woke up to find another patient asleep in the room and a voice told him the man was going to turn into an alligator and eat him up if he didn't either pay the man some money or beat him with his shoe. Hayward said he realized he was wearing a hospital gown and had no money at all, and his only other choice would be to beat the man with his shoe. Then he said he asked himself what in the world was he doing, and said he realized the guy was there for help just like he was, so he didn't do anything to him."

Bissell told doctors during his hospital stay that federal agents had set the fire in his apartment, and said the government had taken away his special powers. His sperm was being extracted and frozen, he said, and was being implanted in women around the world; he claimed to have thousands of children already. Voices were telling him to kill himself, he said, and he wanted to die and go to Heaven.

A Norwalk woman, a former girlfriend who introduced Bissell and Patricia Booher, accused Hayward of threatening her in August of 1999, saying he had called her at home twice. She claimed he told her to watch her back and that he was going to kill her. The confrontation came after Bissell discovered the air had been let out of his tires during the night, and he accused the woman of being the guilty party. When the police asked him to come by the station for a little talk, he denied calling her and said he had never threatened her and had no intention of doing so. The police advised both parties to stay away from each other.

The woman had dated Bissell for three months, but broke it off because, she said, Bissell twice threatened to kill her.

"He was nice in the beginning; then he got mean," she said. "He is evil. I tried to warn Patricia, I tried to tell her he was mean and evil, and he wants to control your life."

While he was a patient at the Norwalk Clinic in October 1999, Bissell got upset because he was unable to get a prescription refilled at a local pharmacy. He called the clinic and said, "If I don't get my meds, I will make a visit to your office and you will be sorry that you ever heard of me."

Needless to say, the clinic staff was alarmed and called the police. The clinic's business manager told officers all threats were taken seriously, and Bissell would no longer be a patient there. A registered letter was sent to Bissell by the clinic informing him that he would no longer be treated there, and in early November he called the clinic apologizing for his previous behavior. He did not mean his statement to be taken as a threat, he said.

During the time Bissell lived in Greenwich prior to the fire that started in his apartment, an acquaintance who visited him at his apartment on several occasions said that Hayward would often hold up an envelope of papers that he referred to as his "crazy papers," and tell people that he could kill someone and get away with it because the papers "proved he was nuts."

The collection of papers in Bissell's envelope undoubtedly grew larger as time passed. He had a long history of seeking treatment at hospitals and clinics, but his family reported that he would usually refuse to take the medication he was given and would ask for early release. And since he would almost always have entered treatment voluntarily, the doctors would have no choice but to release him.

In one psychiatric assessment alone, Bissell was described as "vague, guarded, evasive, suspicious, watchful, delusional, with a bizarre thought process." And yet he was repeatedly released from treatment only to go to another hospital or clinic seeking more treatment, usually only weeks or months later. Clearly, Hayward Bissell had perfected a pattern of seeking help, then refusing to take medication and demanding early release from therapy.

In the days leading up to Patricia Booher's murder on Sunday, January 23, 2000, several incidents occurred that gave clear indications that serious trouble was brewing on the horizon.

Bissell talked to his aunt on Sunday, January 16, and told her he didn't have any friends.

"An angel is talking to me," he said.

He told his aunt about getting engaged in early December, and said that he and Patty had broken up on Christmas Day. Patty had given him back the engagement ring, he said, then she wanted to make love.

Hayward's aunt didn't put a great deal of stock in her nephew's truthfulness, since she had been placed in several unpleasant situations because of his aberrant behavior. On one occasion, he took her credit card and ran it up over $5,000, a bill she had to pay. For years, she had served as his power of attorney and had kept his legal records and paperwork. Then in the summer of 1999, he came to her home and took all his papers with him, carrying them away in a briefcase in which he kept everything of the sort.

Hayward had a history of telling his aunt wild stories that ranged from the bizarre to the downright scary. He said a disk was planted in his head, on which he received secret transmissions from some unnamed mysterious source; he claimed that the actor Paul Newman was his natural father; he said he was an agent for the Secret Service; he claimed to be the biological father of several family members, all of whom who were many years older than he was.

Bissell's aunt never knew if she would get a straight answer or a tall tale from her nephew, so she usually made it a point to ask him as few questions as possible. She was afraid of him, and so were several of his other family members, although they claimed at times not to be.

"I have helped him with food and kept his clothes washed," his aunt said, "but never let him stay with me. He is big and stout and, at times, could bring harm if he wanted to. But he never threatened me. I have tried to keep him with the counseling center in Norwalk, but he got so he wouldn't go anymore."

On other occasions, family members would describe incidents such as once, when he was expected to come for a visit, one relative told her family to be sure and put up some knives that were lying in the sink.

"We don't want any knives lying around while Hayward's here," she told her husband.

On Thursday, January 20, 2000, Bissell visited the Norwalk Police Department and told Sergeant David Light, who had befriended him on several occasions, that he had been to a veterans medical facility in Cleveland a few days earlier and a doctor there had taken him off some of the medication he had been taking. He complained of not feeling well and having pain in one of his legs, and said he had another appointment the following week.

Light told Bissell that he would contact the doctor for him and stop by his apartment the following day to let him know what was said.

When called by Sergeant Light, the doctor confirmed she had decided to let Bissell stop taking some of his medication, but said that if he wasn't feeling well, he should start taking it again. When the officer went to Bissell's apartment to tell him, he came to the door and said he had company and was "busy in the bedroom." He thanked Light for his help and said he would be fine.

The medications Bissell was told to continue taking included prescriptions for pain, an antibiotic, a drug for diabetes and Xanax to be taken twice daily.

The prescriptions Bissell's doctor had decided to let him discontinue, all of which he had been taking three times daily, were Haldol, Cogentin and Prozac. Over the next few weeks, authorities would speculate often about the effects of stopping such a potent daily dosage of those medications and how the sudden decrease of drugs in his system might have influenced Bissell's actions and eventually led to assault and murder.

Around 3:00 A.M. on Saturday, January 22, a cousin of Bissell's ex-wife had an unexpected and rather unnerving visit from Hayward, whom he had not even seen in six or seven years.

The cousin told reporters from the *Norwalk Reflector* that during the early-morning visit, which lasted around an hour and a half, Bissell told him the "government and police had planted a bug in his head to make him do weird stuff. He said they wanted him to murder someone and he wouldn't do it. He said he was hearing voices."

In his statement to police, the man said that Bissell also told him, "I have great demonic powers, but David Light and Mike Ruggles are trying to take them away from me." He said the voices in his head were caused by the pills he was taking, and said that he didn't want to do anything to hurt anybody. He next claimed that a female relative had molested him as a child, apparently attempting to blame that blatantly fictitious incident for some of his later problems.

The man went on to say that Bissell had mentioned that his girlfriend, Patty, was pregnant and said they had broken up, but he also claimed they were going to get married. He was very intense during the entire conversation, but never mentioned anything about plans to leave for Florida in only a few hours.

"He talked mainly about what the cops were doing, though, and hearing voices. I went along with everything he said. I didn't think he was whacked out enough to do anything. I just thought he was talking to be talking," the man said.

Only a few hours later, Hayward Bissell would turn from talk to brutal, bloody action as Patricia Booher's life ended at his hands.

Chapter 12

"She never was a very good judge of character when it came to boyfriends."

While Hayward Bissell visited his friends and relatives, telling them about his discontinued medication and the voices inside his head telling him to kill someone, Patricia Booher visited a local pregnancy test center, where she was overjoyed to learn she was five weeks pregnant with Bissell's child.

Patty had begun to suspect that she might be pregnant. She went to the center on Friday, January 21, for testing and the results of the pregnancy test turned out to be positive, just as she had thought and hoped. She was very happy and excited to find out that she really was expecting, according to the staff of the center, and made plans to come back the following week to begin counseling sessions on parenting and self-care. She also told several friends and her sister, Charlene Booher, the good news and told most of them that Hayward was also pleased about the pregnancy. There were conflicting reports about that situation, however, with some people claiming she told them Hayward did not yet know that she was pregnant and that she planned to tell him on Sunday. Others said she told them Hayward was the person who had driven her to the testing center for her appointment, and that he was pleased with the news of the positive test results.

"When she told me, I asked her, 'How does Hayward feel about it?' She said he was happy about it," Charlene Booher said.

But apartment complex manager Linda Rogers said Patricia had told her a couple of weeks earlier that she planned to break up with Hayward. Rogers told authorities she thought Patty might have told Hayward she planned to raise the child herself, and suspected he might have been displeased with the situation.

Another friend said Patricia told her that she and Bissell were going to break up but remain friends, and that she would still be able to get rides with him. Patty also said she was going to raise the child herself, and talked about her plans to get a two-bedroom apartment before the baby arrived.

Was Hayward Bissell aware he was about to become a father again, and how did he feel about the prospect of paying support for a third child? Did he know Patricia was pregnant before their hurried departure on Saturday morning, supposedly on the way to visit his parents in Florida?

Patricia Ann Booher grew up in a trailer court near the town of Olena, Ohio, playing with her sister, Charlene, and their cousins who lived in the trailer next door. Their life was less than picture-perfect, for Patricia was molested by a relative who was sent to prison for child sexual abuse. Despite this trauma Patricia and Charlene still enjoyed spending hours playing with their Barbie dolls, and they and their cousins all went together to the same school. Patricia was a shy, quiet little girl who loved animals and enjoyed reading, dancing, music and swimming, but her asthma prevented her from taking part in more strenuous athletics.

When her aunt, uncle and cousins moved away to Wakeman, Ohio, Patricia often visited them in the country and they remained close.

"I can't imagine anyone wanting to hurt Patricia," her cousin Rebecca Booher told reporters from the *Norwalk Reflector.* "She was just very kind and sweet."

Rebecca said she didn't see her cousin as often as she would have liked because of her work schedule, but Patricia always came to visit at the holidays and liked to talk to Rebecca and her mother, Betty Booher. She called her aunt often, keeping in touch with her and her uncle and cousins.

Patricia was well liked at Western Reserve High School and in the EHOVE career development program for students with special needs, making many friends among her teachers and EHOVE tutors. But she tended to hang back, remaining quiet and seldom speaking up in class, lacking the confidence and self-assertion of most of her classmates. She often told her friends she wished she could be more like her older sister, Charlene, whom she had always looked up to as a role model. Charlene was so smart and pretty, Patricia said, and she was popular and had lots of friends and knew how to dress well.

After Patricia graduated from high school, she began having recurring bouts of deep depression. During the course of her treatment, she began attending meetings of an organization called the Friendship Club, a support group for young adults with mental and emotional problems. Through the club, she made a number of new friends and gained the self-confidence that would help her to eventually join the Norwalk First Baptist Church. She began volunteering at a local clothing bank, attended church suppers, which she particularly enjoyed, and took part in group activities at the Friendship Club.

As a part of Patricia's therapy, counselors suggested she begin keeping a diary, writing down her thoughts and feelings. Patricia went out and bought a small pink hardbound book with a design of multicolored flowers on its cover and bright pink pages. She began writing sporadically in her book, using the diary as a sounding board and reporting her daily activities as well as the emotional highs and lows she experienced. The entries show her to be a hopeful but insecure young woman who was constantly in search of someone to love, someone who would love her in return. She yearned for friendships and tried, almost too hard sometimes, to cultivate new relationships. With entries scattered from April 1995 until shortly before her death, the diary's pages document Patty's joys and disappointments in life and love.

On April 21, 1995, Patricia wrote enthusiastically about a man she met six months earlier, saying she didn't think she could stand to be without him and didn't know what she would do without him. She said he was really fun to be with, looked good in jeans, was a really good kisser and—best of all—he loved her.

"I'm in Heaven!" she wrote.

She said she hoped she never loved any other person but him and hoped he'd always be hers. He was a really nice guy, she said, and was considerably older than she was.

The diary entries then skipped to June 31, 1997, when Patricia wrote that she didn't understand why something bad was happening to her every time she turned around. She told of living every day in fear of being shot, abducted or raped, but said God must be watching over her, and that He would not have sent one of His assistants if He wasn't. Whether or not this referred to a new boyfriend was not explained.

"I'm in good hands with God," she wrote.

Patty went on to say that she had learned a while earlier not to justify herself to others, then wrote that maybe she hadn't learned after all. She thought her unresolved feelings from the past might be what was causing her to feel depressed, and she said she wasn't doing anything when she was at home but "mope around watching TV."

Around three months later, on September 12, Patricia dashed off a short, two-line entry complaining about feeling stressed when trying to concentrate or when trying to find something she had lost. Then a week later, after a nightmare on September 19, Patty told about the "really scary dream" she'd had the night before. She dreamed her ex-boyfriend walked up to her door nude, she said, adding that she was in no way attracted to him anymore. He was a sex maniac, she said, and he did obscene things in strange places.

"He masturbates and other stuff," she said.

Before he and Patty broke up, he began stealing little things when he came to visit, and Patty said she eventually stopped answering the door when he came around. He found out her phone number, though, and wouldn't leave her alone.

"I think he pranks me sometimes," she said.

Patty told of her fear that she might never have him completely out of her life, and wondered if the dream was trying to tell her something.

"I'm really scared," she wrote.

Two days later, Patty wrote about a girl she met with whom she wanted to develop a friendship. The girl, however, apparently didn't want to be friends. Patty said that part of her still wanted to be good friends with the girl, but the other part of her was learning to give up on friendships that weren't meant to be before she ended up getting upset or hurt.

The entry then abruptly switched to the topic of driver's licenses, with Patty saying she needed help with getting over her sister, Charlene, getting her license first.

"It's eating away at me," Patty wrote.

She said she wished she knew someone who had the time to help her with her driving.

"It's the most important thing to me right now," she said.

On October 14, Patricia was evidently still being troubled by her dreams, reporting she'd had scary dreams about her father and a lot of dreams about accidents. She was going to ask her counselor to tell her the warning signs of stress, she said, so she would know what to avoid. Her counselor told her certain things she wanted her to do, Patty wrote, but said that she had a hard time remembering the details.

The next entry in the diary came on October 27, when Patty wrote that she recently lost a friend because she was afraid of getting hurt. Then she mentioned the Friendship Club directly for the first time, saying she had gone there three times. She had fun when she went there, she said, and was impressed with herself because she automatically made friends.

Then she skipped abruptly to another topic.

"I have a problem I'm dying to talk about with someone," she wrote.

The problem, it seemed, was that she was attracted to one of her new male friends from the Friendship Club. He didn't know, she said; neither did her boyfriend.

"I didn't mean for this to happen," she said.

Patty was unsure of what she wanted, saying she still loved her boyfriend but was scared to tell him about his competition because it would be the end if or when she told him. She had been with him for so long, she said, that it would seem awkward and she needed some advice on wht she should do.

Two days later, on October 29, Patty was off on another romantic tangent and writing about yet another new friend from the Friendship Club.

"He likes me," she said, adding that she told him she was engaged and he still liked her. She told him she'd still be his friend, she said, but confided to the diary that she just wasn't attracted to skinny guys; the other two, she said, weren't really skinny. She went on to say that she had told "the new guy" that if she were single, she would choose him over her boyfriend. That news, she said, brought a smile to his face.

November 15 brought only a one-line entry, saying that Patty had gone to Ponderosa with the Friendship Club.

Four days later, on November 19, Patty wrote that she was "even more depressed than the last time," and had been to see her counselor. The reason for the depression was, she said, that she had finally told her new friend how she felt and he told her he just wanted to be friends. Everything was okay, she said, now that things were out in the open.

On November 21, two days after the previous entry, Patty said she and her boyfriend had decided they should go their separate ways because things just weren't working out for them. He knew everything, she wrote, but wasn't upset like she had thought he would be. Patty, however, said she "got really depressed on Wednesday night. I felt like harming myself. I feel better now."

November 24 brought another rambling entry, which began with Patty saying that she wrote poetry, had written a poem for her friend Cheryl and the

Friendship Club, and had won an award once. Then she jumped to a far more serious topic.

"I think maybe I'll wait and see if my depression increases any more before considering PHP," she wrote, adding that she really didn't think she needed a psychiatrist, since she was already on an antidepressant.

A rather bleak, one-line entry on December 1 stated that Patty had visited her family for Thanksgiving. Then, two days later, Patty wrote that she was scared that whatever she said or did, her new friend was not going to find it interesting. She thought she should tell him, but was afraid that would make things worse. The following day, Patty said her new friend was a very special friend, and whenever she said or did something, she was scared she wouldn't be a good-enough friend. She had started burying herself in work, she wrote.

The entry for December 12 covered several different topics, with Patricia writing that she was no longer upset about her ex-boyfriend coming to see her. Then she said her depression fluctuated from time to time, and lately she had been irritable and had felt like crying for no reason. She wrote about an invitation to go to Curtice, Ohio, for Christmas Eve, then said that her ex-boyfriend's day off would be changing from Thursday to Monday after New Year's. She ended the entry by saying one of her girlfriends had gone with her to open a checking account. Two days later, Patty wrote that she had come close to having another "episode" because she had skipped one day of taking her medicine, and was still feeling very depressed.

"I've had a not so good weekend," she wrote, "and it's all my fault."

Patty said she had fun at Ponderosa on Wednesday, evidently another Friendship Club outing, and said the club was planning a bowling night in January. She also said she got her picture taken on Thursday, December 4.

Patty wrote on December 15 that she had come to realize that she didn't want to "depress" for the rest of her life and was going to work harder at pushing herself out of it. She was going to need help, she said, and didn't know what to do.

Apparently, the approaching holidays were becoming hard to face, for on December 19, Patty wrote that on Wednesday night she had started thinking about all the things her ex-boyfriend had done and on Thursday morning she became very depressed over it and started crying. She had seen the ex-boyfriend at the Friendship Club, and had done okay all day until that night. Then, as an afterthought, she added that she had sent out Christmas cards to friends.

Two days later, on December 21, Patty said she was feeling better. She had decided, she said, that she planned to have a baby between the year 1999 and 2000. Then she said she was going to get her hair cut.

"I feel like I'm going through a lot of changes right now," she said.

Then she wrote about being worried about how she was going to get her Christmas shopping done; her ex-boyfriend, she said, had offered to help her out. Her counselor had called to tell Patty she was going to send her the handouts from the holiday stress group. Patty also said she was going to take karate lessons, and said the Friendship Club had sent her a fruit basket.

"I sent them a Christmas card," she wrote, "and I have one for my girlfriend too."

That was the last entry in Patricia's diary for a long time, until August 1999, when she wrote about having a crush on a man from Sandusky that she met through her work selling Avon.

"I plan on asking him out," she said.

Patty also wrote about her ex-boyfriend, saying he was acting very strange and that his behavior was hurting her. Then she went on to say that she was a lot more assertive than she used to be and was speaking up more. She had a job for a few weeks, she wrote, but had to quit and was selling Avon now.

There was only one entry remaining in Patricia's diary, written on December 20, 1999, after she had been dating Hayward Bissell for a few months. It expressed doubts about their relationship but was also full of determination and hope for the future—a future Patty would not live to see. She wrote that it had been a year since she'd been in the hospital and had only been depressed a few times since then, but was depressed again.

Then she made the only reference to Hayward Bissell to be found in the diary.

"There is a man in my life that I love with all my heart and soul," she wrote, continuing to say that they were not getting along and that she was depressed because it might come to splitting up. Patty then wrote that she was going to start doing some assessments in her life because she wanted to live a better life for herself.

"I can't go on depressed any more," she wrote, saying that she wanted to make some decisions for her future and live each day as it came, following her heart and not taking anything for granted anymore.

"I feel like I have received a wonderful blessing," she wrote. "I am in touch with myself now."

From now on, she said, when she had any thoughts, she would jot them down in the diary. She would think of her needs first and others second, and work on her priorities and at solving her problems. And she said she would learn to accept when someone else wanted to help her.

Patricia had obviously spent enough time in counseling to learn which behaviors were supposed to improve her life, but the rest of the pages in the little pink diary would remain blank. Sadly, at the time she wrote her final entry, she had only a month to live. There was no time left to put her good intentions into practice.

Patricia's diary was filled with accounts of relationships that just didn't turn out quite the way she hoped, and her last entry indicates she felt she was headed toward a breakup with the man she claimed to love with all her heart and soul. Relatives said that previously Patricia always had brought her boyfriends home to meet her family, but they had never met Hayward Bissell.

"She just said she had a boyfriend she really liked, and they were planning on getting married," a cousin told the *Norwalk Reflector.*

"He gave her an engagement ring, but she lost it on the beach last summer. She didn't say he hit her or anything, but he was mad."

Patricia's aunt had watched her niece grow up and had seen several men come and go in Patricia's life through the years. She apparently hadn't been very impressed with any of Patricia's choices.

"She never was a very good judge of character when it came to boyfriends," she said.

Chapter 13

"Get away from him and leave him be."

In July 1999, Hayward Bissell and Patricia Ann Booher were both living in the Firelands Village apartments in Norwalk. Not long after they each moved into the apartment complex, they were introduced by a mutual friend, a girl Bissell had dated previously. The two soon began seeing each other. They made an odd couple—the huge four-hundred-pound man and the tiny woman only a fourth his size who looked young enough to be a middle-school student.

"Of all people, her," said Bissell's former brother-in-law following Patricia's death. "Look at him and look at her. It's like an elephant stepping on an ant."

For others who knew the couple, their concern about the relationship went much deeper than the drastic physical differences between the two.

A Greenwich, Ohio, man and woman who knew Bissell and Booher were both surprised and dismayed to learn the pair were dating.

"We talked to Patty a couple of weeks [before the murder] at the Friendship Club and she told us who she was going with," the man said, "and I told her,

'Take any way you can, get away from him and leave him be, because he is trouble.'"

Patricia called the Greenwich couple around 9:30 A.M. on Saturday, January 22, to tell them about her pregnancy. During the course of the conversation, she told them Hayward was pressuring her to go with him to Florida to visit his parents in Winter Haven.

"She told us that Hayward wanted her to go down and meet his family, go down to Florida to his mother's for a couple of weeks," the woman said. "She didn't really want to go. She said she was excited about having the baby and that Hayward wanted to marry her, but she was telling him no. And she was hesitating about going to Florida with him."

In a statement they gave to Mike James and Johnny Bass, the couple told the investigators that several years earlier, back in 1995, they had a confrontation of their own with Bissell when he lived in Greenwich. They said he tried to stalk the woman, attempting to find out where her apartment was.

"One night when I was up here visiting her, he came up to where some of us were standing at the end of one of the apartment buildings and started in asking her about where her apartment was," the man said. "I told him to leave her alone. I told him, 'She don't want nothing to do with you.' He just acted like he was drunk or something; anyway, I didn't pay much attention to it at the time, but I told him to leave her alone."

On the Fourth of July weekend the following year, at a popular annual event called the Greenwich Fireman's Festival, the couple again had problems with Hayward Bissell. After walking through the festival grounds and spending some time playing bingo, they were returning to their truck when Bissell approached them and once again demanded to know which apartment the woman lived in.

"I said, 'Hayward, it's none of your damn business which apartment I live in and I'm not gonna tell you,'" the woman said, "and he started to go for me and choke me and I said, 'Hayward, back off.' I told him I wasn't going to tell him again, 'Now back off.'"

Randall Kilgore, Greenwich's chief of police, happened to be standing nearby and noticed the heated conversation taking place. He walked over and asked the woman if there was a problem, and she told him Bissell was harassing and threatening her.

"I'm going to get at her and kill her," Bissell announced.

The police chief told Bissell he was going to do no such thing, and he and his assistant chief attempted to handcuff the big man. It took some effort on their part to get the job done, since their prisoner was not cooperating.

"Hayward, you are going to jail tonight," the chief said.

"I'm not going anywhere," Bissell informed him. "I'm going to get out and I'll get her. I'll get her tomorrow night when I get out."

"You won't get within ten feet of that kid," the chief told him.

The officers enlisted the woman's boyfriend to help them take Bissell into custody, telling him to get in the police cruiser and bring them a pair of shackles that were lying on the floorboard.

"I told them I didn't have the authority to get in the cruiser," the man said, "but the assistant chief said he didn't care, get in there and get them. Then the chief said to do it, so I took and done it. I put the shackles on Hayward and he made about one or two steps and fell right back on his face because he was gonna take and try to run."

After a bit more scuffling and wrestling, Bissell was finally loaded into the patrol car and taken to the county jail in Norwalk.

The Greenwich couple were understandably alarmed when Patricia told them Hayward Bissell was the father of her baby. They knew how violent he could be, they told the investigators.

"We told her to stay away from him. You could tell he didn't like kids at all," the man said. "When kids were around him, he'd tell them to get away, cuss and everything."

Patricia told them, they claimed, that she was going to try to stay away from Bissell, but she said he wouldn't stay away from her.

"I'm going to tell him I'm not going on vacation with him," she assured them.

Around a month before the murder, the couple said, Patricia had told them Bissell had threatened to take her somewhere and beat her up and not let her come home alive. They told the investigators she always acted afraid of him. They also said Patricia had come to the Friendship Club in November with bruises, which she told them Hayward had given her. They were not at all surprised to hear of this rough treatment of the small, helpless young woman.

"We know how violent he could be," said the woman.

When Patricia phoned them from her apartment that Saturday morning, only a short time before she left town with Hayward Bissell, she never mentioned any plans to go to Florida.

A Norwalk woman, the mutual friend who introduced Bissell and Booher, told the *Norwalk Reflector* she broke up with Bissell because of his violent behavior.

"That could have happened to me," she told reporters after learning of the murder.

She said that Bissell had tried to get her to go to Florida with him when they were dating.

"He said he would go to Aldi's, buy a bunch of canned food, take it to his parents and sell it so he could get enough money to take me to Disney World," she said.

He also told her to borrow Patricia's bicycle and then sell it for $50 so they would have some spending money at Disney World.

The woman turned down Bissell's invitation to go along on the trip to Florida.

"Toward the end of our relationship, he got violent, hateful and mean," she said. "He tried to control my life, telling me I couldn't hang out with my friends."

The woman also claimed that Bissell had emptied Patricia's $3,000 savings account and took the money she made from her job, selling Avon products, before she could send it in to the company.

"I tried to warn her about him," she said.

The warnings came too late for the small, easily victimized young woman who was both mentally and physically unable to defend herself against the easily angered, six-foot four-inch, four-hundred-pound Bissell. Their on-again, off-again relationship was completely out of her control, and her repeated attempts to distance herself from him were not working.

On December 18, Patty told a friend that Bissell had forbidden her to eat at a local VFW celebration and had taken all her money. The friend, who felt sorry for Patricia, paid for her meal. Investigators later asked the friend if Patty had ever mentioned that Bissell had been physically abusive toward her or if she knew of his use of street-level narcotics. The woman said she had asked Patricia if Bissell ever hit or mistreated her, but Patty was unwilling to talk about it and wouldn't confirm or deny any assaults.

"I never saw any signs of physical abuse, but I suspect he abused her verbally and mentally," the woman told investigators. "I know that he took her money and prohibited her from doing certain things or going places."

"Patty told me she thought Hayward was taking street drugs, but she never had any proof that he was," the woman added.

When Patricia and Bissell broke up on Christmas Day, her friend Janice Timman took her to give back the engagement ring. Hayward was angry; he had earlier called Charlene trying to find Patty, but Charlene did not know where her sister was. He was polite on the phone, Charlene said, and did not sound like he was mad. But when Bissell called Patty's aunt Betty, that wasn't the case. He got angry on the phone, Betty Booher told investigators, and demanded to know where Patty was. Betty had no idea, and told him that she hadn't seen Patty in quite a while.

After Patricia gave back the ring and broke up with Hayward, she began going back to meetings of the Friendship Club. At an Avon meeting on January 13, she told a friend that during the short time she was apart from Hayward, she had dated a young man she met at the club and said that she had fallen in love with him. But despite the fact that Patricia claimed to have rather quickly developed feelings for this new man, she reconciled with Hayward within a week of the breakup.

During the few days the couple was apart, Janice Timman persuaded Patricia to stay with her for a while, because Hayward had threatened Patty, saying she was going to die and he was supposed to kill her.

"Patty was scared of him for the last month, ever since he told her that," Janice said.

A few weeks before the murder, Patricia told another friend that Hayward was "swatting her on the butt," and said "she didn't like it." A couple of days later, however, she told the friend she and Hayward were "friends again."

In a conversation about a week after Christmas, Patricia told Charlene that she was engaged to Hayward again, and she had evidently made up with Hayward on a tentative basis and accepted his engagement ring once again. But she also said Hayward was upset with her because she didn't have any money left to buy Christmas presents. Patricia had complained earlier to Charlene that Bissell was too possessive. He wasn't satisfied with the way she kept house or managed her money. He didn't like the way she washed dishes or kept herself.

"I don't think things are going to work out for me," Patty told Charlene.

One likely reason for Patricia's change of heart and her decision to accept Bissell's ring once again was a note Charlene found in her sister's apartment after her death. The three-page note to Patty, from her on-again, off-again fiancé, was not dated but was obviously written after the Christmas breakup. Charlene turned it over to the authorities as soon as she found it, realizing it was an important piece of evidence.

The note was a masterfully crafted piece of work, designed to tell Patty everything she longed to hear. The note was proof positive that Hayward Bissell was a master manipulator. He chose words and phrases that were supportive, reassuring and loving, and his note gave Patty every reason in the world to want to get back together with him.

Bissell began by writing that he hoped Patty was feeling better; then he said a Norwalk police officer had stopped by his apartment to tell him that the department had received a call that evening from a woman concerned about Patty's welfare. The officer said Patty had talked to the woman about her relationship with Bissell and said she wanted to end things with him.

The officer told him Patty had said she was afraid to break away from him, Bissell wrote.

Bissell then assured Patty she had no reason ever to be afraid of him, and said he could have "handled it fine" if she had broken up with him, and wished she would have trusted him enough to talk with him about it.

He had been very upset for the past twenty-four hours, he wrote, but said he wanted her to know that he was doing okay. He asked Patty please not to worry about him or anything else, and said he would not hurt himself or do anything else to hurt his future. He had come a long way, he said, and he wanted Patty to know all of her love and care had helped him very much in many ways.

Bissell also said in the note that he wanted Patty to know that he had a lot of respect for her always, still trusted her very much and was looking forward to the two of them becoming close friends soon. He hoped she would be able to get over his mistakes, he said.

Bissell also told Patty he would like for her to stop by his apartment and visit him when she was feeling up to it. He knew that she might never love him again, he wrote, and said he was very sorry that their relationship had to end.

"I just want to be your friend always," he said.

Bissell told Patty she was a very wonderful woman and said he was going to miss her love the way it was and that he would never forget all the good times they'd had together. He was looking forward to many more, he said, with her as a close friend.

"Please understand me," Bissell wrote, saying that he cared for Patty and was concerned for her always. He asked her to please let him know if she ever needed a ride or anything else, and said she was more than welcome anytime.

Bissell ended his carefully crafted note by saying, "With all my love, your friend, H.W.B."

What young woman, hoping for true love and longing for romance, would not find her heart warmed by such a note? No guilt, no blame, everything positive and optimistic—how could Patty have resisted? She could not, and Hayward Bissell knew she would not be able to remain separated from him for very long.

Around the same time that he wrote the note, Bissell told one of his friends that Patty was so dumb, she didn't know how to brush her teeth or wash dishes. Those loving, supportive words in the note clashed with the cruel remarks Bissell made to his friend. His tender sentiments in the note were obviously a manipulative ploy, designed to regain control over her and keep her firmly under his thumb, which was just where he thought she belonged. He intended to rule every aspect of her life, and he knew just what to say and do to make that happen.

When Patricia told Charlene about her pregnancy on January 21, she said Bissell was happy about it, but she went on to say they had broken up again. Hayward wanted her back, she said, but they were not going to get back together because of his controlling behavior. Charlene later told investigators Patty had been dating Hayward for around two or three months when she began complaining about not liking his behavior toward her.

A neighbor of Patricia's was also very concerned

about the couple's one-sided relationship and told Norwalk police, following the murder, she had always been fearful for her young friend's safety. Bissell was so overly controlling and possessive, she said, that he even dictated to Patricia about where she should buy her shoes.

A couple of days before New Year's Eve, Bissell contacted his estranged wife, Teresa, and asked her if he could have visitation with their daughter, Brittany. Teresa and Brittany hadn't had contact with him for almost four years until he got in touch around Thanksgiving and asked for a visit. Things had gone well at that visit, but Bissell wanted his daughter for an overnight stay on New Year's Eve.

Teresa initially said no because she was concerned about Brittany's safety, spending that much time with a father she hardly knew. But eventually she changed her mind and agreed to let Brittany stay overnight.

Hayward and Patty had evidently gotten back together by that time, since when bedtime came on New Year's Eve, Brittany stayed overnight at Patty's apartment. The girl later told her mother that both Bissell and Patty had talked to her about being in their wedding.

Bissell had told Teresa earlier about his new girlfriend, and said he didn't have to be lonely anymore, but he never once mentioned getting a divorce from Teresa, to whom he was still married.

During the first week of January, Patricia was admitted to the hospital complaining of gynecological problems. During that time, she told Linda Rogers that she was breaking up with Hayward Bissell. He was very controlling, she said, and was taking all her money. Linda suggested that Patricia should once again return the engagement ring Bissell had bought for her, and told her she should ask him to give back the keys to her apartment. Later, after leaving the hospital, Patricia told Linda that Bissell had returned her apartment keys, and had assured her everything was fine, and it wouldn't be necessary to have the locks changed.

On Tuesday, January 18, Hayward Bissell paid another visit to Norwalk police sergeant David Light, this time at Light's home. He brought Patricia Booher along, introduced her to Sergeant Light, and told him she was "Heaven sent." The two, evidently back together again, snuggled close together on the couch, with Bissell's arm around Patricia and her head resting against his chest. Patricia remained very quiet, occasionally smiling and agreeing with whatever Bissell said, but mostly watching television.

Patricia looked very young, Light thought, and he wondered if she was even as much as eighteen years old. But when Bissell went outside to move his car, Light took advantage of the opportunity to find out how old Patricia really was by asking her if she was still in school. He was very surprised to learn she had graduated from Western Reserve High School several years earlier.

The couple spent around an hour and a half visiting at Light's home, and Hayward did most of the talking during that time. He told Light about a traffic accident he had been involved in a few months earlier, and claimed that he was still having pain in one of his legs. Patricia, he said, was still seeing a chiropractor for muscle spasms she was having as a result of the wreck, and the other driver's insurance company had settled for $500 damage to the rear end of Bissell's car.

Bissell also told Light about the incident that took place a year earlier in Greenwich, when he had fallen asleep while cooking and set his apartment on fire. He described his resulting stay in the mental-health center and said he had tried to leave the facility twice, breaking a door on one occasion, but had gotten caught each time before he managed to get off the property.

After his release, Bissell said, he moved to Norwalk's Firelands Village, where he met Patricia.

Before the couple left Light's home, Bissell asked Patricia to go out and start the car to warm it up, saying he needed to discuss something of a "confidential matter" with Light. The sergeant expected Bissell to ask to borrow some money, but Bissell instead told him that he and Patricia had broken up in December after he called her a bitch. They had just gotten back together, he said, and now everything was just fine.

But the very next day, on Wednesday, Patty told a friend she was afraid of Hayward and was trying to break up with him. She wanted to get back into the Friendship Club, she said.

The Reverend Paul Lamb's secretary and her husband gave Patty a ride home from church services Wednesday night, and told investigators that Patty said she was very glad to be going back to church. She had previously told the secretary that Bissell was pressuring her to leave the Baptist church and go to his church, the Jehovah's Witnesses. Patty also told the woman that she had broken up with Bissell on Christmas Day because he took down the Christmas tree, which upset her. Like several of Patty's other friends, the woman asked her if Bissell had ever hurt her. Patricia remained silent and wouldn't discuss any further details of the Christmas-tree incident or say whether or not she had ever been physically abused by her on-again, off-again boyfriend.

Bissell saw his former brother-in-law on that same Wednesday, and was reported to be unusually quiet. He kept making references to needing friends, and said that he had been asking for help from various social agencies, claiming that nothing was being done for him.

The ex-brother-in-law told Norwalk police that he knew Bissell was on medication for depression and back pain, but said that other than those medications, he did not know of Bissell taking or possessing narcotics such as Xanax or Vicodin. However, he did report that during their conversation, Bissell claimed to be hearing voices in his head.

On Thursday, Bissell came to the police department and said he needed to talk to Sergeant Light. Once again, he made the statement that Patricia was "Heaven sent" and said the two of them had helped each other through a lot of troubled times. He believed he and his tiny girlfriend were meant for each other.

Bissell rambled on, saying he felt he had failed by not reaching his goals in life, and told Light that he was disappointed in himself. He had never gotten his GED, he said, and thought that he ate too much. He talked about going on a diet.

Sergeant Light sensed something else was troubling Bissell, but his visitor wouldn't come out with whatever was on his mind. Light knew about all the mental problems that Bissell had experienced over the years, and asked him if he was okay. He was fine, Bissell said, except for the pain in his leg he had mentioned earlier. Then he finally admitted to Light that his medication had recently been decreased and said he was not feeling well. Light offered to contact the doctor on Bissell's behalf, and asked him if he had enough money and food. Bissell thanked him, saying he had everything he needed, and left.

That evening, while Light was still on duty, the Norwalk police dispatcher received a call from the sergeant's wife reporting that Hayward Bissell was parked in front of their home, sitting in his car. Light knew that he had told Bissell he would be working that night and would not be home, and when the dispatcher radioed to tell him that his wife had called saying that Bissell was sitting there in front of his house, Light was concerned for his family's safety. Since Light couldn't break away from the detail he was working on at that time, he asked the dispatcher to send a marked police unit to his home and have the officers ask Bissell to leave.

Later that evening, Bissell stopped by the department to ask why he had been told to leave from in front of Light's home and to see if Sergeant Light was "mad at him." The officer explained that he was not mad; he just didn't want people at his house when he was not there. Bissell said he understood, and Light told Bissell he would stop by his apartment the following day, Friday, after he talked to Bissell's doctor.

At some point on Thursday evening, a resident at Firelands Village told investigators they had seen Hayward and Patty "fighting in his car." The officers were unable to determine what time this incident occurred, so they were not able to tell whether or not this argument took place before or after Bissell's vigil in front of Light's home.

On Friday as promised, Light and another officer stopped by Firelands to tell Bissell the doctor had said that if he wasn't feeling well, he should resume taking the medications that had been discontinued. He met them at the door, thanked them for coming and said, grinning knowingly, that he had company and was "busy in the bedroom."

That was the last Light would hear concerning Hayward Bissell until Sunday evening, when he was called by the police department dispatcher and notified that

Patricia, the tiny girl who had sat so quietly on his couch only a few days earlier, had been found horribly butchered in Bissell's car on a rural road in Northeast Alabama.

And the big man who had sat in his parked car in front of Light's house on Thursday night, knowing that the officer was not there and that his family was home alone, was in an Alabama jail, under arrest for two vicious assaults and admittedly responsible for Patricia's murder.

Chapter 14

"Her face was red, like she'd been crying."

On Friday evening and Saturday morning, Patricia Booher made several phone calls to family and friends to tell them her good news. She wanted everyone close to her to know that she had been to the clinic the day before and found out that she was pregnant. Patty left messages for several other friends who were not at home, and they reported the phone messages did not sound as though she was upset or that the call was urgent; none of them felt there was any problem when they listened to her message.

Patricia's pastor, Reverend Paul Lamb, told investigators he wasn't aware of any trip she was planning, and said she most likely would have told him if she was going out of town. He, too, had a phone message from Patricia on Saturday morning but was unavailable to contact her, and said he had heard she was pregnant and suspected she wanted to talk with him about the pregnancy.

To those people Patricia spoke with on the phone, she sounded very happy and excited about her positive pregnancy test, but she mentioned to none of the people she talked to on Friday night or the following morning that she might be about to leave for Florida to visit Hayward Bissell's parents.

"No one knew she was leaving town," her cousin said. "Usually she tells someone, either her sister or us. She would have been easy to take advantage of."

The trip was quite obviously unplanned on Patricia's part, for when her apartment was searched by Norwalk police on Sunday night, all of her personal items were there. It is highly unlikely she would have left her apartment planning to go on vacation without taking any extra clothing or even her toothbrush.

Patricia had told several people she did not want to make the trip to Florida with Bissell because she was trying to end the relationship. She would not be comfortable going on vacation with him under the circumstances, she said.

"When she tried to break it off with him, I just think he thought, 'If I can't have you, no one can,'" her cousin said.

Regardless of her intentions, Patricia left the Firelands Village apartments with Hayward Bissell on Saturday morning, shortly after making a last phone call to two of her friends. She took only her purse and coat, and Bissell also left Norwalk with no extra clothes or personal items. He carried nothing but the contents of his pockets . . . and two very long, sharp knives hidden in the backseat of his Lincoln Town Car.

Bissell told investigators that he and Patricia had gotten as far south as Chattanooga, Tennessee, on Saturday, and said they spent Saturday night in the parking lot of a motel near there. A frigid rain was falling and ice was beginning to form on the streets, and it must have been a cold, miserable night during which they got very little sleep. They had only a few dollars in cash, and Bissell knew they would have to get more money in order to keep going.

The next morning, as the weather grew increasingly

Hayward Bissell killed his pregnant girlfriend, Patricia Ann Booher, in the passenger seat of this 1988 Lincoln Town Car. *(Author's photo)*

Soon after he drove into Mentone, Alabama, Bissell attacked Don and Rhea Pirch with a hit-and-run. *(Author's photo)*

James and Sue Pumphrey are lucky to be alive after Hayward Bissell's brutal assault and attempted home invasion. *(Author's photo)*

Pumphrey stands in the front yard of his home where Bissell was first attacked by Pumphrey's two dogs. *(Author's photo)*

Cocoa fought to the death to protect her owners.
(Courtesy of James and Sue Pumphrey)

Reese attacked Bissell, giving the Pumphreys time to get inside their home and lock the door. *(Courtesy of James and Sue Pumphrey)*

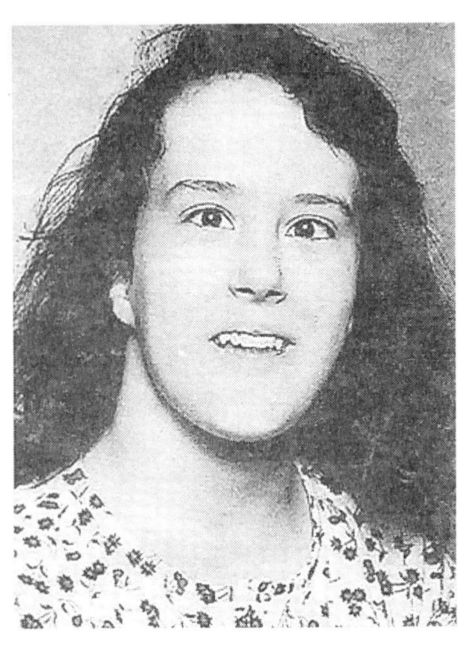

Patricia Ann Booher's high school yearbook photo.

Bissell's driver's license photo.
(Courtesy of DeKalb County Sheriff's Office)

On the morning after Bissell's arrest, TV news crews crowded into Sheriff Cecil Reed's office for a press conference. *(Author's photo)*

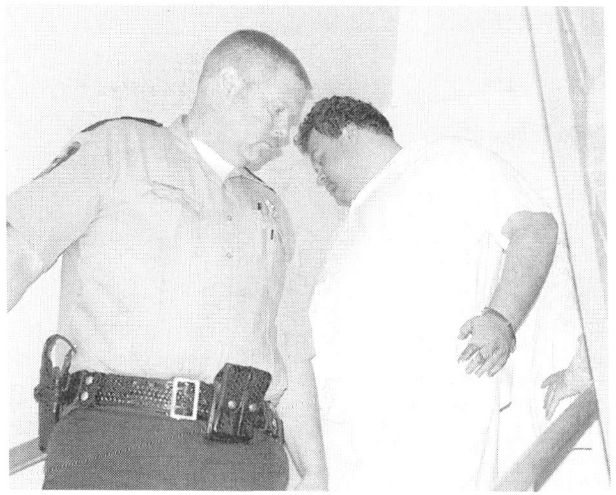

The first photo taken of Hayward Bissell following his arrest. The defense wounds visible on his left hand were from his encounter with the Pumphreys' two dogs. *(Author's photo)*

DeKalb County Sheriff Cecil Reed. *(Courtesy of Scott Turner)*

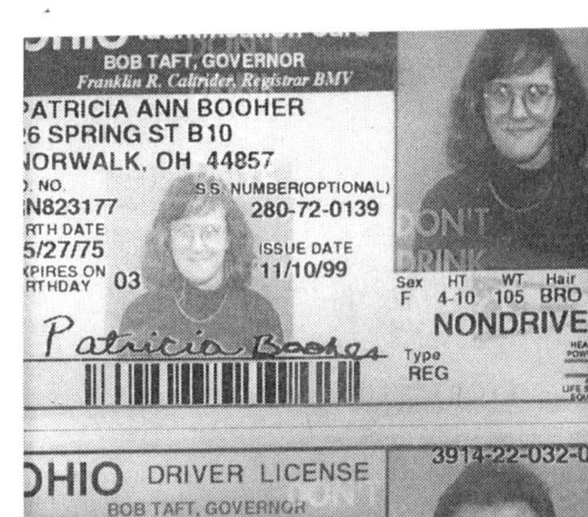

Patricia Booher's ID card and Hayward Bissell's driver's license. *(Courtesy of DeKalb County Sheriff's Department)*

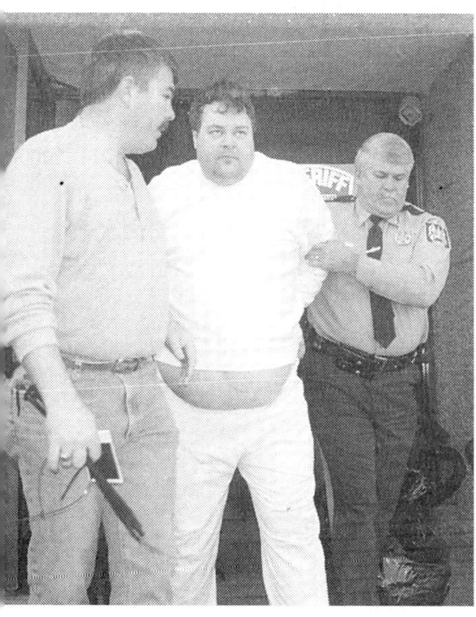

Bissell was taken to a mental facility for evaluation. *(Courtesy of Steven Stiefel)*

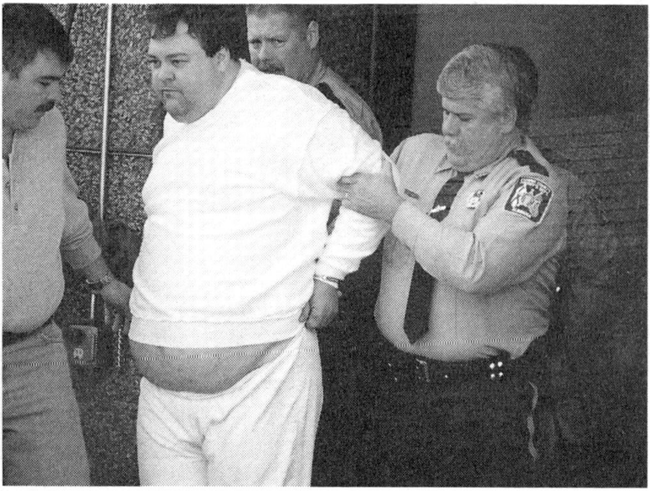

No clothing at the county jail was large enough to fit Bissell, and officers had to search local department stores for something he could wear in jail. *(Author's photo)*

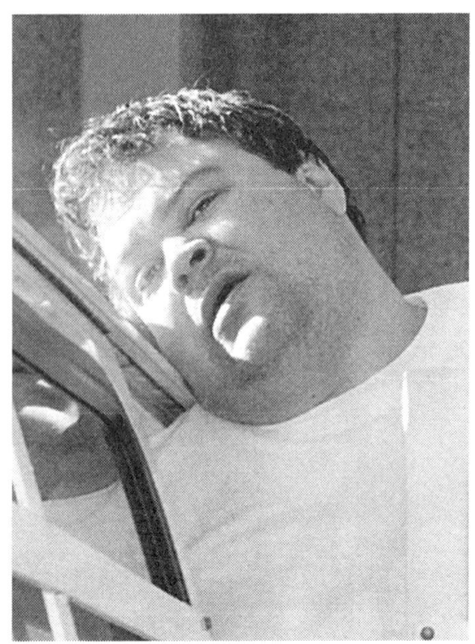

Bissell getting into the van that will take him to Taylor-Hardin Secure Medical Facility for evaluation. *(Courtesy of Steven Stiefel)*

Transporting Bissell required this specially equipped reinforced van, as well as a shock shield and two officers specially trained in dealing with violent prisoners. *(Author's photo)*

Security camera tapes show Hayward Bissell entering the Discount Food Mart in Trion, Georgia, on January 23, 2000, at 2:24 p.m. *(Courtesy of Detective Eddie Colbert)*

Bissell left the Discount Food Mart at 2:32 p.m.
(Courtesy of Detective Eddie Colbert)

At 2:34 p.m., Patricia Booher entered the Discount Food Mart.
(Courtesy of Detective Eddie Colbert)

The last photo of Patricia, taken by the store's security cameras at 2:36 p.m. *(Courtesy of Detective Eddie Colbert)*

DeKalb County Jailer Bill Lands was responsible for Bissell's daily care, feeding and medication for two years. *(Author's photo)*

Bissell's cell was repaired and equipped with new plumbing after he ripped out the pipes and flooded the jail. *(Author's photo)*

When he returned to the DeKalb County Jail, Bissell had lost weight, had short hair and a beard.
(Courtesy of Scott Turner)

WHNT-TV cameraman Brad Hood covered Bissell's return to the DeKalb County Jail.
(Author's photo)

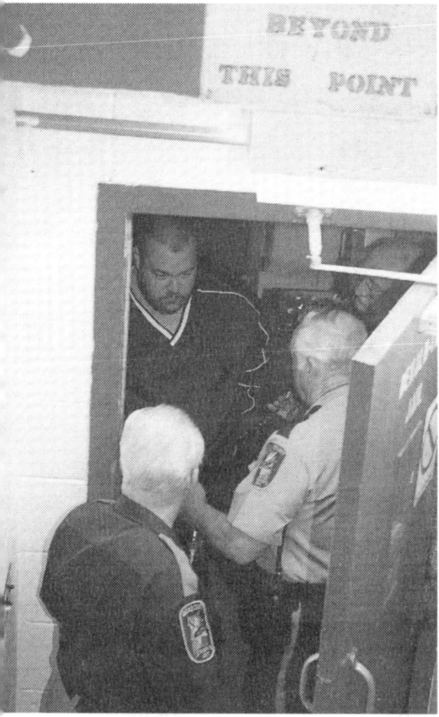

Bissell remained calm and gave officers no trouble as he was escorted downstairs and booked into the jail. *(Author's photo)*

Deputy James Denton prepared Bissell's medication according to instructions from the doctors. *(Author's photo)*

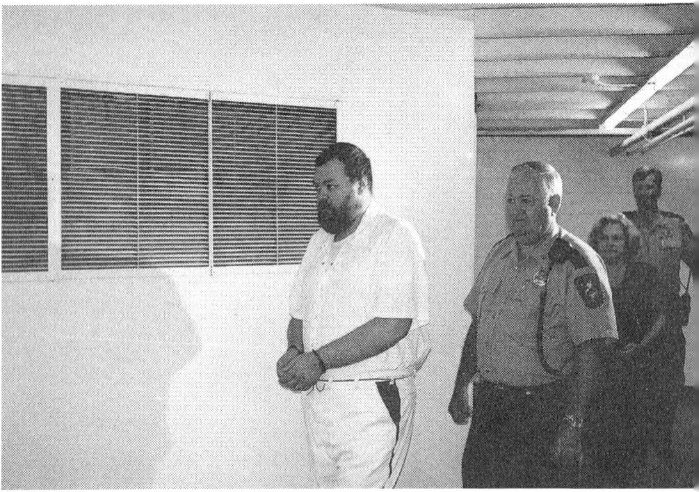

Bissell was escorted to his first courtroom appearance by Chief Deputy Dale Orr. He had lost so much weight that a piece of black cord held his pants up. *(Author's photo)*

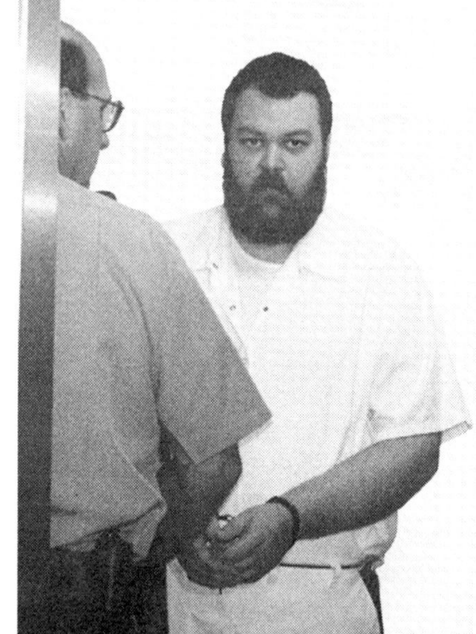

Courthouse Security Officer Stanley Hollingsworth escorted Bissell to the courtroom of Judge Randall Cole. *(Author's photo)*

The Georgia/Alabama prosecutorial team, from left: Chattooga investigator Johnny Bass, Chattooga Chief Assistant DA Grover Hudgins, DeKalb investigators Danny Smith and Mike James, DeKalb Sheriff Cecil Reed, Chattooga DA Buzz Franklin, Chattooga Sheriff Ralph Kellett, DeKalb DA Mike O'Dell, and DeKalb Assistant DAs Scott Lloyd and Bob Johnston.
(Courtesy of District Attorney Mike O'Dell)

District Attorney Mike O'Dell and his staff spent untold hours preparing the Alabama cases against Hayward Bissell. *(Courtesy of Scott Turner)*

Hoyt Baugh was appointed by the court to represent Bissell in his Alabama cases for the assaults on Don Pirch and James Pumphrey.
(Courtesy of Scott Turner)

Hayward Bissell awaiting transfer to Georgia to begin serving his sentence for the murder of Patricia Ann Booher. During his two years in the DeKalb County Jail, he lost almost half his total body weight.
(Courtesy of Steven Stiefel)

James Pumphrey's friends gave him a Lab puppy to help heal the loss of the beloved dogs who gave their lives to save him and his wife, Sue.
(Author's photo)

nastier, Bissell again headed south in the predawn darkness on the interstate. As he crossed the state line from Tennessee into Northwest Georgia, he knew he wouldn't get much further without money for fuel and food. He began to look for an exit where he claimed he wanted to try to find an automated teller or a Western Union, and eventually he left the interstate heading in the direction of the small towns of Summerville and Trion, Georgia.

That Sunday morning, residents of Summerville woke up to find trees and power lines downed by the night's accumulation of ice. Streets and roads were slippery in spots and many were blocked by fallen timber, but some were still passable, and a few gas stations and convenience stores were able to be open early.

Amy Gilliland and her husband, Kevin, live in one of the most pleasant residential sections of Summerville. The streets leading to their house on White Oak Road are narrow and winding and lined with trees and shrubbery that fill in the areas between the comfortable, attractive homes.

On Sunday, January 23, 2000, Amy woke to find her neighborhood had been turned into a fairyland of glittering ice and snow. Unfortunately, there was a downside to the picture-postcard beauty left by the winter storms. Many sections of town, and the neighboring towns of Trion and Lyerly, were without electricity that morning.

Around 8:00 A.M., Amy called to check in with her father-in-law, Bobby Gilliland, who told her he had already been out riding around to see which parts of town still had power, and he told her he had gone to the Golden Gallon store on the Lyerly Highway. It was open and he had gotten some coffee there.

Amy then called Barbara Deering, her grandmother, to see if she had power. The electricity was out at Deering's house, and after Amy hung up, it occurred to her that she could go to the Golden Gallon store and get her grandmother some hot coffee. Amy left home in her 1996 Nissan Maxima and drove to the store, got the coffee, then went to her grandmother's house.

After a short visit, Amy left Barbara Deering's house and drove to Highway 27, which runs through downtown Summerville. She continued through town and made a couple of turns that took her back to White Oak Road. It was then that she first noticed she was being followed.

The car was an older Lincoln, pale blue or silver colored, with a dark blue top. It was a big car, a long four-door model, and it was following her so closely that she could read the Ohio license plate. Amy could see the driver, a big man, and he was coming dangerously close to Amy's car, especially considering the treacherous icy roads. She sped up, trying to move away from him, but he stayed on her bumper, keeping up with Amy as she drove faster along the twists and turns of the road toward her house.

The Gilliland house is only one house away from the dead end of White Oak Road. When Amy turned into her driveway, the driver of the Lincoln pulled in right behind her without any hesitation. Amy parked her car, then sat there for a few seconds, keeping a close eye on the driver in her rearview mirror. She decided she would be safer to get into the house as quickly as possible, so she got out of the car, walked around behind it, and went straight to the doorway leading to the house. The entire time, the stranger in the car watched her every move, and at the same time she was keeping a very close eye on him. He had turned off the motor of his car and was sitting there, staring at her, expressionless.

Amy hurried inside the house and began calling to her husband, Kevin, telling him to get up and come to check on the man who had followed her all the way home and was now parked behind her car in the driveway.

While Kevin was getting dressed, Amy peeped out the blinds looking at the car and the big man behind the wheel. For the first time, she noticed that there was either a small person or a child sitting in the passenger's seat and wearing a seat belt. The person was so small Amy could only see them from the nose up. Maybe this was a man and his child who needed help for some reason; maybe that was why they had followed her all the way home. She really ought to check and see if they were having car trouble or something.

Amy opened the door, staying safely inside the house, and shouted, "Can I help you?"

There was no response from the car.

Amy called out again, "Can I help you?"

The driver opened his door and stepped halfway out, with one foot on the ground, and leaned out and said without any expression, "We're lost."

Amy was able to get a good look at the man, who was only about twenty feet away from the doorway where she stood. He appeared to be in his late thirties to early forties with short, dark hair, a receding hairline and no mustache or beard. He was a very big man, and his face was very red and looked flushed. For some reason, Amy got the impression that he wasn't telling her the truth about being lost. The man got back in the car and shut the door without any further comment.

Amy's cat chose that inopportune moment to dart between her feet and run out the door, stopping by

Kevin's truck, about halfway to the Lincoln. Amy dashed out, snatched up the cat and retreated back to the house as quickly as she could. Her unwelcome visitor then started his car and backed out of the driveway, and Kevin got to the window just in time to see the big Lincoln's Ohio license plates as it pulled away and headed back down the road.

Sometime later that morning on Orchard Hill Road, in a neighborhood on the opposite side of Summerville, a man and his daughter left home on a walking tour of the neighborhood to look at the ice and broken trees. They had not gotten far from their home when Jeff "Coach" Bennett and his daughter, Beth, noticed a large grayish silver car stopped in the northbound lane of one of the streets they passed.

When the Bennetts headed back toward their home, the big car had moved on past their house and stopped again. As they walked closer to the car, Beth could see it had Ohio license plates. Through the front windshield, she saw a small woman or child sitting in the passenger's seat and a very large man behind the wheel. As they walked nearer, Coach thought to himself that it was unusual for a car with Ohio tags to be in his neighborhood, and even more unusual for it to be stopped in the middle of the road on a Sunday morning during an ice storm. He said, "Hi, how are you?" to the driver, but the man didn't respond. The Bennetts walked on past their house to the end of the road, and when they turned around and came back to their home, the car was gone.

Moments later, around 10:30 A.M., two women who lived farther down Orchard Hill Road decided to walk up the road and look at the storm damage. As Connie McCurdy and Rebecca Mickley topped Orchard Hill, they saw the Lincoln stopped in the road with its emergency flashers on.

"Ask those people if they need some help," Connie told Rebecca as they neared the car.

At first, the man and woman inside the Lincoln didn't answer when Rebecca spoke. Then the driver rolled down the window and told her he didn't need any help; he was letting the transmission cool down, he said.

The driver was a very large man with dark hair, and Rebecca could also see the small woman sitting in the passenger's seat. She had dark hair and glasses and was wearing a blue coat, and Rebecca later told investigators, "Her face was red, like she had been crying." Connie was standing by the passenger's-side window and she, too, noticed the woman appeared to have been crying and looked as if she were very upset.

As Connie and Rebecca began walking back toward their home, the Lincoln pulled into a driveway and both women noticed and commented on its Ohio license plates. They, like Coach Bennett, found it highly unusual for a car from Ohio to be cruising their neighborhood on a Sunday morning, especially when the streets and roads were gradually becoming impassable due to an ever-increasing coat of ice.

Chapter 15

"There was a woman with a cat."

The weather had improved enough for Amy Gilliland to make it in to work on Wednesday at the Trion Recreation Center, where she worked as the secretary. That afternoon, she overheard Coach Bennett talking to another employee of the recreation center about "the man from Ohio who had mutilated a woman." Remembering the Ohio license plate on her eerie visitor's car the previous Sunday morning, Amy excitedly interrupted Bennett, asking what he was talking about.

Coach Bennett told Amy about Hayward Bissell's arrest in Alabama with his girlfriend's dismembered body found strapped into the passenger's seat. He told her that he and his daughter, Elizabeth, along with quite a few other people, had seen the man and woman on Sunday morning, stopped in the road in their neighborhood. He described the man and his car, and said several people had seen him driving around in the area or sitting parked in the street.

Amy was almost certain this had to be the same man who had followed her home and pulled into her driveway behind her. Then Coach Bennett told Amy that he had talked to the police, and he and Beth had both given statements. The police had asked the Bennetts, "Do you know of a woman with a cat who lives close by?"

Amy almost started to cry when she realized she was the woman with the cat that they were looking for, and that the killer had been sitting right there in her driveway on Sunday morning, staring closely at her as she walked from her car to the house.

During the course of making some of his many rambling statements to the police, Bissell had evidently mentioned stopping at a house somewhere in the Summerville area.

"There was a woman with a cat," he had said.

The investigators had been searching in the wrong neighborhood for the woman with a cat. They had been asking about the woman in the same area where the Bennetts lived, in the Orchard Hill Road area west of Summerville. But Amy lived on the opposite side of town. In the course of his travels on Sunday, Bissell must have followed Amy to her house, gotten lost when he left her neighborhood, then crossed all the way through town and found himself in another, very similar neighborhood where he was spotted by several other people.

Coach Bennett told Amy that the *Chattanooga Times Free Press* had a photo of the murder suspect in that day's edition. Amy immediately went out and bought a copy of the paper. When she looked at the photo that accompanied the article, showing a large, bushy-haired man in shackles being led down a stairway by a uniformed deputy, she felt sick to her stomach and went weak with shock. She said to herself, "That's him. That's the man in my driveway!"

In the following weeks, Amy would come to realize just how lucky she was. Someone else looked out their window later that day and saw a big man in their driveway. Like Amy, James Pumphrey asked the man if he needed help. But James Pumphrey was not fortunate enough to keep Hayward Bissell at a distance. Amy's home had two stories, with the garage on the first floor. She looked out at Bissell from the safety of an upper level. But James Pumphrey was an easy target, standing on his small front porch. If Amy had not gotten quickly into her house first, then asked from a safe vantage point if Bissell needed help, he might have gone into his killing frenzy a few hours earlier that day. And "the woman with the cat" could very well have become his first victim.

Chapter 16

"She's deader than hell."

No one will ever know exactly what happened between Patricia Ann Booher and Hayward Bissell on January 23, 2000, in the final hours leading up to her death. No one knows but Bissell, and the truth is locked inside his mind and will likely remain there, untold, for the rest of his life.

Investigators in Alabama and Georgia spent countless days piecing together fragments of information gathered from Bissell's own statements, accounts from witnesses and autopsy findings. Gradually a clearer picture of Patricia's last moments of life began to emerge. However, authorities could only speculate about the fear, betrayal and disbelief the young woman must have felt in that final instant when she realized the man shc had loved, whose child she carried, was about to become the instrument of her death.

On Saturday morning, January 22, Patricia Booher had just finished talking on the phone to a couple of her friends, sharing with them the happy news that she was pregnant and asking their advice about the best places in the area to go shopping for baby clothes. She told them her baby's father was Hayward Bissell, a man they had repeatedly warned her not to continue seeing. She wanted to break off the relationship, she said, and had tried several times to do so, but each time Hayward convinced her that he loved her. He always seemed to know just the right things to say to make her change her mind and take back his engagement ring one more time. This time, she swore to herself, it would be different. It meant a lot to her to have a boyfriend, but she was beginning to believe that things were never going to work out with Hayward. He was too controlling and critical, and he hit her sometimes, and recently he had threatened to do much worse. She was afraid of him. They would break up but still be friends, and she would raise their baby herself.

Patty told her friends Bissell was pleased about the pregnancy, but assured them that she did not intend to marry him and did not want to go with him to Florida to visit his parents. He had been pressuring her to go, she said, but since she intended to break off their relationship, she would not feel comfortable making the trip with him.

Only a short time after the phone call ended, Patricia left her apartment to go for a ride with Bissell. He had talked her into taking a ride; a nice overnight ride, he later told an inmate at the DeKalb County Jail. She didn't know she was going to Florida, he said; she left with only her coat and purse. Patricia's sister and friends apparently were right when they kept insisting they didn't believe she left for Florida of her own free will without telling them; according to Bissell, she didn't go on the trip of her own volition. She was deceived by him.

Patty must have been quite upset when it dawned on her that the short ride she believed she was taking, to go shopping or perhaps to the library, was going to be much longer than she had planned. And there seemed to be nothing she could do to stop it; no matter how she begged and pled, Hayward refused to turn around and take her back to her apartment.

The couple got as far as Chattanooga that day, then stopped to spend the night at a motel on the outskirts of the city. They didn't get a room, however; neither of them had enough money. They spent the night in the parking lot, sleeping fitfully in the car while a cold rain fell outside.

Patricia woke long before dawn to find a thin coating of ice on the trees and power lines around the motel. She again begged her boyfriend to take her back home to Ohio, but Bissell ignored her pleas and got back on the interstate, headed south regardless of the worsening weather conditions. He crossed the state line into Georgia and began watching for an exit leading to a town. He told Patricia he intended to find a Western Union or automatic teller so his family could send him money to continue the trip. He was angry with Patricia because she said she had no money in her purse. They barely had enough to get coffee and some breakfast.

Eventually Bissell came to the Ringgold exit on I-75 and turned left at Highway 27, driving in a direction he hoped would lead him to a convenience store or other business that would be open early on a Sunday morning during such poor weather. He ended up in the small town of Summerville, Georgia, where he pulled into a Burger King restaurant's drive-through at about 7:30 A.M.

Bissell ordered two cups of coffee and breakfast biscuits, and he pulled to the window and talked to the waitress as he and Patricia got their coffee and waited for their breakfast order.

"I hear y'all have a big Trade Day around here," he said to the woman at the drive-through window.

"We have one," she said, "but it's not open on Sundays, only on Tuesday and Saturday."

"Can you buy weapons, guns and knives and stuff, at the Trade Day?" he asked.

"I don't think they sell them up there," the waitress replied, "but you could probably get some at the pawnshop."

Bissell shook his head.

"That takes too long. How do you get to the I-59 Flea Market over in Alabama?"

The waitress told him she didn't know for sure, but said that she could give him directions on how to get to Alabama, by turning to the right when he pulled out of the Burger King driveway and following Highway 48 into Alabama.

"When you get to the top of the mountain, someone at the store up there will be able to tell you how to get to the I-59 Flea Market," she said.

The waitress smiled at Patricia, who sat huddled miserably in the passenger's seat.

"Do you need that coffee to wake you up?" she asked.

"I need something to wake me up this morning," Patricia said. She looked tired and very frail, the waitress said, and she seemed to be unhappy.

Bissell paid for his order, then pulled out of the drive-through, turning left toward Trion, Georgia, instead of going to the right, the way the waitress had told him would take him into Alabama. He drove through the town's rather tricky intersection near the Chattooga County Courthouse, turning west on Highway 114. The road took him past several used-car lots and convenience stores and brought him to the far eastern side of Summerville.

Bissell drove around aimlessly for a while before another vehicle attracted his attention. He began following the woman driving the green Nissan Maxima as she drove through town into a residential area.

Bissell followed the woman closely, keeping pace with her as she sped up in an attempt to move a safe distance away from the Lincoln. When she turned into her driveway, he pulled in directly behind her and watched her as she got out of the car and went into the house.

A moment later, she opened the door and shouted, "Can I help you?"

Bissell did not answer at first. When she asked a second time if he needed help, he leaned out of the car and said, "We're lost," then got back into the car and closed the door. He saw the woman's cat dash out of the house into the snow, and watched the woman as she hurried out, grabbed the cat and quickly went back inside the house.

Bissell sat there for a while, trying to think what to do, then started the Town Car and backed out of the driveway, heading back the way he had come. He was becoming more angry and frustrated by the minute. All the streets looked alike, and all the houses looked the same.

Bissell continued wandering through the neighborhood, stopping frequently because of fallen trees and limbs that partially blocked some of the streets. He was not sure where he was, and did not know how to get back to a main highway. He couldn't decide which turns to take and Patricia was upset and crying, which only added to his anger and frustration. Eventually he found his way back to the road he had been on earlier, Highway 114, and went back through Summerville to the western side of town. He found himself in another residential district with more of the same small, winding roads that had frustrated him so much when he followed the woman in the Nissan into her driveway.

By this time, Bissell had gotten himself thoroughly lost. He was driving aimlessly around in circles throughout the area and was seen by a large number of residents. These folks later reported they had seen him stopped in several different locations and he looked as if he were trying to decide what to do.

He stopped once again in the middle of an icy street, trying to get his bearings, and a man and his daughter, who were out walking, said, "Hi, how are you?" as they passed by. Bissell ignored them and waited until they walked farther up the road; then he started the Town Car and drove a short distance farther down the road before he stopped once again, disoriented and very annoyed.

Two women, also out for a walk to look at the storm damage in their neighborhood, walked up beside the car a few moments later.

"Do you need some help?" one of the women asked.

Bissell did not respond at first, but then he decided to answer and rolled the window down.

"No, I don't need any help," he said. "I'm letting the transmission cool down. We're traveling."

Both women got a good look at Patricia while the window was rolled down. She didn't speak to them, but her face was red, they said, and she seemed upset and looked like she had been crying. As soon as the women walked on past the car and continued down the road, Bissell started the car and pulled into the driveway of a nearby house, where he sat until the women were out of sight. Then he pulled back out into the road again and continued on.

After more time spent driving around searching for a road leading out of the residential neighborhood and toward a business district, Bissell finally ended up at a stop sign on the outskirts of the small town of Trion, Georgia, where he turned left. He stopped and parked in front of a store in town for a few minutes, arguing with Patricia and shouting at her as she cried and begged him to take her home. Then, without explanation, he tried to force her to get out of the car, threatening to put her out on the side of the road and leave her there. Patricia, upset as she was, found the idea of being abandoned in rural Georgia during an ice storm even more terrifying than staying in the car with her angry boyfriend. She refused to get out of the Town Car and kept crying as she begged to go home. Her pleas were ignored, and Bissell drove another fifteen or twenty minutes farther to a Discount Food Mart on the Trion/Teloga Highway west of town. It was one of the few stores in the neighborhood that had electricity, and Bissell parked the Lincoln at the end of the building around noon, waiting for the store to open.

The Discount Food Mart's manager later reported to police that the car remained parked there until she opened the store at around 1:20 P.M.; then Bissell pulled into the blue gravel parking lot beside the store and parked the Lincoln close to the road and facing the store.

Around midafternoon, a Trion man drove to the Discount Food Mart to wait for two other men, who wanted to talk with him about a job. As he waited, the man saw Bissell's car sitting in the lot away from the store. He thought that the driver must have car trouble of some kind, to have parked so far away from the gas pumps.

"I saw a big man in a brown jacket leave the store," the man said. "As he walked down the sidewalk across the front of the store, he looked at me, started staring at my truck and at me, and walked over toward my side of the truck."

Bissell stood close outside the truck's driver's-side window and stared in at the man for fifteen or twenty seconds, but he didn't say anything. This began to make the man uneasy, and he rolled down his window and said, "Whatcha say, man?"

Bissell didn't answer; he just kept staring. Then finally he broke eye contact with the man, turned away, walked back around the truck and on to the Lincoln, opened the driver's-side door and got in, leaving the door standing open.

A minute later, the man in the truck saw a small young woman walk out of the store. From the drawn, worried expression on her face, he thought she might have car trouble and need some help, but she walked on past his truck to the Lincoln, opened the passenger's-side door and got in. She, too, left the door open.

The man thought it was unusual that the two people who had just gotten into the Lincoln had left both of the car's doors standing wide open, even though it was bitterly cold outside. About that time, the two men he was waiting on pulled up and parked beside him, and he pointed the Lincoln out to them, telling them about the people inside the car and how the driver had, for some unknown reason, tried to stare him down. He also mentioned to his friends about how strange he thought it was for the people in the car to have left their doors open in such cold weather.

After the three men talked awhile and exchanged information about their upcoming job, the man in the truck prepared to leave the store's parking lot. As he glanced over again at the Lincoln, he noticed something that looked like a woman's purse had been set on the ground outside the car. Both of the big car's doors still stood open as the man drove away.

Security tapes from the store's surveillance cameras show Hayward Bissell as he entered the front door at

2:24 P.M. He was a huge man who all but filled up the doorway, and he appeared to be fairly neat and well dressed. His hair was combed, and he carried himself with a haughty, arrogant bearing.

At 2:32 P.M., after going to the bathroom then wandering around the store for a while, he went back to the door and opened it halfway, standing there and looking out at the parking lot. He must have been watching his girlfriend as she walked toward the store, for in a frame of the film timed at 2:34 P.M., the tape showed Patricia Booher coming inside the building. Her appearance was a dramatic contrast to Bissell's, since she was such a diminutive young woman that her head reached only a short distance above the door's handle.

Patricia came into the store tentatively, looking around like she was afraid she would be punished for coming inside. Her face looked pale and she appeared to be very tense. At 2:36 P.M., she stood at the door and looked out toward the Lincoln sitting in the parking lot. Her hand rested on the door handle, and she seemed to be deciding whether or not to go outside. She, too, went to the rest room, then left.

After Hayward Bissell and Patricia Booher returned to the Town Car, the situation between them went from bad to worse. Bissell began screaming furiously at Patricia, accusing her of being either a black witch or a double agent. She was dismayed and terrified to hear her boyfriend making such wild accusations, and she didn't know how to respond. She was afraid of saying the wrong thing and making matters worse.

Hayward tried to get Patricia to tell him which of the two she was—a witch or a spy—for about an hour, he said, but she was scared to talk to him.

Bissell claimed that all the while he was trying to force Patricia to get out of the car, he was hearing voices in his head telling him he had to kill her. He said that he believed he was either "007 or the Devil."

Bissell told a jail inmate, "I told Patty she was a double agent and a black witch. Then I asked her, 'Do you know where you are, Patty?' She said, 'Georgia.' That was the last word she said. I reached into the backseat, got the knife, and cut her throat.

"I was just following orders," he said. "I was her supervisor. She was lying, so I terminated her."

The end must certainly have come with sudden, merciful speed for Patricia, with the first strike of the knife more than likely the cause of her death. Hopefully, she didn't have time to realize fully what was happening to her before she quickly lost consciousness and slumped over into the seat.

After cutting Patricia's throat, Bissell told the inmate, he "went on a rampage." Considering the terrible carnage that followed, his words were a gross understatement. He said he cut Patricia's hand and leg off "so she couldn't come back at me"; then, as falling rain and sleet partially obscured the view through the windshield, he continued his vicious mutilation of her dead body.

Autopsy findings listed multiple sharp-force injuries as the cause of Patricia's death. Her lower right leg was amputated at the knee, and her left hand was removed at the wrist. Portions of her left lung, heart, liver and stomach were removed, and extensive stab wounds were noted.

According to the autopsy report, a group of approximately thirty stab wounds were inflicted to both of Patricia's eyes and the bridge of her nose. Another four stab wounds were found on the left side of her neck below the left ear.

The sharp-force injury that was the first to be inflicted, and was most likely the cause of Patricia's death, was a fifteen-centimeter incision across the right side of her neck that completely severed her right carotid artery and jugular vein. The wound also transected her epiglottis and completely severed the top of her esophagus.

Another sharp-force injury was centered in the chest area, a large incision from which the left lung and most of the heart were removed, along with sections of the liver and stomach.

"A person doesn't bleed as much as you would think," Bissell later confided to another inmate. "She bled just enough to soak my hands good."

The interior of the Town Car was also blood soaked, according to the forensic examination that took place in Huntsville, Alabama, following the murder.

Forensic scientists found bloodstains on the outside of the car on the hood, driver's rearview mirror, driver's window and post, the driver's-side rear door and the trunk. Inside the car, bloodstains were found on the front and rear passenger's floor mat and carpet, the front passenger's door, seat and headrest, the driver's seat, the driver's door, steering wheel and gearshift knob. Blood spatters were found on the front passenger's window, and a total of twelve cuts were noted in the upholstery of the front passenger's-seat area. Four were on the seat near the driver's side, four were on the attached seat cushion, and four were underneath the cushion.

There was a fair amount of traffic at the Discount Food Mart that afternoon due to the weather conditions, with most of the other stores in the area without power, but Bissell had plenty of time to finish his bloody work without being interrupted. He was going to take the body to a hospital morgue, he later claimed, and "file his report." But before he could start the Lincoln's engine and leave, another vehicle, which was parked a short distance away from the Town Car, backed out and began to drive past. The two men inside were there to meet another man to talk about a job, and after they finished their discussion and their coworker pulled out of the parking lot, the two men also began to pull back out. As they drove past the Lincoln, they noticed its driver was staring at them in a very strange, almost challenging, manner. The car doors were open and they saw a girl was lying in the seat.

Then the big man reached down and pulled Patricia Booher's head up within their view, holding it up by the hair as they drove by, as if to show the two men his handiwork—as though he were proud to display what he had done. When he let go of her, the men said she "melted down into the seat." There was no expression on her face, and her eyes were closed and sagging down.

As the men watched, horrified but unsure of exactly what it was that they were seeing, Bissell cranked the Town Car and "kicked it" out of the parking lot and down the highway.

The two men were momentarily shocked into silence; then one of them spoke finally.

"She's deader than hell," he said.

Investigator Johnny Bass has a theory that differs from Bissell's account of what happened on the day Patricia was killed in the convenience store's parking lot. Because of the extensive number of wounds, the two amputations and the careful rearrangement of Patricia's clothing and the refastening of her seat belt, Bass believed the initial killing blow, when Bissell cut her throat, was struck in the parking lot. But he believed the other horrible wounds inflicted on her body may have been done in another location. Bass believed that the two witnesses saw Patricia's body after the first fatal blow had been struck. Then, he speculated, instead of continuing on his self-described "rampage" and dismembering his girlfriend's corpse in the parking lot of the Discount Food Mart, as he had claimed, Bissell may have shown the two men what he had done, then sped down the highway a very short distance from the store to a dirt road that turned off into a field.

"I think he went out to that field road and turned in, out of sight from the highway, and mutilated Patricia there after killing her quickly in the parking lot of the store," Bass said.

"Then he may have come back out to the road and drove back past the Discount Food Mart and on to Menlo, Georgia, then turned right and ended up in Mentone, Alabama. He would have been on the road that went to Menlo and would have had to make only one turn to get to Mentone. And he had been asking people about the I-59 Flea Market, which is in Hammondville, so he had that location on his mind. At some point, Bissell found out about Collinsville Trade Day as well as the I-59 Flea Market. He was into flea markets and things like that."

Bass said he believed that Bissell had probably killed Patricia at the Discount Food Mart parking lot, but would have had to take her someplace else to mutilate her in such a horrific manner. That, he said, would have taken some time to accomplish; then Bissell would have had to have time to re-dress Patricia's body and strap it into the seat.

"I don't think he could have done so much to her while he was sitting there in the parking lot; the place where the car was sitting was up close to the road, facing the store. There were quite a few people coming and going, since that was one of the few stores in the neighborhood that was open and had electricity that day. I think he must have had to take her somewhere else to finish what he did to her."

When Bass developed his theory that the mutilation had taken place in a different location, somewhere in the field off the dirt road near the store, he brought in a team with trained dogs to check out the area for any traces of blood. The dogs and their handlers went over every inch of the field where Bass believed Bissell might have parked the car while he mutilated Patricia. It had been several weeks, however, since the murder. By that time, the weather had successfully erased any traces of blood evidence that might have been found there earlier. The dogs were unable to detect any scent of blood in the area.

"I still think that's where it happened," Bass said.

Wherever the desecration of Patricia Booher's dead body took place, it was a horrible, tragic ending to an all-too-short life. Patty only wanted to be loved, but sadly, the man whom she claimed to love with all her heart and soul turned out to be her brutal executioner. And the heart she so freely gave to him was carved from her chest and left lying on the floorboard of his blood-soaked car.

Chapter 17

"I'm not exactly normal."

When Hayward Bissell arrived for treatment and evaluation at Taylor Hardin Secure Medical Facility in Tuscaloosa, Alabama, he was described by hospital personnel as appearing to be "dazed and confused." He had behaved fairly well on the trip from the DeKalb County Jail, according to the deputies who brought him to the hospital, except for one minor incident when he began demanding for them to stop and buy him a Sprite. He grew quite insistent about his immediate need for the soft drink, but he didn't get it until later, when the van stopped for fuel. Then the deputies brought him his Sprite and he was quiet once again, remaining pacified for the rest of the trip.

Once Bissell arrived at the hospital, he talked very little, but was relatively cooperative and still believed himself to be a Secret Service agent who had been "contaminated by the Devil."

Several courses of medication were tried during the following weeks and eventually a combination of drugs seemed to begin working effectively. Bissell gradually became more alert and oriented, but claimed that he still occasionally continued to experience delusions. Patricia's ghost sometimes visited him in his cell and talked with him, he said. As time passed, he began reporting less hallucinations and was able to hold rational conversations with staff psychiatrists about his legal situation.

On one occasion, Bissell was asked if he realized that he had problems with mental illness.

"Yes," he replied. "I'm not exactly normal."

While Bissell was being evaluated at the institution in Tuscaloosa, Investigator Bass and Detective Colbert made a trip to Ohio to gather evidence in the case against him. They arrived in Norwalk on February 7, and were welcomed by what Bass described as "one of the sharpest, best police departments I've ever seen." Norwalk police chief Mike Ruggles and Sergeant David Light went out of their way to assist the two Georgia officers, and Bass and Colbert were treated like visiting royalty by the local authorities and the press.

"The Norwalk Police Department couldn't have been any nicer, more cooperative or more professional," Bass said, "but they have never had to deal with any cases like Bissell's. Their area is fortunate in that they seem to have a very low crime rate, especially when it comes to murders or even accidental deaths. They and the news media in that area were all really excited over the situation. It was something they hadn't experienced previously."

Norwalk, in fact, was a town that was accustomed to enjoying a great deal of positive publicity instead of being touted as the home of a crazed killer and his helpless victim. The town was named 1998's "Safest Ohio City" in its population class by the FBI, and presented an almost picture-perfect image of the ideal all-American town. In December 2000, the city became one of Ohio's Mainstreet Communities, largely due to the high quality of services and opportunities provided by its city government, including its outstanding police and fire protection.

Chief Ruggles and his department may have been unaccustomed to dealing with a large number of major crimes within their jurisdiction, but they went all-out in their efforts to assist Bass and Colbert during their stay in Norwalk. On February 8, 2000, Ruggles obtained a warrant to re-search Bissell's apartment, and Bass and Colbert got the chance to go over the premises again thoroughly and look for any additional evidence they might be able to find.

The search yielded a few minor items that proved interesting, but provided little new information. A "to do" list was found in the bedroom, with mundane daily activities planned in a regimented manner.

"It was everyday stuff like 'get up, brush teeth, get dressed, eat breakfast,' things like that," Bass said.

"Bissell had written some notes to a lot of people," said Colbert, "telling them stuff like how he was going to go away for a long time. He tore them up in little pieces and threw them in the trash, and we fished them out and fit them back together like jigsaw puzzles. But they didn't amount to anything of any real importance to the case."

After driving for hours to several small towns in the area of Norwalk to locate and interview countless acquaintances and relatives of both Hayward Bissell and Patricia Booher, Bass and Colbert returned to Georgia on February 9. They brought with them a great deal of evidence that would prove to be of primary importance when jurisdiction of the murder case was finally decided.

Bass returned from his trip to Norwalk and the surrounding area with some colorful descriptions of the Ohio countryside with which he had become so familiar in such a short time. After driving around the region for hours on end during the three-day trip, searching out cousins, coworkers and friends to try to interview for information on the case, Bass described the area for his friends in the Chattooga County District Attorney's Office.

"That place is flat, flat, flat," he said, comparing the farmlands and countrysides of rural Ohio to those of the gently rolling northwestern Georgia hills.

"And they've got some big-ass barns up there."

Toward the end of March, Bissell was evaluated as being logical and without any obvious symptoms of mental illness. He claimed to have no current problems with depression or psychosis, and was described by doctors as neat and clean, with an IQ above average. He had a good-enough understanding of the charges against him and the functioning of the court and the trial process, according to his primary psychiatric examiner, who believed Bissell would now be able to assist his attorney with his defense and get a fair trial.

"It is my opinion that he can move forward with the trial process at this time," the examiner informed the court.

In early April, Sheriff Cecil Reed got a phone call he would have preferred not to receive. Bissell was ready to return to his cell in the DeKalb County Jail.

"They're sending him back," Reed grumbled to Chief Jailer Bill Lands. "Let's get his cell ready."

Circuit court clerk Jimmy Lindsey was officially notified on Tuesday, April 11, that the Taylor Hardin Secure Medical Facility had completed their evaluation and treatment of Hayward Bissell, and they were now ready to return him to the custody of DeKalb County authorities. A court order to that effect was requested, and was issued that same day by circuit judge Randall Cole.

Cole's order required that Bissell would be transported from Taylor Hardin to the DeKalb County Jail by the sheriff's deputies, and that arrangements would be made through the local mental-health center or other treating physician for Bissell to receive whatever follow-up care was recommended by the clinical staff at Taylor Hardin.

"Mr. Bissell shall remain on his current medication regimen while housed in the DeKalb County Jail to ensure psychiatric stability," the order stated. It went on to list the prisoner's current medications: Diabeta (for his type 2 diabetes), Haldol, Prozac, Vistaril and Cogentin to treat his mental and emotional difficulties, and Zantac for his stomach problems.

Reed and his staff began making careful preparations for Bissell's arrival. Remembering his behavior in the jail before his transfer to Taylor Hardin, both the jailers and the inmates dreaded his return.

"We're putting him back in the same cell he had before," Lands said. "We've got all new plumbing in there, and I hope we don't end up having to replace it again."

A small group of reporters and photographers were allowed into the jail to take pictures of the cell and its new pipes and fixtures, which had been installed to be as sturdy as possible. It was obvious, however, that Bissell would be easily capable of ripping the plumbing out once again if he took a notion to do so.

"We don't really know what to expect out of him," Lands said. "We're just going to try and be as well prepared as possible."

On Thursday, April 13, a group of deputies traveled to Tuscaloosa to bring Hayward Bissell back to the DeKalb County Jail. Sheriff Reed told reporters he expected that the prisoner would remain in his custody for some time to come.

"I'm still convinced the homicide happened in

Georgia," Reed said, "but the state of Georgia has not yet filed murder charges against him. The only charges against him at this time are our assault cases here in DeKalb County, so unless that situation changes he will be housed here in the county jail awaiting trial in the circuit court sometime this fall.

"We haven't heard from the authorities in Georgia lately. There haven't been any updates. The last we heard, they were still actively investigating."

Reed said Bissell would be alone in his cell for security reasons, and would be constantly monitored by security cameras and checked on frequently by jailers.

Early on Thursday afternoon, a county patrol car pulled up to the back entrance of the jail. A crowd of TV cameramen, reporters and photographers were waiting for Bissell's return, along with almost all the sheriff's department personnel on duty at the time. No one knew what to expect from the notorious prisoner, but they were all in for a shocking surprise.

The man whom deputies helped out of the backseat of the patrol car was practically unrecognizable to those who had, only three months earlier, gathered to watch him leave the jail under heavy guard in a specially reinforced transport van.

Hayward Bissell was a drastically changed man. He had lost over forty pounds during his stay at Taylor Hardin and was wearing handcuffs, but no leg irons. His hair was cut short, he had grown a short beard, which was neatly trimmed, and he was wearing a navy-and-white jogging suit instead of prison whites.

The greatest change, however, was in his behavior. He appeared calm and clear-eyed as he walked steadily toward the jail entrance. He showed no reaction at all to the waiting cameras and microphones of the press.

One new and slightly inexperienced television reporter, who had earlier expressed a great deal of nervousness about coming face-to-face with the notorious prisoner, hung back at the rear of the pack of news personnel. His cameraman prodded him to move in and get close enough to the action so that he could at least get some footage suitable for the evening news, and the rookie finally mustered up the courage to dart closer to Bissell and thrust a microphone into his face.

"Do you have anything you'd like to say to your victims?" the nervous young man asked in a shaky voice.

"No comment," Bissell replied without even glancing in his direction.

The reporter's colleagues teased him unmercifully for several months about the speed with which he backed away out of arm's reach following his brief and unsuccessful attempt at a jailhouse interview.

Bissell and the deputies accompanying him walked down the stairs into the jail, where his handcuffs were removed. He sat quietly in a chair beside the jailer's desk during the booking process and remained calm and cooperative, occasionally glancing around the room while he waited for his transfer paperwork to be completed. His huge packet of prescriptions was carefully logged in, and the dosage schedule was checked and double-checked by a jailer as Bissell continued to sit quietly, clear-eyed and calm. His behavior, so dramatically changed, was going to come as a tremendous relief to the staff of the DeKalb County Jail and to Bissell's fellow inmates.

This time, perhaps, having Hayward Bissell in residence at the jail might not cause the other prisoners to lose their visiting privileges and leave them wading through an inch or more of filthy water.

While things remained quiet and orderly at the jail the following week, word came that charges against Bissell in the death of his pregnant girlfriend were apparently beginning to move forward in Georgia.

When contacted by the press for a statement, Chattooga County District Attorney Herbert "Buzz" Franklin said that his office did indeed plan to charge Bissell in the case.

"At some point, he will be charged with the murder of Patricia Booher," Franklin said. "The laboratory last week confirmed that the blood found in the parking lot of a convenience store in Trion, Georgia, was that of Ms. Booher."

Franklin said Bissell, at some point during the investigation of the murder, had stated he had killed Booher at that location.

"We will be conferring with Alabama authorities at some point," Franklin said. "The Chattooga County Grand Jury meets in August, and we will likely present the case to them at that time."

Sheriff Reed confirmed Franklin's statement that Bissell had told his DeKalb County investigators the location of the murder site and they, in turn, had led Chattooga County authorities to the evidence.

"That's why I've remained convinced the murder occurred in Georgia," Reed told reporters. "I was present at the scene with my investigators when we initially found the blood evidence in the parking lot."

The news that Georgia planned eventually to file murder charges against Bissell came as welcome news to DeKalb County district attorney Mike O'Dell. Regardless of what Georgia authorities might do or when they might do it, however, O'Dell felt he had a great responsibility to Bissell's Alabama victims. Two of his county residents had been assaulted without provocation and had suffered serious and traumatic injuries, and Mike O'Dell was determined that Don Pirch and James Pumphrey would receive the justice to which they were entitled.

O'Dell's greatest worry was the possibility that, if for

any reason Georgia didn't proceed with the murder case, Bissell's insanity plea might be upheld in the assault cases. Then Bissell could conceivably walk the streets a free man in a relatively short period of time if he was able to convince his doctors at some point that he was "cured."

That possibility, to Mike O'Dell, was completely unacceptable. He suspected that Bissell might not be nearly as unstable as he appeared, and that his ability to play the role of a mentally ill person could have been easily perfected during his years of visits to psychiatrists and counselors.

O'Dell and his staff continued to press forward with their own investigation, preparing to present their cases against Hayward Bissell to the DeKalb County Grand Jury at its next meeting. And Sheriff Cecil Reed and his staff continued to house the prisoner in the county jail, with most of the other inmates taking great pains to avoid any contact with the big man they still feared.

There was, however, an exception. The relationship one jail trusty developed with Hayward Bissell would eventually provide some of the most valuable information Mike O'Dell and the DeKalb County investigators could ever have hoped for—information that helped to back up Mike O'Dell's theory about Bissell's true mental state.

Chapter 18

"A person doesn't bleed as much as you would think."

Todd Graves was a well-liked young man in his hometown of Collinsville, Alabama. His extended family was one of the oldest, largest and best known in town, and it included scores of aunts, uncles and cousins. Todd also had a wide-ranging circle of friends throughout the county, with a steady stream of visitors dropping by his house at all hours for parties and backyard barbecues. Todd was a husky, good-natured guy who happened to be an excellent cook, and he loved to feed and entertain his guests.

When the opportunity to sell a little marijuana on the side presented itself, the money-making prospect was just too great to turn down. Todd succumbed to the old-as-sin temptation of easy money, and his business began to grow.

Before long, Todd was handling a fairly large volume of product, and as in most small towns, word began to get around and the competition began to get jealous. Eventually, as with all get-rich-quick schemes, the bubble burst and Todd was arrested, the first time in his life that he ever had been in any sort of trouble. He was sentenced to the DeKalb County Jail after a conviction on marijuana-trafficking charges; he began serving his time in autumn 1999.

Todd had several friends among the ranks of the county deputies, including some from the Collinsville area who had known him all his life. On his first day in jail, he was made a trusty and was put to work as a cook. Jailhouse meals immediately took a drastic change for the better. The likable young man became as popular inside the jail as he was on the outside, and the deputies, jailers and inmates started looking forward to mealtimes. Instead of ordering out at lunchtime or going to one of the local restaurants, deputies on patrol often stopped by the jail to see what Todd was cooking that day.

Like the other inmates, Todd Graves heard all the commotion when Hayward Bissell was first brought to the county jail. Along with everyone else, Todd waded through the murky water standing on the floors when Bissell ripped out the pipes in his cell and flooded the jail, and he could hear the prisoner screaming obscenities all the way to his workstation in the jail kitchen. And he heard all the rumors and stories that circulated throughout the jail population, rumors that were even more lurid than the reality of Bissell's crimes.

Despite his own size and his considerable ability to defend himself, Graves was just a bit on edge when he first began delivering meals to Bissell's cell after the prisoner's return from evaluation and treatment at Taylor Hardin. Although there had not been a single problem since then, those flooded floors, canceled family visits and shocking rumors remained vivid in everyone's memory.

Todd Graves was, by nature, a very friendly and talkative fellow, and in spite of his uneasiness, he just couldn't find it in himself to be rude to Bissell. He always spoke politely to the big, silent man when he brought meals around to the cells. At first, Bissell didn't reply, but after a while, he began occasionally making small talk with the good-natured trusty whenever he came around.

In mid-May 2000, Todd Graves sent word to Investigator Mike James by way of his deputy friends that he had gotten hold of some information they might be able to use in the Bissell case. A few days later, an interview was arranged with Todd Graves, Mike James, Eddie Colbert and Johnny Bass. The men met in James's office and Todd told them what he had learned from his talks with Bissell.

Bass began by asking Todd about a conversation he'd had with Bissell earlier that week.

"We went out on a yard call and they let him come out with us," Todd said, "and when he came out, he made a beeline straight over there to me and started talking to me."

"Why do you think he may have come to you?" Bass asked.

"I guess because I've served him meals and talked with him then, and he would talk about the food and stuff like that. He said that he liked the meals on Sundays and he likes the peanut butter and jelly sandwiches we made and stuff like that. He just commented about how good some of the food was and some of it wasn't."

Bass asked Graves if Bissell was coherent and able to carry on a decent, logical conversation, and Graves said yes. Bass then asked Graves if he had seen inside Bissell's cell, and what it looked like.

"Real clean, neat, everything in its place," Graves answered. "He's got a top bunk and keeps his stuff on it and it's all in neat order and, you know, everything in its own little place."

"What about his personal hygiene," Bass asked, "does he brush his teeth?"

"He's real clean, brushes his teeth, and everything," Graves said, "and his clothes are real neat and clean."

Bass asked about the day and time of the conversation in the exercise yard, and Graves told him it took place on Tuesday of that week around 6:00 P.M., and that Bissell commented on enjoying being outdoors in the pleasant weather, the sun and fresh air.

Bass asked if Bissell had ever had any kind of outburst with anyone while he was out on the yard, or if anyone else had any words with him, and Graves said no.

"He was fine about that," Graves said. "They were shooting basketball and the ball came to him several times out there and he would grab it and throw it back to them and stuff, you know. He was just fine."

Graves told the investigators he and Bissell talked for around an hour, and the conversation began with Bissell's concerns about his car.

"He was wondering if he would be able to get the car back or not and talked about it being in the impound yard, and then he got to talking about where the murder happened in Georgia," Graves said. "Then he talked about him leaving Ohio with her and about him killing her in the car, and just wondering [again] if he was going to be able to get his car back or not."

Bissell told Graves he had been planning to go to Jacksonville, Florida, and claimed that his father worked there. He never referred to Patricia Booher by name, never called her his girlfriend, and didn't mention her pregnancy, Graves said. Bissell also never mentioned hearing voices, being a Secret Service agent on a secret mission, and never claimed that a part of his mission was to terminate Patricia. He did, however, tell Graves several other details about the murder.

"Did he say that he killed her in the front seat of the car?" Bass asked.

"Yes. He didn't say what he killed her with, but he was talking about having knives in his car. He called them toothpicks, and I said, 'Yeah, Texas toothpicks.' That's a long, slender knife."

"What did he say about the things that happened in Alabama?" Bass asked.

"He said that he wasn't worried about that because his doctor told him that he was insane about what happened here in Alabama and his doctor is going to testify on his behalf on that. So he wasn't worried about the charges here, but he was worried about the ones in Georgia because he said the murder happened in Georgia, in his car in Georgia. He was worried about whether that doctor could go to Georgia and testify on his behalf—being from Alabama like this—or if he would have to get another doctor, or something like that."

Bass asked Graves if he thought Bissell had talked with his lawyer about the doctor's testimony.

"He said he had, and that his lawyer told him that he had a paper where the doctor said he was insane and was going to testify on his behalf."

"So, he was saying that's how his defense is going to be, that he was insane?" Bass asked.

"Yes," Graves said, "that's basically what he said."

"And he talked with you coherently about that defense? He didn't hesitate about it or act like he was hearing some kind of voice telling him that or anything?"

"No, he was fine," Graves said.

Colbert then asked Todd if he had any more information about Bissell's knives.

"He was talking about him having a knife collection back home and he got rid of all of them but the ones that he had in his car with him," Graves said. "He was talking about them being those toothpick knives and I collect knives, too, and I told him I had some Texas toothpicks and he said yeah, he said that's what they were."

"So, he was worried about getting the car and the knives back?" Colbert asked.

"Yeah, he was real worried about the car and the knives," Graves said. "He really wasn't too concerned about the other stuff, the way he talked. You know he said the murder was in Georgia. It happened in the front seat of his car in Georgia and he thought his car would probably have to go to Georgia because of that."

The investigators asked Todd if Bissell had acted normally since he'd been having contact with him, and if he seemed to have a clear understanding of what was going on around him. Todd told them Bissell seemed to be fine, and that he had said he'd like to have a television in his cell, since he liked to watch TV occasionally. He also said he had seen Bissell reading newspapers and playing solitaire.

"So, he knows what's going on in the world around him?" Bass asked.

Graves said he believed so, and said he and Bissell often had brief, general conversations when he brought meals around to thc cells, but on the day in question they had talked in detail about the murder and his defense.

"And he talked about what his intentions were about claiming to be insane, or the doctor's saying he was insane?" Bass asked.

"Yes," Graves said, "he said he thought that's what was going to get him out of this in Alabama and he was hoping that the same doctor, you know, could testify over there in Georgia and that the same thing would happen over there."

The information Todd Graves was able to provide for the investigators painted a new and very valuable picture of Hayward Bissell's mental state at the time of the murder and subsequent assaults. Details that Bissell previously had claimed remained cloudy in his memory were now being described to Graves during the yard calls with gruesome clarity. Some of Bissell's casual remarks during their conversations were horrifying to Graves, and they burned themselves into his memory.

"I'll never forget this one thing he said about killing the girl," Graves said. "He was acting like he didn't think killing her was any big deal, and he wasn't worried about it. He said, 'A woman gets killed every fifteen minutes in this country,' just like it was nothing."

For some time, Mike O'Dell's belief had been that Bissell was, to a certain extent, manipulating his doctors by playing the well-learned role of a paranoid schizophrenic. He'd had years of practice, and countless medical and psychiatric professionals on which to hone his performance, O'Dell thought, but now he was beginning to tip his hand at last. Bissell's jailhouse conversations with Graves and other prisoners about his crimes were drastically different from the carefully worded accounts he had given to the mental-health personnel and investigators he had talked to.

Todd Graves was very willing to help with the case in any way, and he began keeping precise, detailed notes on his increasingly frequent talks with Bissell. He always listened carefully, then returned to his bunk and wrote down each conversation as accurately as possible, with the date, time and place noted.

Only a few hours after his interview with Bass, Colbert and James, a group of inmates that included Bissell and Graves went on yard call from 6:00 to 7:00 P.M. and the two had time for another long and very productive chat. More and more details continued to emerge about Patricia Booher's death and the hours leading up to it.

Bissell told Graves he initially got off the interstate to find a Western Union so his family could send him money to continue the trip to Florida. Then, he said, he drove across Georgia.

Bissell related how he stopped at a convenience store in Georgia, which he described as having two gas pumps with a blue gravel drive and a parking lot, also blue gravel, beside the store. The Georgia Bureau of Investigation was wrong about finding blood on the gravel, he told Graves, because he killed Patricia in the car and he didn't believe any blood was spilled from the car.

Bissell also told Graves that Patricia was dead before he mutilated and dismembered her, and added that it was raining and that if any blood had gotten out of the car, it would have washed away.

"A person doesn't bleed as much as you would think," he said, shocking Graves. "She bled just enough to soak my hands good."

Bissell went on to say he shouldn't have gotten off the interstate. He went on a rampage, he said, and thought that he had gone only twenty to thirty minutes after killing Patricia when he stopped at the Pumphrey home in Mentone. Then he showed Graves the bite marks on his hand and arm that the Pumphreys' dogs had made in their attempt to defend their owners.

"I got even with the dogs," he said. "I cut one's throat and then I cut the second one. Then the man got in my way, so I cut him, too, because he was in my way."

Bissell told Graves that he had asked the doctor to take him off his pills because he wasn't schizophrenic, so the doctor put him on Xanax and Prozac.

The conversation then turned to the knives that were in Bissell's car, and then to Patricia's family. Amazingly, he remarked that his girlfriend's family was probably upset at him. But he had not met them, he said, and said he was a "little to blame" for her death. He told Graves he wanted to talk to him about the murder, and said it helped him to talk about it. At the end of yard call, when the inmates returned to their bunks, Graves carefully wrote down the conversation to the nearest of his recollection.

Graves had a chance to talk to Bissell again the following evening, and he pulled a metal folding chair up to the bars of the cell and sat in the hallway, listening as Hayward talked about what he expected the outcome of his case to be. Bissell speculated that he might get twenty years for murder.

Bissell told Graves he would accept a manslaughter charge, but not murder, and claimed he would get off on an insanity plea. If he had to do twenty years in prison, he said, he would be fifty-eight years old when he got out. He also talked about his two daughters, telling Graves that one of them was nine years old.

A few days later, Graves sent another note to investigators with more details about Patricia Booher's murder. Bissell had told him during another yard call that when they were stopped at the convenience store, he was screaming at Patty and she was scared to talk to him.

"If she had said something to me, I wouldn't have killed her," he told Graves.

Bissell told Patty she was a double agent and a black

witch, he said. Then he asked her, "Do you know where you are, Patty?"

She answered, "Georgia."

That was the last word she said, Bissell told Graves. He then said that he reached in the backseat of the Town Car, got the knife and cut her throat. He repeated again that the last word Patricia ever spoke was "Georgia."

Bissell told Graves that he had packed the knife to show to his father when they got to Florida. He started to leave it at home, he said, but wanted to show it to his father.

Graves also noticed that Bissell occasionally spoke to a few of the other inmates, and he, along with jailer Michael Toombs, enlisted them in the efforts to collect details of Bissell's crimes for the investigators. Several of the men reported back to Todd and Toombs with valuable tidbits of information, which they passed along.

One man reported hearing Bissell say he killed Patricia in Georgia, and that his intention then was to kill someone and rob them. He said the dogs "messed it up." He told the man he was irritated at the dogs, because he was going to finish dismembering Patricia and scatter her body parts up and down the interstate.

Another inmate said Bissell was bragging that the doctors had certified him as being crazy, and claimed he would do six years for his crimes and be back on the street.

Still, another man reported that Bissell acknowledged that Patty did not come on the trip with him on her own. He said he talked her into taking a ride, a nice overnight ride, and said she did not know she was going to Florida when she left her apartment with him that Saturday morning.

Bissell also told other inmates that when he ran Don

Pirch down on the highway, he just wanted to keep Patricia's body from being noticed. On stopping at the Pumphrey home, he said, he needed money. And he didn't say "the voices" told him to.

Perhaps the most intelligent comment came from an inmate in a nearby cell, a man who was waiting to be transferred to the state prison for the murder of his wife and mother-in-law for insurance money. He had spent much of his time listening to what Bissell had to say, starting with his first night of screaming and cursing in jail, then after his return following evaluation and treatment. After analyzing and observing Bissell at close range for several months, the inmate stated, "This guy's smart, not crazy."

Graves continued to pull a metal folding chair up to the bars outside Bissell's cell occasionally and sit in the hallway, talking to him for a while in the evenings. One night, during a thunderstorm, Graves was sitting in the hall next to the bars of Bissell's cell when the power suddenly went out and the lights in the jail momentarily went dark. Prisoners began to shout and bang on the bars of their cells, but the loudest sound that echoed through the jail that night was the ear-splitting screech of the metal chair against the cement floor as Graves hurriedly scooted back out of Bissell's reach.

"I didn't want to take any chances of him trying to grab me through the bars while it was dark," Graves said. "You never know what somebody like that might do."

A moment later, Graves said, Bissell began to scream.

"He was yelling, 'Get out of the halls! Get out!' It was enough to make your hair stand up, the way he was hollering," Graves said. "But he did that sometimes at night; he'd be talking to the Lord one minute and the Devil the next."

With the exception of his single marijuana-trafficking conviction, Todd Graves had always been a young man who tried to do the right thing. He had a mother and twin sisters, whom he loved dearly, and it wasn't easy for him to sit and listen, trying not to react, while Bissell described his horrific mutilation of Patricia Booher. It could have been his own brother or father instead of Don Pirch on that road in Mentone, or his beloved grandparents instead of the Pumphreys who might have looked out their front windows to see Bissell walking up their driveway with a long knife in his hand. Todd couldn't keep from being very ill at ease while he was spending time talking with Bissell, but he was determined to do his best to help. He did whatever he could to aid the deputies and investigators; after all, it was the right thing to do.

The information Todd reported to the investigators and the tips that he helped to collect from other inmates provided a great deal of validation for O'Dell's theory about Bissell's alleged mental state at the time of his crimes. And, like Mike O'Dell, Mike James, Eddie Colbert and Johnny Bass, Todd Graves believed that Hayward Bissell was crazy like a fox, attempting to use his long-documented mental problems to get himself out of trouble.

Chapter 19

"We've exhausted all our personal and family resources."

While Hayward Bissell spent his days sitting leisurely in jail, having his meals delivered, his laundry done, and sharing his accounts of going "on a rampage" with Todd Graves and a few other of his fellow inmates, the DeKalb County victims of that rampage were suffering a very different kind of punishment.

"We didn't ask to be victims, but we live with it every day, with every limp Don makes because of his injured knee," Rhea Pirch said in April.

"Although he didn't suffer any broken bones that day, Don just had surgery to repair some torn cartilage in his right knee as a result of the attack. We thank God Bissell didn't stop and do more damage than he did to Don, and we look forward to the day when it will be a faded memory."

As time passed, however, the memories didn't fade quite as quickly as Don and Rhea had hoped that they would. They, along with James and Sue Pumphrey, were beginning to learn that the problems of assault victims don't end when the perpetrators are arrested and charged. Victims remain victims long after the crime is over and the case is settled.

"We see the damage of the ice storm every day on the mountain and it always brings back memories of January twenty-third," Rhea said. "We're happy to see the trees turn green this spring, not only because we welcome springtime, but because it will help cover up some of the reminders of the ice storm."

In addition to his continuing knee problems, Don Pirch was also experiencing a recurrence of the post-traumatic stress disorder he suffered after serving a tour of duty in Vietnam. The terrifying images of the hit-and-run attack, with Bissell's eyes staring at him through the windshield of the Lincoln Town Car as it sped down the highway, continued to haunt him day and night.

"I've got a vindictive attitude at times about what has happened," Pirch said, "but understanding the circumstances might help me feel some sympathy toward Bissell if lack of medication was partly responsible for his behavior."

Bissell's return to the county from Taylor Hardin in such a changed condition made Pirch believe the attack might not have occurred had Bissell been on the proper medication. For a time, both the Pirches and the Pumphreys considered the possibility of hiring attorneys and bringing suit against Bissell's Ohio doctors if investigators determined the halting of some of his medication was a likely cause of his ensuing crimes. They took no action, though; the difficulty and expense of retaining attorneys out of state was great, and the stress would have been more than they were able to deal with at the time.

In addition to his physical and emotional difficulties, his nightmare encounter with Hayward Bissell left Don Pirch with some equally serious financial problems.

"We've been in contact with the Crime Victims'

Compensation Commission, but it's taking a long time to get assistance and our financial situation is in dire straits," Pirch said. "Our insurance limit has been exhausted. I had my knee surgery two weeks ago and the doctor has indicated I may get a percentage of disability, but I had some broken ribs on January fifth and was just getting ready to go back to work when this happened. I've had a total of forty-five minutes of work so far this year, and we've exhausted all our personal and family resources."

Despite their own situation, Don and Rhea Pirch were very much aware they were the luckiest of Bissell's Alabama victims that day. They were sad that their friends James and Sue Pumphrey had to suffer such serious injury and emotional trauma when Bissell attacked them in their home after leaving the hit-and-run scene.

"We've worked with James and known them both for a long time, and they're wonderful people," Don said, "and we regret that James was Bissell's final victim."

The Pumphreys fared even worse than Don and Rhea Pirch in the aftermath of Bissell's attack. Months after the assault, James continued to have nagging muscle spasms and a great deal of pain from his surgery, and he kept regular appointments with a counselor. James had hoped to be able to return to work, and after a few months of recovery, he tried to start back to his job at a local hosiery mill, on light duty and on a part-time basis. His injuries were not sufficiently healed, though, and within a few days, he realized, to his great disappointment, that it would not be possible for him to continue.

Sue's employment literally had gone up in smoke a couple of weeks before the attack when a local landmark, the Rock Castle Cafe in Hammondville, burned to the ground on January 3. Ironically, the Rock Castle had stood for decades at the same intersection where Bissell was intercepted and arrested only a couple of weeks after the café burned. Sue had worked there as a cook, and she woke up the morning after the fire to find herself out of work. That situation—added to the emotional trauma she had suffered during Bissell's attack—left her as much a victim as if she, too, had been physically wounded. The horrible memories of seeing James critically stabbed, and her beloved dog Reese being slaughtered in his final attempt to defend her, just wouldn't go away.

Both the Pumphreys made regular visits for counseling, and both applied for disability, but they had no resources that would enable them to get by until James began to receive his disability payments. As a result, they lost their cozy, attractive mobile home and had to move into a noisy, crowded subsidized housing project in downtown Fort Payne. In a way, though, their home had been lost to them on the day Hayward Bissell came walking up their driveway carrying a long, sharp knife.

"Every time I looked out front, I'd see him standing there," Sue said. "I saw him everywhere I turned, especially out front. I'd always imagine him out there, and I just couldn't get past it."

The loss of their home wasn't the end of financial problems for the Pumphreys; while they waited for the disability checks to begin, they had to start selling many of their personal belongings a few at a time in order to get by from one month to the next.

"The Lord God knows, we are in a financial bind right now," James said. "A lot of people have pitched in and helped us in a lot of ways, but it's been hard making ends meet when both of us have been out of work this long. People want their payments whether you've been able to work or not."

"There's a lot of people who have really helped, and we wouldn't have made it this far if they hadn't," Sue said. "We've had a lot of people, even people we didn't know, who helped us. We had no idea so many people cared. There's no way we could ever thank everyone in person, but I want them all to know how much their help meant to us. We could never thank them enough."

The Pumphreys didn't realize how highly they were regarded by many of the people who knew them, but their loving, Christian attitude toward their friends and neighbors was the reason that everyone rallied to their aid. James and Sue Pumphrey lived according to the Golden Rule, and that accounted for the help they received when they needed it so badly. A statement Sue made shortly after the attack clearly showed her attitude toward those around her, and especially toward the neighbor children.

"People have asked why Bissell came here, to our house, to do what he did, and that's one thing I can't answer," Sue said. "But these people next door had three or four little kids, and they had just left about an hour before then. He could have seen those little kids playing outside and might have gone there instead of coming here. People might take this wrong, but James and me, we don't have any kids, you know what I'm saying? I just thank God it wasn't those kids next door that he went after. It was better that he came here.

"At first, I hated that man. I wanted him dead. But after I got calmed down, I don't hate him anymore. I forgive him for what he's done to us, but I can't forget it."

The Pumphreys weren't ready to deal with all the media attention that came their way following the attack, and initially they didn't speak to the press. There were many calls to James's hospital room that went unreturned, and Sue was reluctant to talk to the reporters who doggedly tracked them down after James was released from the hospital.

"We've had people call from newspapers I've never heard of in other parts of the country," she said, "and the *National Enquirer* and talk shows, and we couldn't deal with it then. We had more than we could handle. I understand they just wanted to get the story, but we couldn't handle it right at first."

Later on, in the months of recovery and rehabilitation, the Pumphreys welcomed some of the publicity they received. An account was set up with a local bank in an effort to keep them from losing any more of their possessions, and when their financial plight was publicized, donations to the account came from several states in addition to all those from local contributors. When some county officials realized the seriousness of the victims' situation, they began contacting politicians with enough clout to be heard by state and national agencies.

Social Security red tape appeared to be one of the main things delaying the start of James Pumphrey's disability payments, so a member of the DeKalb County Commission hand-delivered a letter about the Pumphreys' situation to DeKalb County's congressman in Washington, DC. Representative Robert Aderholt then personally contacted Social Security officials to request the agency act with all possible speed in helping these constituents who were in such dire financial straits. Thanks to Aderholt's help, the paperwork began to move through the system a bit faster.

Alabama's state senate pro tem, Senator Lowell Barron of DeKalb County, joined in the effort and helped to secure funds for both Don Pirch and James Pumphrey from the Alabama Crime Victims' Compensation Commission. Barron, an icon in Alabama politics for decades, was keenly aware that the overwhelming support of the voters in his district had made him one of the most powerful figures in state government. He enjoyed such solid popularity because, for his entire career, he had made his constituents his first priority in all matters. When he joined in the effort to get state compensation for Pirch and Pumphrey, the ball began rolling a great deal faster. The financial requests of both men were finally approved, with Barron's help, after months of work by District Attorney Mike O'Dell and his staff in trying to secure financial aid for the two victims.

"I am glad I was able to assist Mr. Pirch and Mr. Pumphrey in their efforts to receive compensation," Barron said. "Both were unfortunate victims of Hayward Bissell's gruesome and vicious crime spree in DeKalb County. Although there is no way to ever fully compensate them for the pain and horror they and their families have endured, it provides some comfort to know they will receive financial compensation from the Alabama Crime Victims' Compensation Commission for what they have suffered.

"Mike and the other dedicated attorneys at the district attorney's office worked tireless hours 'to secure financial compensation for Mr. Pirch and Mr. Pumphrey," Barron said in a press release announcing the approval of the requests.

"They are to be commended for the selfless work they do to secure justice for the citizens of Alabama. DeKalb County is fortunate to have such committed law enforcement officials working on our behalf."

O'Dell thanked Barron for his help in expediting the matter.

"As district attorney, I see firsthand the physical and financial devastation that crime inflicts on our victims," he said. "I am very pleased the commission has approved the financial requests filed by my office on behalf of these victims.

"I am especially pleased with the interest shown by Senator Barron in the plight of these particular victims, Mr. Pumphrey and Mr. Pirch, and in his efforts to speed up the processing of their claims. Senator Barron has proven himself to be a friend of law enforcement and he has always been available to me and my office to assist us in any way he could. He is not only a special friend to me personally, but he is also certainly a friend to all the citizens of this county."

The Alabama Crime Victims' Compensation Commission was created by the Alabama Legislature in 1984 to provide financial aid to victims of violent crime. It provides the only substantial financial relief to crime victims and their families by assisting with medical expenses, loss of earnings and other necessary expenses. With its help, and with the assistance of Representative Aderholt in expediting the processing of James Pumphrey's Social Security disability claim, Hayward Bissell's victims gained a small measure of relief.

Even so, the nightmares and physical problems continued for the Pirches and the Pumphreys, and the financial aid they ultimately received wasn't nearly enough to cover their needs. While his victims did without things that many would consider necessities, Hayward Bissell sat comfortably in the DeKalb County Jail with everything he needed being provided to him at the expense of the citizens of the county.

With time continuing to pass, District Attorney O'Dell fretted that Georgia authorities were taking their own sweet time charging Bissell in the murder of Patricia Booher. Although Georgia apparently was not in a hurry to assume custody of the prisoner and move forward with a murder case against him, a court date was set in DeKalb County for the entry of Bissell's plea on charges of attempted murder and attempted burglary. O'Dell wanted as few delays as possible in bringing Hayward Bissell to trial. He knew that no amount of financial compensation for the victims could equal the relief that the closure of a conviction and sentence would bring, and he was determined somehow to make that closure a reality.

Chapter 20

"The look in his eyes tells it all."

The legal process moves more slowly in some cases than in others, and the cases against Hayward Bissell seemed at times to be moving at a snail's pace, if they were even moving at all.

On Monday, June 26, 2000, despite numerous postponements and delays, Bissell's first actual in-person appearance in a DeKalb County courtroom was finally scheduled. Bissell was set to enter his plea in the cases against him in the courtroom of circuit judge Randall Cole, but this time no one anticipated the court appearance turning into the same sort of circus that took place at Bissell's initial bond hearing held in the flooded jailhouse basement. Since his return to the county jail, Bissell had been a model prisoner and had not given the jailers or his fellow inmates one moment's trouble.

A much smaller group of the press was waiting to cover the court appearance that morning than had been present for Bissell's dramatic return from Taylor Hardin Secure Medical Facility. Those of us who stood in the sheriff's lobby waiting for the prisoner to be brought upstairs were mostly "regulars" on the county crime beat, a group of friends who worked well together and helped each other despite the rivalries of our employers. We knew we stood a good chance to get a few pictures of the notorious inmate as deputies walked Bissell through the underground tunnel that connected the sheriff's office with the courthouse.

Around 11:15 A.M., we heard the heavy jail door open and a group of people started up the stairs. Then Assistant Chief Deputy Dale Orr called out, "Hold on there, boys, wait a minute!"

Orr hustled upstairs and into his office, then came back out carrying a length of heavy cord, which he took back down the steps. A few minutes later, he stepped back up to the landing.

"What's going on, Dale?" I asked.

"His pants was falling down," Orr said, "and I had to get something to tie 'em up with."

Orr disappeared back down the stairs before we could ask him why Bissell's pants weren't staying up, but we soon found out. The deputies came into view leading a man none of us would have recognized. Hayward Bissell had made yet another drastic physical change; he was considerably thinner than when we had seen him last on his return from Taylor Hardin following his mental evaluation. His hair was still neatly trimmed, but he was wearing it slightly longer. It was thick and glossy, and he had a full beard, dark and neatly trimmed. He looked fit, healthy and well groomed, and he was calm and alert. His prison whites fit loosely, and his pants were held up with a makeshift belt fashioned from a piece of Deputy Orr's heavy cord.

As the deputies quickly led Bissell through the lobby and to the doorway leading into the tunnel, Brad Hood rushed behind them with his WHNT-TV camera on his shoulders. His footage would be used that night on the channel's evening news, and much of Northeast Alabama would be amazed at the sight of the notorious prisoner's continuing physical transformation. I managed to dash into the tunnel ahead of the group, and got several pictures as they moved down the hallway toward the elevator going to the upper floors of the courthouse. Monia Smith brought up the rear of our small press contingent, no doubt remembering how Bissell had looked when she saw him before in his cell, during the infamous hearing in the basement. Much to her relief, this time he was fully clothed.

When Bissell reached the elevator, he was escorted inside by courthouse security officer Stanley Hollingsworth. I got one last shot of the prisoner before the elevator doors slid shut, and once again the camera caught Bissell looking directly at me. He might have undergone great physical changes in the five months he had been in custody, but his eyes still held the same blood-chilling, mesmerizing look they'd had when I first encountered him coming down the staircase in the sheriff's department on the morning following his arrest. He continued to stare straight through the camera's lens at me until the elevator doors closed, and I was relieved when the panels of brushed steel rolled shut and cut off our eye contact. I was certain he remembered me, and it wasn't a comfortable feeling.

Those of us covering Bissell's court appearance waited in the tunnel and took the next elevator upstairs to Judge Cole's second-floor courtroom. Other than court personnel, the only other people present for the hearing were the two couples whose lives had been so severely impacted by the man who was about to come into the courtroom and enter his plea. James and Sue Pumphrey sat with Don and Rhea Pirch, waiting for their first face-to-face meeting with the man who had wreaked such havoc on them—physically, emotionally and financially. James and Don were still having nagging medical problems, and it was continuing to be a long, hard recuperation for both men. They and their wives had been terribly traumatized by Bissell's attacks, and they all clung to each other for support as they waited together to face the man who had done them so much damage.

I had become close to both the Pirches and the Pumphreys while covering the Bissell case, and Sue Pumphrey called me the day before the scheduled court appearance to make sure I would be present in the courtroom. She dreaded the confrontation with Bissell and wanted to be sure she'd have the support of a friend. Sue saw the man regularly in her nightmares, but she was afraid that seeing him in person would only increase the terror she had experienced for the past five months.

The proceedings were about to begin, and Judge Cole and the court reporter took their places as the bailiff sent for the prisoner. When Bissell entered the courtroom, his victims gasped audibly. Even though they had seen photos in the newspaper of Bissell on his return from evaluation, they were still shocked at the drastic change in his appearance since the assaults. Hoyt Baugh, Bissell's attorney, is a very tall, well-built man, and as Baugh stood beside his client, the two men were almost an exact match for height and weight.

Judge Cole called the proceedings to order and read the two charges of attempted murder and one charge of attempted burglary against Bissell. He and Baugh stood together facing the judge and Baugh answered the charges.

"Your Honor, my client respectfully enters a plea of

not guilty by reason of disease or mental defect at the time of the alleged incident," Baugh said.

Judge Cole told Bissell and Baugh the case would be set for trial during an upcoming week of jury trials, most likely in the month of August. The judge asked Baugh if further evaluation of his client's mental state would be requested, and the attorney replied that he felt no additional evaluations would be necessary. Both the prosecution and the defense had requested and received countless reports from Ohio hospitals and clinics, and the information from Taylor Hardin was also on file with both parties. Since these previous evaluations had been received, the defense felt they were sufficient to prove its case.

As the hearing concluded and Bissell and his attorney turned to walk out of the courtroom, Don Pirch reached his limit. He could keep still no longer. He stood up and shouted at the man who had thrown him from the hood of his speeding car into an icy ditch.

"Hey, Bissell!" Don shouted. Rhea and the Pumphreys tried to quiet him, but Don would have none of it. He wanted some kind of acknowledgment from the man who had assaulted him so viciously.

"Hey, Bissell!" he shouted again.

Hayward Bissell didn't even glance in Don's direction. He didn't indicate in any way that he heard anyone calling his name. He and his attorney walked swiftly out of the courtroom and he was whisked downstairs to the tunnel and back into his cell in the jail without ever uttering a single word to anyone.

As the Pirches and Pumphreys left the courtroom, they stopped to speak to the reporters waiting to get their comments. They were highly emotional, and they had all clearly been shaken by the experience of being in the same room with Hayward Bissell. The memories were still too painful for Sue Pumphrey. She was crying as she walked out of the courtroom toward the elevators. She stopped to hug me tightly.

Monia Smith of the *DeKalb Advertiser* asked Sue how she felt about Bissell invoking the insanity plea.

"I don't want him to be set free; he has to be punished for what he did," Sue answered, sobbing. "The look in his eyes tells it all."

Don Pirch agreed.

"Just look at him today," he said when he was asked if he believed Bissell was sane enough to stand trial for his crimes.

As Bissell's victims left the second-floor courtroom, District Attorney Mike O'Dell's staff readied themselves to shift their preparations for trial into high gear. They had received their copy of Bissell's plea of not guilty, and much of the space in their fifth-floor suite of offices would soon be filled with stacks and boxes of files and correspondence concerning the *State of Alabama* v. *Hayward W. Bissell.*

Matters were proceeding very slowly in the Georgia case; too slowly, O'Dell felt. He decided not to wait, but to press ahead with preparations for what would undoubtedly prove to be the biggest jury trial in the county since the sensational Judith Ann Neelley murder trial early in O'Dell's career.

That trial was largely responsible for forging Mike O'Dell's lifelong commitment to seek justice for the victims of violent crimes. O'Dell is an emotional man who does not attempt to hide his feelings and the fact that he feels great sympathy for those he is sworn to protect and defend. Neelley's murder of thirteen-year-old Lisa Ann Millican affected him greatly. O'Dell's participation in Neelley's prosecution left him determined to be a strong advocate and protector of the innocent victims he would encounter so often during the course of his career.

There would be justice for Hayward Bissell's DeKalb County victims, O'Dell determined. Their suffering would not go unpunished, no matter the cost in time and effort.

Chapter 21

"When Hayward's on his medication, he's as sane as anybody else."

The month of August 2000 came and went with no jury trial on the docket for Hayward Bissell. An extremely crowded court calendar delayed his trial along with scores of others, and the case was scheduled, rescheduled and scheduled again. A date of April 2, 2001, was finally set, and defense attorney Hoyt Baugh planned to argue that because of the discontinuation of his medications in November 1999, his client did not realize what he was doing when he murdered Patricia Booher and assaulted Don Pirch and James Pumphrey.

If and when the case finally reached a jury, it would be left to those people to decide whether they believed Hayward Bissell was really insane or if they thought he was conducting an award-winning performance in order to avoid life in prison. If he was found not guilty by reason of disease or mental defect in the Alabama cases, it would be up to doctors, not the courts, to decide when Bissell was well enough to be released. The possibility existed that he would someday be sufficiently improved, in a psychiatrist's opinion, to be discharged from treatment and walk the streets once again as a free man, and that was a possibility Mike O'Dell and his staff simply could not accept.

The mounting evidence of Bissell's awareness of his actions, like the information provided by Todd Graves and other inmates, became even more important to O'Dell's case.

As a part of his defense, Baugh filed a motion before Judge Randall Cole to establish travel expenses so the defense could travel to Ohio to ask Bissell's doctors there why his antipsychotic medication was discontinued. Baugh told the *Times-Journal* his client was sorry for what he did, and blamed Bissell's murderous frenzy on his lack of proper medication at the time.

"The medication he is on now subdues him, but he's scared to death," Baugh claimed. "He's remorseful and would do anything to go back and change what happened. He didn't know how bad his condition could get. There are evil folks who kill because they like it and then there are people like Hayward who go off their medication and do evil things."

Baugh said he was horrified by the crimes that had been committed by his client, but said he did not think of him as a monster.

"Hearing what he did sent chills down my spine as well," Baugh said. "Monster might be a good way to describe what a person with a mental disorder becomes when he gets off his treatment. When Hayward's on his medication, he's as sane as anybody else. He's been fine since he returned to the county jail. It's scary to know there are people who are average until they get off their medication, then they do pretty bizarre and horrible things. Hayward remembers some of what happened, like the voices in his head, but other stuff he has blocked out. He had no control over his actions. The voices sent commands, and he reacted the same way as you eat when you are hungry or instinctively pull your hand out of a fire."

Baugh told the *Times-Journal* he realized jurors might not be easily convinced that someone who appeared as calm and as sensible as Bissell had become since his arrest could commit such horrible crimes without being a cold-blooded killer. Some people would believe it was all an act, he said, that Bissell had faked insanity in order to get away with murder. But Bissell's repeated mention of his "crazy papers," both years earlier to his friends in Ohio and more recently to his fellow inmates in the jail, did a lot to reinforce that perception. Then there was the widely reported incident that took place at the back door of the Pumphrey home, when James and Sue managed to lift a rifle and point it at Bissell when he came around the house and attempted to resume his attack on them.

"Don't shoot me, I'm leaving," he had said to them before he turned and ran away, a reaction which Mike O'Dell and his investigators claimed clearly indicated that the prisoner was well enough in touch with reality at the time of the assault to recognize the danger a firearm posed to him.

"I've been practicing criminal law for many years and people think a defense of mental defect is used all the time," Baugh said, "but this is the first time I've used it. His behavior was not a feigned thing to get out of prison. The inmates at the DeKalb County Jail were absolutely scared and horrified when he was first arrested."

Baugh said Bissell's Alabama cases had been on the back burner because everyone was waiting to see what Georgia would do concerning charging his client with Patricia Booher's murder.

"It's a tough call," he said. "People will not want

someone who did what he did out in public again. If he wins in court, he will be hospitalized. It could be for ten months or ten years, however long it takes until the doctors say he is no longer a threat. The dilemma is, how can we ensure that a person will take his medication for the rest of his life?"

The answer to that question was clear to Mike O'Dell. After reviewing countless medical records documenting Bissell's long history of failing to complete treatment, checking himself in and out of institutions and refusing to continue his prescribed medication, O'Dell believed there was no way Hayward Bissell would ever be willing to continue on a program of psychiatric treatment of his own volition.

As April 2, the date for Hayward Bissell's jury trial neared, a number of DeKalb County residents began receiving postcards informing them they had been selected to report for jury duty. Most did not realize they were being called as potential jurors for the sensational Bissell trial which was the only case on the docket for that session. When, a few learned what case it was that they might be called to hear, they knew all too well what they could be in store for.

"Oh my God, I've got to get out of this somehow," said one panic-stricken woman when she learned of the possibility she might serve as a Bissell juror. "I just can't do this, I can't do it; there's no way. I'd have to look at the pictures of that poor little girl after she was killed, and I just couldn't. And I'd be scared to death that Bissell might get out someday and come looking for me. I don't know what I'm going to do."

Her fears were put to rest shortly before the trial date, for calling jurors for duty on the Bissell case became unnecessary when another postponement was announced. Hayward Bissell would spend a few more months in the DeKalb County Jail while both the defense and the prosecution continued to gather additional information in the case. The trial was rescheduled for October 1.

During spring and summer 2001, work on trial preparations for the Bissell case kept summer interns in the DA's office sorting through a mountain of paperwork. One intern, Shaunathan Bell, devoted his entire period of employment to carefully collecting and assembling Bissell's huge medical history. The information obtained and filed by Bell filled up several large file boxes, one after the other, and Mike O'Dell enlisted Assistant District Attorney (ADA) Bob Johnston to sort the enormous log of statements, reports and evidence into a manageable case file.

ADA Johnston was an ideal choice for the job. In addition to his excellent organizational skills and legal scholarship, he was a calm, easygoing man whose steady disposition was equaled by his patience and persistence. By putting in countless extra hours at work, he was able to present O'Dell with all the materials he needed to finish preparing his case for trial by jury.

O'Dell had spent a great deal of time carefully developing arguments in support of his belief that Hayward Bissell was malingering. O'Dell was convinced that Bissell was, to a great degree, skillfully acting the part of a paranoid schizophrenic, and he felt that Bissell was not nearly as mentally ill as he had led many of his psychiatrists to believe. In reviewing the enormous case file prepared by Johnston, O'Dell had discovered countless contradictions concerning Bissell's mental state, and he included them in his reviews of the prisoner's psychiatric and medical concerns.

O'Dell noted that Bissell's medical history and physical examination, dated January 27, 2000, said that the patient had a long history of substance abuse, including prescription Xanax and marijuana. Bissell had no specific physical complaints at that time, and said that he was in no acute distress, with no mention of experiencing any chronic back pain, for which he had repeatedly sought pain medication in the past. He was cooperative, the report said, and responded appropriately.

Much of Bissell's psychiatric evaluations relied on what is known as "self-reporting," or information Bissell himself gave to the examiners.

"He did not present as a very reliable informant," O'Dell said, "since much of what he provided was later proven to be untrue."

For example, Bissell at first told the interviewer that his mother was dead, when, in fact, she was not.

"That proved to be false," O'Dell wrote in his summary, "therefore you have the verifiable claims—the life of his mother—versus the unverifiable, his claims of hearing voices in his head, commanding him to do certain specific things. Do Bissell's claims become more believable because they cannot be verified? That is the inherent problem with unverifiable self-reporting from an individual who has been described by the admissions staff as an unreliable informant."

O'Dell noted that the doctors who examined and evaluated Bissell also seemed to form much of their opinions from information based on media reports, hearsay and other sources, which in some cases were also less than reliable. One doctor admitted to having read newspaper accounts and Internet stories about Bissell's crimes prior to Hayward's being admitted for evaluation. Many of those stories, despite some of the extreme inaccuracies they contained, seemed to play a role in forming the doctor's opinion of the case before he ever even interviewed Bissell for the first time.

Bissell's long history of mental illness was recounted in the assessment, along with the fact that he denied ever having had any legal problems. Records, however, showed that he had multiple previous arrests for assaults, menacing and other charges, with no mention made of his claiming to hear voices during those incidents.

Bissell told one doctor, who asked him if he knew why he had been admitted for evaluation, "I don't know. I really don't know why I'm here." But in his initial statements to Investigator James and the two Secret Service agents who interviewed him, he seemed quite clear on what he had done that would have caused him to be sent for mental evaluation. He was able during many interrogation sessions to describe in accurate detail exactly what had happened when he murdered Patricia Booher and assaulted Don Pirch and James Pumphrey. If he was able to do that immediately after the crimes, there is no logical reason why he should not be even more lucid a week later, O'Dell felt.

Bissell's assessment mentioned his self-reported claims of being a double agent and "agent #666 for Satan." It also stated he had assaulted two officers while in the county jail; in reality, at no time did Bissell behave violently or threateningly toward any officers from the time of his arrest, during interviews, during transportation to the hospital or while in jail. The only occasion during which he acted out was in his cell during his bond hearing; he really performed then, O'Dell said, but the rest of his disruption after his arrest was not in the form of threats or violence toward others, but rather abuse to himself and to the plumbing in his cell.

"The allegation that Bissell assaulted two officers is

blatantly and completely false," O'Dell said. "Bissell had no problem 'calming down' and was quite passive from the moment of his arrest, except for the one occasion when the judge conducted his initial appearance hearing. At that time, and at that time alone, Bissell acted out, stripping off his clothes, turning his back on the judge, shouting obscenities at him and appearing to masturbate. It is alleged that he ate his own feces, but no jail official could confirm that. Shortly after the judge, the attorneys, jail officers and an army of press who were privileged to view this performance left the cell area, Bissell returned to his 'docile, passive' self."

Bissell's evaluation stated that in 1999, records showed he tried to commit suicide by taking an overdose of Xanax, for which he required hospitalization. O'Dell's review of all the records of this incident showed it was not a suicide attempt at all. It was, in fact, the well-documented incident in which Bissell reported he had smoked marijuana and taken Xanax, got drowsy, passed out, and left a pot on the stove that caught fire and resulted in his being burned during the ensuing apartment fire. When taken to the hospital, he told the staff that he had been ordered by the FBI to kill himself by taking an overdose of Xanax.

"It is important to note that local law enforcement agents, including the District Attorney, were looking at prosecuting him for the illegal street drugs taken from his apartment that day, but they decided not to pursue charges against him due to his alleged mental state," O'Dell said in his summary. "My theory is that he has consistently used his reported mental illness as a 'get out of jail free' card."

One of Bissell's family members also had told the evaluators that Bissell had a long history of fire-starting behavior and delusional beliefs about being an agent for the CIA.

O'Dell also noted that in Bissell's history of domestic abuse, there was never any mention that his behavior was the result of "hearing voices" directing his acts, but his spousal abuse appeared instead to result from raging anger and sheer meanness.

The report stated that during his hospitalization for his initial assessment, he exhibited some bizarre behavior such as putting his hands in the commode, dropping food on the floor, lying on the floor, shaking the door and engaging in constant delusional conversation. O'Dell noted that most of those incidents were not seen by the observers who were posted outside Bissell's door on a continuous basis, keeping a constant watch on him and making fifteen-minute entries on their observations.

The report also stated that Bissell had been assaultive to the staff of many of the hospitals to which he had been admitted. O'Dell and his staff carefully combed through all the submitted records from those hospitals; they could find no evidence whatsoever of this claim.

Bissell's family reported to social workers that he was difficult to deal with and combative, and "gets angry and loses control."

"This does not mean he does not know right from wrong," O'Dell said, "or is unable to appreciate the wrongfulness of his conduct."

The family also reported that Bissell had abused drugs since the age of twelve, starting with marijuana. They said he had used drugs extensively while in the United States Army, and since then had used marijuana, crack cocaine, alcohol and other street drugs. The family members reported that he was a crack cocaine abuser, and claimed that many of his problems were either caused by or closely connected to his use of crack cocaine.

Bissell stated that he had never been a sexual abuser and had himself never been abused, but he claimed to his ex-wife's cousin during his early-hours visit on January 23, 2000, that he had been the victim of a highly improbable sexual assault by one of his relatives when he was a child. He also volunteered during his assessment that he was "in denial of maybe being a pedophile."

"Is this another attempt by Bissell to sensationalize his alleged illness?" O'Dell wrote. "This seems to be much like his report concerning the January 1999 fire, when he stated the FBI told him to urinate in his milk and drink it before committing suicide by overdose."

O'Dell also pointed out that Bissell was reported to have complications secondary to the injury to his back, and his family reported those injuries had become chronic.

"And yet, he didn't report any complaints about his back when undergoing his medical exam," O'Dell wrote. "Further, review of the 15 minute observation entries shows an absence of back pain or other complaints until later in his stay at the facility. He then began demanding frequent pain medications. Was he malingering for drugs?"

Bissell told the evaluators, "I don't know why I'm here, I didn't do anything." A family member, however, said, "Hayward got off his medication and got on drugs again and I think he was using crack cocaine. He is difficult to deal with and he is combative. All I can say is watch out, he is slick."

O'Dell said that, according to countless hospital records reviewed by his office, Bissell was reportedly given a diagnosis of generalized anxiety disorder in 1985 and was treated with Xanax.

"The course of Bissell's treatment history is not entirely clear," O'Dell said in his written summation. "He has received additional diagnoses of Chronic Depression, Mood Disorder, Polysubstance Dependence and Paranoid Schizophrenia, but the treatment records dating to 1998 provide little information about the symptoms of his thought disorder."

On one occasion, O'Dell wrote, Bissell was interviewed during evaluation and refused to get out of his bed. He seemed irritated, defensive and hostile, and stayed in the bed with his eyes closed for most of the interview; nonetheless, the evaluators reported that his responses were relevant and his speech was easy to understand. When he was asked how he had been feeling, Bissell said, "I am not exactly happy, but not sad." He denied feeling stressed and said his sleep, appetite and energy levels had been average.

This is in direct conflict with other statements, when Bissell claimed he hadn't slept in seven days. He also denied having any current suicidal or homicidal feelings, and said he had never tried to kill himself in the past. This conflicted with Bissell's many prior self-reports at a number of hospitals and clinics, when he sought treatment because he claimed he was having suicidal thoughts.

Bissell said he had been treated previously in Ohio and had been given a diagnosis of paranoid schizophrenia because he heard voices. But he also said he currently was not hearing voices and that he couldn't remember the last time he had heard voices. According to the statements he had given to Mike James, the Secret Service agents and others, though, he had heard voices on a massive scale less than a week earlier, when he was receiving detailed orders from "signals" on his "implant" directing him to kill Patricia Booher, run down Don Pirch and stab James Pumphrey.

Bissell said he did not feel anyone was out to get him, and he said he had no special talents. Yet only a week earlier, he had told his ex-wife's cousin that he had "great demonic powers" and that "Mike Ruggles and David Light wanted to take them away" from him. When Bissell was reminded during the interview that he had claimed earlier that week that he was a special agent for the Secret Service, he said, "I don't think that anymore."

He had also claimed, "They are trying to kill me. I'm the richest man in the world. I'm going to be leader of the new world."

"These statements are clearly self-reported and unverifiable," said O'Dell, "and in addition they contradict some of Mr. Bissell's other admission statements, even in the same report."

O'Dell again questioned the accuracy of Bissell's self-reporting, since he claimed to hear voices and experience delusions at the time of his admission for evaluation, then within days denied having any hallucinations at all. Then a short time after that, Bissell told his doctors, "I have a problem making the right choices. I'm dyslexic. I have double depression. I have hallucinations. I'm in denial of maybe being a pedophile. I have a problem dealing with anger. When I'm under stress I hear voices and especially when I don't take my anti-anxiety meds."

In March 1999, a doctor renewed Bissell's prescription for Haldol, a medication to help stop hallucinations and delusions, among other uses. In May, Bissell told the doctor the Haldol was not helping. He was then given a prescription for Prozac and Xanax, and was allowed to leave the clinic with follow-up visits left up to him. He did not see the doctor again until November 1999, when he was reported to have "no psychiatric symptoms" and was told to return in two to three months.

During evaluation, Bissell said voices instructed him to run over and kill a man he saw getting out of a pickup truck in Mentone, Alabama, which he attempted to do but failed to accomplish. A short distance down the road, according to Bissell, he was told to enter a house, which he again failed to do, and kill two dogs, which he did. But Bissell earlier had told police he was to go to the house and kill the man, not the two dogs. Was this an example of contradictory self-reporting, or did the evaluator interpret it this way from accounts he had read of the incident? Also, Bissell claimed he was instructed by the voices to "plow into a schoolyard full of kids." He tried, he said, but ran into a ditch before he got to them. The event occurred on a Sunday, when schools were not in session, and during a major ice storm, when roads were barely passable. Bissell never mentioned the schoolyard story to anyone other than the evaluating physician, and O'Dell speculated he could have been fabricating the incident to make his condition seem worse.

O'Dell was skeptical of Bissell's continuing claim that he heard voices at the time he murdered Patricia Booher and attempted to murder Don Pirch and James Pumphrey.

"Is there objective evidence of the voices, or just what he self-reports?" O'Dell asked. "Does this not make it easier for him to fake his illness? And what capacity did his evaluator assume from the very beginning? Did he not assume Bissell's diagnosis prior to his arrival at the mental facility? The law says the jury must presume the defendant to be sane, but this particular doctor, on the other hand, appears to have presumed Bissell insane.

"Even if all the facts and evidence provided by Bissell were true, and his mental illness existed as the evaluating psychiatrist has concluded, with voices commanding Bissell to act, how can he conclude Bissell was unable to appreciate the wrongfulness of his acts?" O'Dell questioned. "Just because the voices 'told him to do something,' there is no indication that what he was told to do, if the voices did exist, indicated an inability to distinguish right from wrong."

O'Dell cited the Nuremberg Defense—"they were told to do it"—when refusal could have meant the loss of the defendants' own lives.

"In this case, we have no indication that Bissell believed he was subject to any consequence for refusal," he said.

"The evaluating psychiatrist would respond that it is all a part of Bissell's illness, while I would maintain it is a significant part of his malingering and deception—his sham on the system to try to avoid prosecution and being held accountable for his horrendous actions," O'Dell concluded. "It is absolutely outrageous that he would assume the role of a mentally ill person to avoid accountability, but clearly he has used this ruse in various forms for years now."

O'Dell continued to uncover more and more discrepancies in Bissell's psychiatric history as he fine-tuned his case in final preparations for trial.

"Bissell reported visual hallucinations during his first evaluation, which involved his talking to and seeing his dead girlfriend," O'Dell wrote. "He expressed remorse for her death once he was stable; in fact, he was said to be extremely remorseful, saying he loved her and wanted to be with her. But the doctor stated he had to tell Bissell his girlfriend was dead. This doesn't make sense, since it was Bissell himself who told the investigators repeatedly and in great detail that he had killed Patricia Booher. Is this another attempt by Bissell to present himself as crazy?"

Doctors claimed Bissell had a thought process disorder, with nonsensical reasons for doing some of the things he did. But O'Dell felt Bissell had deliberate reasons for his acts. When he set them down on paper, O'Dell's arguments were impressive:

"Hayward Bissell killed Patricia Booher out of anger and rage toward his pregnant girlfriend who was breaking off their relationship. He cut her heart out because she had 'pulverized his,' as he claimed, and he tried to gouge her eyes out, perhaps so she couldn't look at anyone else. And the cut deep into her abdomen—was it intended to cut out the baby?

"His attempt to kill Don Pirch was an effort to eliminate a potential witness to the body being in the car. Bissell was fearful that Pirch had seen the body. How much sense does it make that Bissell 'heard voices' telling him to 'ram a truck and run over the driver'? Are we to believe that the CIA or Secret Service are omniscient and omnipresent? These things don't make sense and are not believable. What he did was to attempt to cover up or hide his actions. He had no way of knowing there would be a truck up ahead until he caught up to it. Besides, he rammed the passenger, not the driver, who was a woman; was the Secret Service wrong?

"Additionally, how does the act of 'giving Pirch the finger' while he's hanging onto the hood of a speeding car for his life fit into the Secret Service directives? This is an act of anger and rage consistent with his state of mind during the killing. At any rate, by trying to run over Pirch, he was consciously trying to protect himself from detection, which is a 'rational' mental operation he initiated while in flight from the scene of his crime. The same can be said of his attempt to mow down the others in the road assisting Pirch.

"Instead of 'being told by the voices' to go further down the road and either kill an old man, as he told Investigator James, or go into a house and kill two dogs, as he reportedly told his evaluating psychiatrist, what Bissell was doing was going up to the house to rob someone because he had only $5 on him and he needed money for gas and food as he continued his escape from the crime scene. He stopped at the house because it was at the end of a dead end road. He may also have intended to dump the body in the pond in pieces, but the dogs began barking. As he walked up to the house, one or both of the dogs attacked him and bit him on the hand. This enraged Bissell, who was already in a highly agitated and angered state. He cut the throat of the first dog; most likely, so savagely that he severed the esophagus which he kept as a 'trophy.'

"Think about the medieval barbarians who regularly severed limbs and heads from their victims and kept them and displayed them. Or what about the American Indians and the scalps they regularly took and displayed with pride. Think about Booher's heart; was this not his 'trophy'? She had to pay for 'pulverizing his heart,' and also, she wouldn't be able to 'give her heart to anyone else,' or her eyes wouldn't be able to 'look at another man' since she had scorned him.

"As Bissell got closer to the house and Pumphrey came out and confronted him about the dog, he slashed Pumphrey in the gut without any provocation. As Pumphrey retreated to his front door, yelling to his wife for assistance, Bissell followed him up on the porch and, as Pumphrey made it into the house, Bissell grabbed his wife by the collar. He most likely would have stabbed her as well if not for the second dog coming to her aid.

"As Bissell killed that dog in his raging anger, the wife was able to shut and lock the door. Bissell continued around to the back to pursue his prey, this despite the fact that both dogs were now dead. This would have 'completed his mission' for the Secret Service, if that had been true, and he would have left the residence for his next mission command.

"However, if his 'orders' were to 'kill an old man,' then his pursuit of them would have been consistent with his actions. The only problem with this theory is that when he got to the back, the Pumphreys were coming out the back door in an effort to seek assistance for Mr. Pumphrey. They were armed with a rifle that accidentally discharged and struck their freezer. When they confronted Bissell in the back yard, they threatened to kill him if he did not leave. Bissell threw up his hands and pleaded with them, 'Don't shoot me, I'm leaving.'

"This is inconsistent with Bissell being compelled to follow orders from the voices; he would have pursued them until he had completed his mission, or died trying. Instead, his actions and words display a man making a deliberate decision to save his own hide, a rational decision of self-preservation. His pursuit of them, to kill them, was again, to eliminate potential witnesses and to rob them in order to get 'traveling money.'"

O'Dell spent considerable time reviewing the records that indicated there was a great likelihood that Bissell was capable of faking his mental illness to the extent that he was able to convince doctors his condition was real. One of his primary evaluating physicians made the statement to O'Dell that schizophrenics can fake best "because they know what to say." The doctor has to rely on what the patient says, or self-reporting.

Visual hallucinations are uncommon in schizophrenics, but on several occasions Bissell reported them; did he do this, O'Dell wondered, to make his condition seem even worse? Perhaps he did not know that visual hallucinations were not a common part of his so-called illness and were not a symptom he needed to present in order to be more convincing.

For the most part, Bissell knew exactly what was expected of him as a schizophrenic. He had been educated about his alleged mental illness on countless occasions by the doctors and psychiatrists he had seen, and he knew precisely what they were looking for when he talked to them.

O'Dell ended his notes with a summary he planned to present to the jury:

"Bissell's actions could easily be explained as his attempt to display power and control over his victims. They were acts of savagery, barbarism and power. The evidence clearly depicts a man exercising power and control over those he came in contact with, until he found himself in a situation where he saw he could not win, for instance the Pumphreys with their rifle, and Assistant Chief Wooten who pointed his weapon at Bissell at the final traffic stop. At that point, and from then on, Bissell became the passive and docile 'pussycat.'"

O'Dell was ready to take the case to trial. This time, perhaps, when Hayward Bissell played his "get out of jail free" card, it would not be accepted by a DeKalb County jury.

While preparations for Bissell's October 1 trial were taking place during summer 2001, some very welcome news began to circulate throughout the sheriff's department and the district attorney's office. At last, Georgia's case was gaining momentum and it appeared charges were about to be filed against Bissell in Chattooga County, Georgia, in the death of Patricia Ann Booher.

On July 25, superior court judge Ralph Van Pelt of the Lookout Mountain Judicial Circuit issued a court order for the psychiatric evaluation of Hayward Bissell in order to determine his competency to stand trial for Patricia's murder and to determine the degree of his criminal responsibility. Two forensic psychiatrists from Northwest Georgia Regional Hospital traveled to Fort Payne on August 1 and interviewed Bissell in the jail.

At first, the prisoner said that he did not want to talk to the doctors without consulting his attorney. But after the doctors spoke with Hoyt Baugh, who strongly advised his client it would be in his best interest to cooperate fully with the evaluation, things began to go somewhat more smoothly.

After Baugh's intervention, the two doctors interviewed Bissell and later described him as being alert and seemingly free of psychotic symptoms at that time. He told them he was not feeling nervous or depressed, and he held a normal conversation with the doctors that was described as rational, coherent and logical. He was able to organize his thoughts, they said, and seemed to be of average intelligence.

The two doctors recommended that Bissell spend two weeks at Central State Hospital in Milledgeville, Georgia, for an intensive psychiatric evaluation and observation, as well as a neurological examination.

On August 9, superior court judge Kristina Cook Connelly of the Lookout Mountain Judicial Circuit of Georgia issued a consent order for the mental evaluation of Hayward Bissell. He had already signed a double waiver of extradition, agreeing to be transported to Georgia for evaluation, then returned to the DeKalb County Jail upon its completion.

At 5:00 A.M. on August 10, Hayward Bissell left the DeKalb County Jail for the trip to Georgia. It was an eerie scene as he was led upstairs from the basement and out the back door of the jail, where a Chattooga County, Georgia, patrol car waited in the parking lot to take him to the hospital at Milledgeville. A severe summer thunderstorm was looming, and the oppressive heat and humidity weighed on the few people who came out at such an early hour to get a look at the notorious prisoner. Heat lightning flickered in the cloudy predawn darkness and thunder rumbled in the distance from the storm moving in from the west, adding to the ominous atmosphere as well as to the nervous anticipation of those who waited for Bissell to appear.

When Bissell reached the top of the stairs and stepped outside, he had undergone yet another amazing physical transformation. His hair and beard were much longer and appeared more sparse and slightly lighter in color than before, and his clothing hung loosely on a much-thinner frame. Bissell had lost even more weight, and his only restraints were a pair of standard handcuffs that loosely fit his wrists. He was very quiet and glanced around disinterestedly while he waited to get into the patrol car, answering a few questions with "yes" or "no" or simply nodding.

After the car carrying the prisoner pulled out of the parking lot, Sheriff Cecil Reed told reporters the transfer had taken place on orders out of the Chattooga County Court as part of the investigation of Patricia Booher's murder going on in that county.

"Once he is evaluated, he will be returned to my custody here at the jail to hold for further orders of the court," Reed said. "His trial here has been scheduled for October first, and he has been here in my jail since last January, except for two months spent at the Taylor Hardin Secure Medical Facility in Tuscaloosa. I'll be glad when someone else takes permanent custody of him."

Chief Jailer Bill Lands was asked about the chang in Bissell's appearance, and Lands confirmed that Bis sell had lost a total of around 160 pounds since hi arrest.

"He probably weighs under two hundred now, Lands said. "He hasn't given us one minute of troubl since he got back from Tuscaloosa . . . but then, h spends a lot of his time sleeping."

Chapter 22

"His plane was grounded and not allowed to fly to Georgia."

On August 30, 2001, Hayward Bissell was discharged from Central State Hospital in Milledgeville, Georgia. The following day, he was returned to DeKalb County and the jail cell he had occupied since his arrest. The doctors from Milledgeville scheduled a final interview with Bissell to be held in the DeKalb County Jail during the week following his return; then their report would be prepared and the final evaluation presented to the Chattooga County authorities as requested.

Mike O'Dell and his staff were ready to go to court and prosecute the DeKalb County cases as planned on October 1, but then the world changed overnight. Two hijacked jetliners flew into the Twin Towers of New York's World Trade Center on September 11, 2001, bringing the two buildings crashing to the ground with thousands of people inside, and another hijacked plane ripped into the Pentagon, killing hundreds more. A brave group of patriots sent a fourth hijacked plane headlong into a field in Pennsylvania, giving their lives to thwart the terrorists aboard their flight and saving another American landmark from certain destruction. Along with every other aspect of life in the United States, Hayward Bissell's Alabama trial was impacted by the 9/11 terrorist attacks.

A press release was issued by District Attorney O'Dell on September 24, announcing that the trial of Hayward W. Bissell, scheduled to begin on October 1, had been postponed by circuit judge Randall Cole after the prosecution and the defense counsel filed a joint motion to continue the case.

According to O'Dell, the continuance had been requested earlier by both sides when they learned about Bissell's psychiatric evaluation in Georgia.

"Clearly, Mr. Baugh and I are both very interested in the outcome of the psychiatric evaluation conducted by the Georgia psychiatrist," O'Dell said. "We were aware that the evaluation was being conducted, and we had hoped that it would be completed in time for us to obtain copies of the results for review and examination prior to the scheduled trial date. Unfortunately, the tragedy in New York had an adverse effect even on the Bissell trial, in that the psychiatrist who was to do the exam happened to be flying back into the States on the fatal Tuesday that the attacks occurred. His plane was grounded and not allowed to fly to Georgia. As a result, his timetable for conducting the exam scheduled for early September was set back at least a week, and we were informed that a final report would most likely not even be available until after the start of the trial on October 1. Obviously, this was not workable for either side. Bissell's mental status is very important in this case, and both the prosecution and the defense felt that such a report would be important and material to our cases."

O'Dell and Hoyt Baugh scheduled an appointment to meet with Judge Randall Cole to discuss the matter, and it was mutually decided that a continuance was the best route for both sides to take under the circumstances.

"Neither side wanted a continuance in this matter," O'Dell said, "but we really had no choice but to request it. Neither Hoyt nor I wanted to begin a trial of this importance without being armed with all the relevant and material information available. We also felt we would need sufficient time to review and examine the report in order to adequately prepare for trial."

Both attorneys expected the cases to be reset as soon as possible after the report was received by them, and Judge Cole signed an order keeping Bissell in jail pending the setting of a new trial date.

When Sheriff Cecil Reed got word of the postponement, the third trial delay since Bissell had taken up residence in the county jail, the veteran law officer heaved a big sigh, threw his hands up and shook his head in disgust.

"Whenever they finally get him in court and get him tried," he said, "I'm going to have a patrol car sitting at the back door with the motor running, waiting to take him out of my jail to wherever he gets sent to. We've had Mr. Bissell here long enough."

Only two days later, on September 26, the Georgia psychiatrists issued their final evaluation report to the court of Judge Ralph Van Pelt, advising the judge that their belief was that Bissell was competent to stand trial and able to assist his attorney in any other legal proceeding.

Bissell's Central State Hospital evaluation reported having no trouble from the prisoner, but offered much information on his psychological profile and his competency to stand trial. He was described as being depressed, anxious and agitated, getting angry easily and not seeming to care what happened to him. He was calm and cooperative during his hospitalization, but kept to himself and had little contact with others. Difficulties with concentration and lack of self-confidence were mentioned, and it was noted he seemed to dislike having people around him and usually preferred to be alone, spending most of his time by himself.

As far as his condition at the time of Patricia Booher's murder, Bissell told doctors that he had been out of his psychiatric medications, Prozac and Xanax, for around two weeks before the murder. He had not taken his other prescribed antipsychotic medications for the previous year because, he said, his outpatient doctor had told him he did not need them. He was able to describe the murder and the events leading up to it, saying that he started hearing voices telling him Patricia was either a "black witch" or a "double-agent spy." When she would not say she was either of the two, he said the voices told him he had to kill her.

He said he cut her throat, then cut off her hand and leg "so she couldn't come back at me." He did this, he said, because the voices told him it would ensure that she couldn't come back to life and attack him while he was driving. Then, he said, he went in search of a hospital morgue to turn in the body and "give my report."

The report continued by saying it appeared that, at the time of Hayward Bissell's self-described "rampage," he was likely suffering from a delusional compulsion that overcame his ability to resist committing his murderous attacks. It was questionable, the report said, that Bissell understood the wrongfulness of what he did at the time, and the doctors recommended close monitoring of his condition and a continuation of his currently prescribed psychiatric medications.

As far as his comprehension of his legal situation, Bissell understood the charges against him in both the

Alabama and Georgia cases and the doctors believed that he clearly understood the trial process and his rights. He would be able, they felt, to assist his attorney capably in his defense.

"It does appear that he is competent to stand trial," the report concluded.

Chapter 23

"Guilty but insane."

With Hayward Bissell judged by psychiatrists as being able to stand trial, Buzz Franklin and his staff in the Chattooga County District Attorney's Office decided it was time for his case to be presented to a grand jury. Mike O'Dell and the DeKalb County District Attorney's Office didn't press for a new court date to be set on the Alabama assault and attempted burglary charges. O'Dell hoped that Bissell would be convicted of murder with Georgia's guilty but insane charge. If so, a trial in Alabama for assault and attempted burglary might be unnecessary. DeKalb County had already footed the considerable bill for Bissell's upkeep in the county jail for almost two years, and if he were sentenced to life in prison in Georgia, the county could be spared the additional expense of a long and very costly jury trial.

O'Dell's main concern, however, was obtaining satisfactory closure for Bissell's Alabama victims. The lives of the Pirches and the Pumphreys had been devastated by their experiences at Bissell's hands. Whatever the outcome of Georgia's prosecution of the murder case, O'Dell was determined that those victims, whose welfare he felt so responsible for, would have a say in the disposition of Bissell's Alabama charges.

After so many delays, postponements and rescheduling in DeKalb County, and after such a long wait for murder charges to be brought against Bissell, once things started moving in Georgia, they moved at lightning speed.

On Tuesday, February 5, 2002, only a few days after the second anniversary of Patricia Booher's murder, Hayward Bissell was indicted for murder and felony murder by a specially assembled grand jury in Chattooga County, Georgia. That afternoon, he left the DeKalb County Jail to be transferred to the Chattooga County Jail in Summerville, Georgia.

Following a waiver of transfer appearance before Judge Randall Cole, the prisoner was quickly loaded into a patrol car and taken to the Alabama/Georgia state line, near the site of his assaults on Don Pirch and James Pumphrey two years earlier. There, Chattooga County deputies waited to take him the rest of the way to Summerville.

This time, Bissell left the DeKalb County Jail with no members of the press on hand to see him off. Sheriff Reed always had been extremely fair and open with the press, notifying the "regulars" well ahead of time about any developments in his office that they needed to be present for. Bissell's quick transfer, however, was not staged to prevent the media from being present. It was actually an attempt on the part of DeKalb and Chattooga County authorities to beat a fast-approaching winter storm.

According to Mike O'Dell, no one wanted to run the risk of ice coating the roads and causing highways to be closed, preventing Bissell from getting to court the following morning. At long last, after more than two years of legal wrangling and delays, Hayward

William Bissell was about to enter a plea of guilty but insane, and DeKalb County officials were going to see to it that he didn't miss his Wednesday-morning appointment in the Chattooga County Courthouse.

"There's something really ironic about the fact that Bissell first rode into the county almost two years ago to the day during a winter storm," O'Dell said, "and he was transported back to Georgia Tuesday under the same weather conditions."

O'Dell, Sheriff Reed and Investigators Mike James and Danny Smith planned to make the trip to Summerville in the early-morning hours on Wednesday, despite sleet and freezing rain. There was no way they would fail to be present for Bissell's court appearance scheduled for 8:00 A.M.

"We'll go in a four-wheel-drive vehicle if necessary," O'Dell said. "I intend to be there no matter what the circumstances."

O'Dell felt Bissell's plea of guilty but insane to Booher's murder was the best solution for everyone involved in the case.

"It will enable us to put him away for a long time," O'Dell said. "This way, he'll have a long time to think about what he wreaked on his victims and their families, and the people of DeKalb County and Georgia."

The plea of guilty but insane would place Bissell in a hospital facility or state prison in Georgia on a long-term basis, as opposed to Alabama's plea of not guilty by reason of mental disease or defect, which could have led to Bissell's eventual release if doctors became convinced his mental condition had improved.

"A commitment under those circumstances could have been as short as a few weeks or could last for several years; however, Bissell would not be held accountable for his acts as he is under the Georgia statute," O'Dell said. In other words, if found guilty but insane in Georgia, Bissell would be held accountable for his crime and would serve his sentence even if he was pronounced "cured" of his mental illness. In Alabama, he would have been sent to a mental institution, then released if his doctors recommended it, with no sentencing to prison for his crime.

When the press learned Bissell had been transferred to Georgia to enter a plea on the murder charges there, they immediately descended on Sheriff Reed for his comments.

The sheriff was delighted to oblige.

"This nightmare has been going on for us for over two years now, and I am glad Bissell is finally going to be brought to justice," Reed said. "I'm even more glad that I will soon be rid of him from my jail. We have housed and fed him long enough, and now he will be Georgia's responsibility. After two years of supervising Bissell, I'm glad to bid him good riddance."

Bill Lands and his jailers were even more enthusiastic about Bissell's departure. In fact, they were jubilant.

"Looks like the old boy's headed out of here," Lands said, grinning. "He's finally on his way out of this jail, and it's about time."

On Wednesday morning, Hayward Bissell stood in front of Judge Kristina Cook Connelly and entered a plea of guilty but insane to charges of murder and felony murder in the death of Patricia Ann Booher. Mike O'Dell and his DeKalb County contingent made the trip safely and arrived in plenty of time to witness Bissell's plea and his sentencing to prison for the rest of his natural life. They said the prisoner seemed fairly somber as he stood with his Georgia defense attorney, Ken Bruce, and answered the judge's questions directly and clearly.

Buzz Franklin said the plea allowed the Georgia Department of Corrections to make sure special attention would be paid to Bissell's mental-health needs, including medication and a suitable environment.

"I think the plea agreement was appropriate under the circumstances," Franklin said. "At this point in time, Bissell might be considered for parole in about fourteen years, but his release would be up to the Georgia Board of Pardons and Paroles."

Franklin added that the possibility of parole in Bissell's case would be extremely unlikely. "Under the current state of affairs in Georgia, prisoners don't parole on the first go-around very often."

Moments after Bissell was sentenced, the group of men referred to by Mike O'Dell as the "Alabama/ Georgia Prosecutorial Team" stepped out into the courtroom foyer for a group picture. The district attorneys, sheriffs and investigators from both DeKalb and Chattooga Counties posed for the camera to commemorate their successful collaboration and the conclusion of a long and difficult case.

"That's a picture I'm proud of," O'Dell said.

When O'Dell arrived back at his office, he immediately went to work on a press release he had been waiting for two years to write—the announcement that Hayward Bissell had been found guilty of felony murder and sentenced to the Georgia State Penitentiary for the rest of his natural life.

"We have all worked very hard on bringing Mr. Bissell to justice," O'Dell wrote. "District Attorney Buzz Franklin represented the State of Georgia in this case, but I think it would be fair to say this plea was the culmination of two years worth of hard work on behalf of a great many people in at least three states. I am truly grateful on behalf of the people of my circuit for the willingness of Buzz and his staff to pursue this matter as vigorously as they did."

O'Dell said it took numerous telephone conferences and at least a half-dozen face-to-face meetings between Alabama and Georgia authorities to discuss adequately the facts and circumstances of Franklin's case and the DeKalb County cases and finally arrive at a fair and satisfactory resolution.

As is often his custom, O'Dell took advantage of the opportunity to give credit to those whose hard work had been instrumental in ensuring Hayward Bissell would remain safely behind bars.

"Buzz's lead investigator, Johnny Bass, my major crimes investigator, Danny Smith, and DeKalb Sheriff's investigator Mike James, have spent literally hundreds of hours collecting evidence and putting this case together," O'Dell wrote. "They made at least two trips to Ohio to interview witnesses and gather information and potential evidence. We have six huge boxes of materials that we have pored over for the past eighteen months. These cases have been on all our minds virtually every day since Bissell was first arrested."

O'Dell also credited ADA Bob Johnston for the long hours of hard work that went into assembling the case for his office to present to Georgia prosecutors.

"Bob burned the midnight oil on many occasions to take the reams of papers and sort them into a workable case file," O'Dell said. "He was assisted by a summer intern, Shaunathan Bell, who spent his entire term of employment cataloging Bissell's vast psychiatric history.

"I appreciate Buzz letting us work with him to bring this plea to fruition. There was a true spirit of cooperation among the law enforcement officials and the defense lawyers from both states. Because the circumstances of their murder case were intimately intertwined with our cases, it brought us all together to seek a just resolution. I believe we accomplished that task, and I look forward to concluding our matters soon."

Sheriff Cecil Reed was a bit more succinct with his statements concerning what he considered to be Georgia's not-too-speedy handling of the case.

"I applaud the efforts of our district attorney for his persistence," Reed said. "He has expressed all along that Georgia had the more serious of the cases, and should have taken a more active role in the prosecution from the beginning, but we were aware that Buzz Franklin had his plate full with some very difficult capital-murder cases that needed trying before he could turn his attention to Bissell. This plea represents the most we could have hoped for in disposing this case. This nightmare has been going on for us for over two years now, and I'll be glad to turn Bissell over to someone else."

It would be another thirty days before Sheriff Reed would finally be rid of Bissell, however. The prisoner was ordered to be returned to DeKalb County's custody until the time expired for him to file an appeal of his murder conviction; then he would be returned to Georgia to start serving his sentence. After two years, Reed and his staff could easily stand another thirty days of Hayward Bissell's company as long as they knew he would be gone forever at the end of that time.

There were still the two attempted murder charges and one charge of attempted burglary pending in DeKalb County to be considered, and O'Dell planned to reassess those charges after consulting with Don Pirch, James Pumphrey and Hoyt Baugh.

"We've had preliminary discussions concerning Bissell's Alabama charges, and we're contemplating our next step," O'Dell said. "There are some procedural matters to consider, and I am in the process of contacting Mr. Pirch and Mr. Pumphrey to inform them of Bissell's plea in the Georgia case. Both of these gentlemen have recently moved out of state, which may impact their decisions on how these cases should be handled. Once all parties have had time to consider the fact that Bissell has received a life sentence, we will get together with Judge Cole and discuss the handling of the cases here."

Later, in his office, O'Dell confirmed that after time for an appeal expired, Bissell would be transported back to Georgia and it was likely his Alabama cases would be disposed of and he would not have to return to Alabama ever again. He explained that Bissell's plea in Georgia was unusual and quite different from anything that exists under Alabama law.

"Bissell entered a plea of guilty but insane, which exists under Georgia law. By doing this, he was adjudicated guilty of the murder and sentenced to life in the state penal system or such other institution as the commissioner of the Georgia Department of Corrections may direct. This could include a mental hospital, if necessary.

"Alabama does not have such a law. The best we can do with a defendant that exhibits severe mental problems is a plea of not guilty by reason of mental disease or defect. Under such a plea, the defendant would be ordered to our state mental hospital until such a time as he was competent to be released.

"There was a chance that such a sentence could have put Bissell back out on the streets in a very short time, if he could have convinced his doctors he was well," O'Dell said. "That was a chance I just wasn't willing to take."

Chapter 24

"I thank the Lord God he'll be locked up . . .
where he can't hurt anyone else."

One of Mike O'Dell's few enjoyable duties in regard to the Bissell case came on the day of the Georgia conviction and sentencing, when he had the great pleasure of calling James Pumphrey and Don Pirch and informing them of the outcome of the Georgia murder case.

James and Sue Pumphrey had been unable to shake the memories of their experience with Bissell. There were reminders waiting at every turn, sights and sounds that brought back the trauma of their attack. Finally, in an effort to distance themselves from the past, they had moved out of state several months before Bissell's conviction in Georgia and headed north into the Appalachian Mountains, where a number of their family members lived. The couple had suffered such physical, emotional and financial devastation as a result of their encounter with Hayward Bissell that they were unable to remain in DeKalb County without seeing him in their minds' eyes at every turn. They had moved from the subsidized housing project in Fort Payne to a lovely home in a neighboring town, but they were still unable to put their traumatic experience behind them and get on with their lives.

The move was a good decision. It not only put them near a close-knit, supportive group of friends and relatives, it also gave them a new lease on life. There were children in the family to enjoy the love James and Sue had to lavish on them, and the couple felt useful and needed. The rural area where they now lived teemed with wildlife, even the occasional bear in the backyard. It was a beautiful area in which to live, and things were quiet and restful in their new home. Despite James's continuing physical problems as a result of the attack, the Pumphreys finally began relaxing, reclaiming some peace of mind, and learning once again to enjoy their lives.

When they received Mike O'Dell's call, with the news that Hayward Bissell would be in a Georgia prison for the rest of his natural life, the couple was overjoyed to hear the case was about to come to a conclusion after such a long, hard time.

"I thank the Lord God he'll be locked up for the rest of his life, where he can't hurt anyone else," James Pumphrey said. "We are so thankful we can finally begin to put this behind us."

Don and Rhea Pirch had also moved out of state, to a tiny resort town that was high in the Colorado Rockies. The little village had a storybook quality, with only three hundred year-round residents. Don and Rhea soon became a part of the community, and they lived every day surrounded by beautiful mountain peaks capped with snow. In moving from the mountain resort of Mentone, Alabama, to an even smaller town in such a distant location, the reminders of Hayward Bissell should have been left far behind. However, Don continued to be haunted by memories of the hit-and-run attack and was constantly plagued by nagging pain from his knee injury.

Like the Pumphreys, Don and Rhea Pirch were thrilled to hear the verdict in Bissell's murder case.

"I am satisfied with the outcome," Don said, "and I feel that justice has been served in a way that is appropriate for what has been done. Bissell's victims have finally come to the end of a long road, and now we can get on with our lives."

Both the Pirches and Pumphreys agreed that, since their assailant would spend the rest of his natural life in prison, their cases would not have to come to trial in order for them to feel they'd been dealt with fairly by the judicial system. O'Dell told them the state of Alabama would wait approximately a year to determine if Bissell would appeal his Georgia case; then, if not, a motion of nolle prosequi would be filed in the Alabama cases and they would be closed permanently. The two couples would never have to return to Alabama to face the memories of pain and terror and the dreaded prospect of a lengthy trial.

On the day following the Georgia verdict, Sheriff Cecil Reed was still celebrating.

"Yesterday was one of the best days I've had in a long time," he told reporters, leaning back in his office chair and grinning broadly. When asked when Bissell would return to Georgia to begin serving his sentence, Reed said that it couldn't happen soon enough to suit him.

"We'll soon be rid of him," he said. "It looks like he'll be out of here for good before too much longer."

A month later, the sheriff finally got his wish. Hayward Bissell was about to leave the DeKalb County Jail once again, and he would not ever be coming back this time.

"The agreement with Georgia authorities was that

Bissell would stay here until the time ran out for him to file an appeal in his conviction for the murder of Patricia Ann Booher," Reed said. "That time has expired, and no appeal has been filed, so he will be leaving our jail and will be taken to Georgia, possibly to stay for the rest of his life."

Reed was glad to see his most notorious inmate leaving the jail for good. He had stated on several occasions that he'd have a patrol car waiting with the motor running, ready to carry Bissell out of the county, but as things turned out, that wasn't necessary.

"They're coming to pick him up right here at the back door," Reed said. "We're finally going to be rid of him, and that will be the end of that chapter . . . maybe."

That afternoon, Chattooga County deputies arrived to take Hayward Bissell to their jail in Summerville to begin the process of serving his sentence. Again, in a fairly short period of time, his appearance had changed dramatically. The man who had been booked into the jail over two years earlier at four hundred pounds had lost over half his total body weight while in jail. He was clean shaved and his hair was shorter, but it looked dry, very thin and brittle, and it seemed to be much lighter in color.

As he reached the top of the stairs, Bissell walked out without handcuffs or shackles. He was very cooperative with the deputies, but he seemed slightly bewildered as he looked around. His ruddy complexion, which had been described as "flushed" during his initial months in jail, was now quite pale, and he looked frail and stooped. He moved slowly and stiffly, like an old, old man.

Hayward Bissell no longer looked as though he had enough strength or energy to do harm to anyone, not even himself.

Sometime after Bissell was pronounced guilty and

received his life sentence, Buzz Franklin wrote to the Georgia State Board of Pardons and Paroles advising them of the seriousness of his crimes and asking them not to consider him for parole. This was likely a move on Franklin's part to have plenty of documentation in Bissell's file at such time in the future as he should become eligible for consideration, since Franklin had already stated it was highly unlikely Bissell would be a candidate for parole when he finally qualified for such consideration.

On December 10, 2002, the director of the Georgia State Board of Pardons and Paroles answered Franklin's letter, reassuring him that Bissell was unlikely to be going anywhere, even if he were eligible to be considered for parole.

"Bissell is not eligible for parole consideration until February 2016," the director wrote. "However, this does not mean that parole will be granted. Because he has a life sentence, he, in fact, is not entitled to be released from prison at any time, only that his case be considered in accordance with Georgia law."

Mike O'Dell had the Alabama charges against Bissell placed on administrative hold; then almost a year later, he moved to enter a nolle prosequi of those charges.

"The State and Defense counsel, on behalf of the defendant and with his approval, entered into a plea agreement whereby the DeKalb County cases would be nolle prossed upon the defendant's plea to murder in his Georgia murder case," O'Dell's motion said. "He entered that plea in early February 2002, was found guilty of murder and sentenced to life in prison.

"The plea agreement was entered into with full knowledge and approval of the victims in the DeKalb County cases. It was the desire of these victims not to have to come back to this jurisdiction for prosecution purposes. Both victims have moved from this state in order to put these matters behind them and to start new lives. The decision to enter into the plea negotiations and settlement were based in large measure on the various statutes in both states dealing with the issue of mental illness and insanity. It was believed that Georgia provided the best avenue in the pursuit of justice.

"By agreement, the State of Alabama would wait approximately one year before requesting this action by the Court to determine if the defendant was going to appeal his Georgia case. Since he has not, the State is prepared to move forward and complete the agreement."

On January 28, 2003, circuit judge Randall Cole signed an order to nolle prosequi the Alabama cases against Hayward Bissell. It had been three years and five days since Bissell first drove into Alabama, leaving his bloody mark on so many lives.

Chapter 25

"All I can tell you is watch out, he is slick."

Despite the fact that Hayward Bissell was determined to be guilty but insane according to Georgia law, and was sentenced to spend the remainder of his natural life in either a state prison or a mental institution, his true mental condition will always remain in question with many of the people who dealt with him.

Was he really that mentally ill, or was he a skilled actor, a master manipulator, who was faking mental disease in order to get away with a string of crimes, beginning in his youth with minor incidents and ending years later with brutal murder?

Was Hayward Bissell's paranoid schizophrenia, like his diabetes, so improved by regular medication that his symptoms virtually disappeared, then recurred when he failed to continue treatment as directed? Doctors during his initial evaluation believed his self-reported accounts of hearing voices that ordered him to slaughter and dismember Patricia Booher and assault Don Pirch and James Pumphrey. Bissell's evaluating psychiatrist said he gave "a very believable narrative" due to his corroborating symptoms. But could these symptoms have been faked skillfully enough to convince scores of trained professionals that Bissell suffered from paranoid schizophrenia and was therefore not responsible for the crimes he committed?

Schizophrenia is a mental disorder that distorts thought and perception beyond reality, causing people to experience auditory and visual hallucinations. It is not caused by poor parenting, which so often is credited wrongfully as the cause of most aberrant behavior, but is believed instead to be caused by an error in brain development that may be genetic in nature. The disease occurs in about 1 percent of the population, typically appearing during adolescence or later, but occasionally paranoid schizophrenia can begin to manifest itself as early as childhood.

When talking with investigators about Hayward's childhood, one of Hayward Bissell's relatives speculated that he may have shown signs of the disease at an early age, when he was reported to have claimed that he "got down on his knees and saw a bright light." Perhaps he did; or perhaps, like many children, he invented the incident in order to get the attention of his family.

At the onset of schizophrenia, friends and family may notice the symptoms before the patient. Confusion, nervousness, withdrawal, indifference, anger and argumentativeness can indicate an oncoming problem. Other symptoms that may develop gradually are changes in eating or sleeping habits, energy level or weight, and a withdrawal from friends, work or school.

At times during his imprisonment in the DeKalb County Jail, Bissell seemed completely lucid and talked at great length to certain of his fellow prisoners about his crimes, recounting them in gory detail. On other occasions, Bissell was lethargic and withdrawn, unwilling to interact with anyone and spending most of his time asleep on his bunk.

Some of Bissell's lethargy was attributed to fluctuations in his blood sugar levels, for which he was treated while in jail. A counselor from the local Mental Health Center, who visited Bissell regularly, noted in March 2001 that he looked physically ill and recommended that he should be checked out immediately by a doctor. His illness was discovered to be diabetes-related, his medication was adjusted, and he quickly improved.

Bissell's lengthy police record shows several incidents testifying to his problems with anger and argumentativeness, ranging from disagreements with his landlord to complaints filed against him for spousal abuse. His extreme weight loss over the course of his imprisonment was well documented, and he went from claiming he "hadn't slept in seven days" to sleeping during the majority of the time he spent in his cell.

Once schizophrenia progresses, the symptoms also progress. Hallucinations, delusions and distorted thinking and behavior can occur, along with delusions of persecution or grandeur, but the most common symptom of paranoid schizophrenia is hearing voices. Bissell claimed his actions were being directed by the voices in his head, which he received, he said, from a satellite that broadcast his instructions to an implant located behind his left ear. The voices, he said, told him to terminate Patricia and then run down a man in the road, then go to a house and kill an old man.

Bissell, however, seemed to have had a problem keeping his stories straight from one interview to the next. On one occasion, he said he was instructed to go to a house and kill two dogs, not an old man. During another interview, he said the voices told him to kill the pickup truck's driver; Don Pirch was the passenger in the truck, the driver was his wife, Rhea, and Bissell had followed the pickup closely for a long-enough time to see plainly which of the two was behind the wheel. These conflicting accounts of what "the voices" said was one of the things that convinced Mike O'Dell that Bissell was malingering, and was not as mentally ill as he presented himself to be.

Another common symptom is known as a deadened emotional syndrome, which causes the patient to speak in a monotone voice and show a flat, masklike facial expression. In countless medical files, as well as accounts from witnesses who spoke to him on the day of Patricia Booher's murder while he was stopped on the roads in their neighborhoods, Hayward Bissell was described as speaking in a monotone voice and having a blank-faced stare. He might have conveniently adopted this behavior prior to several of his episodes, perhaps in order to have it witnessed by others.

Some schizophrenics believe people can hear their thoughts, control their feelings and behavior, and are plotting to harm them. They sometimes see visual hallucinations, and experience burning or itching sensations without cause. Patients also experience hallucinations that cause them to smell nonexistent odors. Bissell's main complaint consisted of hearing voices, transmissions from a "secret source" that came to him inside his head via satellite. Other schizophrenics have believed they received directions from televisions and radios; in the case of David "Son of Sam" Berkowitz, from a neighbor's black dog.

Schizophrenics often have delusions of grandeur, and Bissell frequently made statements like "I'm the richest man in the world," "I own all the stores" and "I'm going to be the ruler of the new world." He also claimed to have had his sperm extracted and implanted in women around the world, by which he fathered thousands of children. Did Bissell really have these beliefs, or did he know that delusions of grandeur were a frequent symptom of schizophrenia, and one that he could easily display?

A schizophrenic may have more than one symptom, but rarely do they have all of them. In the periods between flare-ups of the disease, schizophrenics can lead relatively normal lives, but patients diagnosed as "chronic" seldom fully regain normal functioning even during these interim periods. Hayward Bissell met Patricia Booher at a time when his alleged paranoid schizophrenic symptoms were seemingly under control, but also during the time of their relationship, he stopped taking some of the drugs he had been prescribed.

Haldol, along with Thorazine and Risperdal, can control symptoms in four out of five patients. But without medication, schizophrenics can experience severe delusions and hallucinations that make them a danger to themselves and those around them. When a person is not receiving effective treatment, it is possible for them to become violent. This is usually the result of their belief that they are being threatened or that they are being directed to take some type of action by the voices they hear.

After Bissell murdered his pregnant girlfriend because he claimed his voices told him she was a "black witch" and a "double-agent spy," whom he had to terminate, he cut off her left hand and right leg because, he said, he feared she would try to "come back at him" while he was driving. Was he really hearing voices directing him to murder Patricia and mutilate her body, or was he "on a rampage," as he told Todd Graves, and in the grip of a killing frenzy resulting from a fit of rage?

The use of alcohol or street drugs by schizophrenics in an attempt to "self-medicate" can contribute to the possibility of violence. Hayward Bissell's use of marijuana began, according to family reports, in his early teens and continued during the following years on a regular basis. His crack cocaine use was also credited by the family for causing much of his violent behavior.

In Bissell's case files are documents from at least nine hospitals and clinics where he sought treatment over the years. During that time, talking to all the countless doctors, psychiatrists and mental-health counselors who treated him at those hospitals and clinics, could he have learned what behavior was expected from a paranoid schizophrenic? Bissell was a skilled manipulator, judging by the letter he wrote to Patricia in an attempt to win her back after a breakup. He knew exactly what to say, and how to say it, to reassure her that he was completely sincere in his professions of love for her.

"He knew how to push her buttons," one investigator said.

If he was that good, could Bissell not have convinced his doctors that he was unable to control his behavior because of being a paranoid schizophrenic? Perhaps he knew how to push their buttons, too. A member of his family may have given some excellent advice when they said, "All I can tell you is watch out, he is slick."

Chapter 26

"He's not a damn bit crazier than I am."

A few days after Hayward Bissell left Alabama to begin serving his sentence in a Georgia prison, officers and jailers stood outside the back door of the DeKalb County Jail swapping stories about their dealings with him and speculating on whether or not he was really as mentally ill as he had sometimes appeared to be.

"Why, hell," one of the deputies said, "he's not a damn bit crazier than I am."

The deputy's colleagues ribbed him unmercifully for that comment, but in all seriousness, there continued to be questions in the minds of all those who had dealt with Bissell during his time in their custody.

If it had been determined that Bissell killed Patricia Booher just over the state line into Alabama, how different might the outcome of his case have been? Could he have been found not guilty by reason of insanity?

The insanity defense has been around since the mid-1800s, when a man who attempted to assassinate the British prime minister was found not guilty by reason of insanity. Currently, less than 1 percent of criminal defendants have used insanity defenses, and very few are found not guilty. Most of those few, however, have ended up spending far less time in mental institutions than they would have spent in prison, had they been convicted without the insanity plea being involved.

At least twenty states, including Georgia, have adopted the plea of guilty but mentally ill as an alternative for defendants who have clearly committed the crimes they are accused of, are obviously mentally ill, but are not ill enough to excuse their crimes.

Those found guilty but mentally ill are required to serve out their sentences whether or not they are pronounced "cured" by their treating psychiatrists. If they had been found not guilty by reason of insanity, however, they would have been released from commitment in a mental institution as soon as they were deemed no longer to be a threat to society.

Some critics of the plea believe there are too many differences in available mental-health treatment from one jail or prison to another, and defendants may not actually receive the treatment they need while serving their time. Others feel the verdict of guilty but insane guarantees the defendant will get the help they need while paying the debt they owe to society for the crimes they have committed.

The trial of John Hinckley, who shot President Ronald Reagan in 1981, did a great deal to draw public criticism of the insanity defense. People were outraged when Hinckley was found not guilty by reason of insanity, despite the overwhelming proof of premeditation of the crime. People feared that those found not guilty of violent crimes by reason of insanity could conceivably be released too soon from the institutions in which they were confined. Then, back on the streets and once again a part of society, they might pose a threat to the safety of the public.

After the Hinckley trial, twelve states adopted the verdict of guilty but mentally ill, nine states limited the substantive test of insanity, and five states abolished the insanity defense completely. In those states that still recognize the insanity defense, the burden of proof is now placed upon the defendant, who must persuade the jury of his insanity at the time the crime was committed.

In insanity cases, the jury must decide whether the defendant was able to differentiate right from wrong, and whether he chose intentionally to break the law or was mentally incapable of making the choice. In the case of Andrea Yates, the Houston, Texas, mother who drowned her five children, psychiatrists said she acted in the belief that her children only could be saved from Satan by taking their lives. She felt she had been a poor mother and the children were destined for hell unless she killed them. Despite a long, well-documented history of mental illness, including treatment for schizophrenia, postpartum depression and psychosis, the jury found Yates guilty. She received a life sentence, and is currently serving that sentence while she receives psychiatric treatment.

Doctors say Yates may have realized killing her children was illegal, but her illness caused her to believe that drowning them was the right thing to do. She is reportedly improving, and with that improvement comes an increased realization of what she has done. At the time of her sentencing, she said in a handwritten note, "I regret that this illness brought me to a place where I was capable of killing my own children."

If Hayward Bissell was faking his mental illness in an effort to escape punishment, his effort failed. He, too, will spend the rest of his life in prison; for this time, his "get out of jail free" card had reached its limit. His "crazy papers" didn't keep him out of trouble.

Malingering is defined by the psychological community as faking a psychological or physical problem to avoid a responsibility, pretending to have a symptom or disorder to avoid an unwanted situation, or intentionally producing symptoms to evade consequences.

If Bissell was not malingering and was really insane at the time of his crimes, and has since responded well to treatment, he will still be locked up for the entirety of his life sentence. But he will face a far greater punishment than going to prison; he will have to live with the realization of what he did to the young woman who loved him and was carrying his unborn child. The guilt that Hayward Bissell must bear for his actions will leave him trapped in a private hell from which he can never escape.

Chapter 27

"[Darrell Glen Smith] told his sister he could kill his mother and get away with it."

Looking into the files of other, remarkably similar cases of paranoid schizophrenics who have murdered loved ones and acquaintances, there are many that parallel the Hayward Bissell case in countless ways. Most have concluded with the defendants pronounced guilty, and sentenced according to the laws of the particular state where the crime occurred. In almost every case, the prosecution argued that the defendant was malingering, and most of the juries in those cases agreed.

At a trial in Cocke County, Tennessee, a forty-eight-year-old man was convicted of first-degree murder after he killed his seventy-five-year-old mother, claiming she was trying to poison him and had sold him into "white slavery." Three mental-health professionals testified on behalf of Darrell Glen Smith, saying he was legally insane when he repeatedly struck his mother in the head with a short-handled ax and a section of steel rebar.

"He told a Tennessee Bureau of Investigation agent that he hit her in the head a bunch of times because 'she wouldn't go down,'" Assistant District Attorney General Jimmy Dunn said.

"And he told his sister, the evidence shows, that he could kill his mother and get away with it."

This statement is much the same as Hayward Bissell's claim, as he held up his "crazy papers," that he could kill someone and get away with it because the papers proved he was insane.

But the jury ruled that Smith was able to understand that his actions were wrong, and after just over ninety minutes of deliberation, they found him guilty of murdering his mother.

At one point, the jury sent the judge a note asking, "If we find the defendant not guilty by reason of insanity, what assurances do we have that he will be institutionalized for a long period of time?"

Circuit judge Ben Hooper called the jury back into the courtroom and told them he couldn't answer their question because it had to do with sentencing, not guilt or innocence. After the jury entered their verdict, Hooper sentenced the man to life in prison, "at whatever facility they deem it best for you to be placed in."

One of the doctors who testified in Smith's favor said the man believed he was put here to destroy his mother, whom he viewed as the Devil incarnate. When asked by the prosecution if Smith was malingering, the doctor said it was unlikely, since the man had been diagnosed as a paranoid schizophrenic for over fifteen years, and had been displaying symptoms for more than thirty years.

However, the doctor agreed with the prosecution that just because a person is mentally ill, that does not mean he cannot tell the difference between right and wrong.

Smith, like Bissell, had been hospitalized several

times and had been involved in several domestic disturbances over the years. His last hospitalization ended with his mother's death taking place only hours following his discharge, and a subsequent suicide attempt in which he stabbed himself in the side and chest with a pocketknife.

Both other doctors who testified at his trial said they could not say that Smith was unable to understand the wrongfulness of his actions. At the time of the incident, they said, they believed he could recognize that assaulting another individual was wrong.

In another similar case, a Texas man was sentenced to death in October 1995 for murder. James Colburn had an extensive history of paranoid schizophrenia, which was first diagnosed when he was seventeen years old. At the time of the murder, Colburn was being treated irregularly on an outpatient basis. He said he had auditory hallucinations that told him to murder his victim, Peggy Murphy, claiming he experienced a flash that he was going to hurt her, and an impulse came over him to kill her and he couldn't stop himself.

A court-appointed psychologist pronounced him to be both sane and competent, but a psychiatrist reviewed the records and said there were serious questions and concerns about Colburn's competency to stand trial due to the fact he was sedated with Haldol and frequently nodded off during court proceedings.

In Portland, Maine, a man shot and killed a cabdriver, and at his murder trial, a state psychologist said Derek-Finn Wilhelmsen's mental condition had deteriorated so much that he was incapable of using thought to control his actions. Wilhelmsen's schizophrenia so consumed him, his defense attorney said, that at the time of the killing he could not appreciate the wrongfulness of his actions.

Wilhelmsen had not taken his medication for months, stopping in fall 2001. Just after that, he met a woman and fell in love with her, much the same as Hayward Bissell started a relationship with Patricia Booher shortly after he stopped taking some of his prescriptions. When Wilhelmsen's girlfriend broke off the relationship, he began to obsess about killing her and bought a pistol, which he believed had magical powers.

Wilhelmsen shot the cabdriver seven times with the pistol, and a psychiatrist testified at the trial that he saw his girlfriend's face superimposed on the cab-driver's when he fired the shots. This instance of self-reporting is similar to Bissell's claim of seeing the face of the Devil and seeing Patricia in his cell during his mental evaluation. Mike O'Dell speculated that Bissell may not have realized that visual hallucinations were a symptom of schizophrenia until he was asked about them at the hospital. He may have added the story about the face of the Devil in order to make his case seem more extreme.

In a widely publicized case that occurred only around two weeks before Patricia Booher's murder, a Haverhill, Massachusetts, man killed seven of his coworkers after the company that employed them told him his wages would be garnished by the IRS for back taxes.

Michael "Mucko" McDermott took four guns and a large supply of bullets to his job on December 26, 2000. Prosecutors said the shootings were planned ahead, but the defense claimed he was a schizophrenic and did not appreciate the wrongfulness of his conduct.

Like Bissell, McDermott offered no resistance when police arrived to arrest him, remaining silent except for a single statement. Bissell's only words at the time of his arrest were "My foot is broke"; when officers took McDermott into custody, he said, "I don't speak German."

The defendants in these cases were determined to be schizophrenic based largely on their self-reported symptoms. And the prosecution in each case, for the most part, took issue with their psychiatric evaluations, claiming that despite their mental status at the time of their crimes, they were still able to distinguish right from wrong. But in each of the cases, even if the defendants were able to appreciate the wrongfulness of their actions, that did not stop them from taking the lives of their innocent victims. Like Hayward Bissell, they each "went on a rampage" that resulted in tragedy.

Chapter 28

"Patricia was afraid of Hayward for the last month of her life."

Many of Patricia Booher's family members and friends were worried that she might be experiencing physical and psychological abuse at the hands of her boyfriend, and several of them questioned Patricia about possible violence in her relationship with Hayward Bissell. But Patricia almost always denied any domestic abuse or refused to discuss the matter any further once she was questioned about her welfare.

However, she did admit to a few of her friends that Hayward had hit her, particularly on one occasion when she showed up at the Friendship Club with visible bruises, which she said he had given her. He had also threatened to kill her, she said, and one of her girlfriends said that Patricia was afraid of Hayward for the last month of her life. Patricia also complained to another friend that Hayward had been "swatting her on the bottom," and said she did not like it, but she later downplayed the abuse, when she and Hayward reconciled.

Was Patricia Booher a victim of domestic abuse?

Without a doubt.

Did she realize that she was being assaulted and intimidated by her domineering boyfriend?

It's possible that like so many battered wives and girlfriends, she never considered their relationship to be abusive.

Although she was a high-school graduate with good grammar and spelling skills, Patricia was considered to be a "special-needs student" during her school years and seemed to be very mildly mentally retarded. Sadly, over 90 percent of mentally retarded persons will experience abuse at some time in their lives, and Patricia was no exception. She was a victim of child abuse early in her life, and from that experience it is likely she learned compliance, hesitation to tell authority figures she was experiencing abuse, and fear of not being believed.

Patricia was made to order to be victimized by a bullying, controlling manipulator like Hayward Bissell, and even though he professed his love for her when it suited his purposes, he practiced a number of behaviors in the relationship that are consistent with almost every indicator of domestic violence and abuse.

Bissell attempted to isolate Patricia by discouraging her attendance at the Friendship Club, and in the weeks prior to her death, he was pressuring her to leave her church and attend his own church instead. This would have left her with virtually no social contacts of her own outside the relationship, and would have given her fewer opportunities to speak to anyone else about the treatment she was receiving at his hands.

Patricia was often told by Hayward that he didn't like the way she kept house, washed dishes, kept herself or managed her money. He intentionally left her with the feeling that she was lucky to have a boyfriend, fortunate that he wanted her, and should devote all her time to doing things in a way that pleased him. He blamed her slight mental disability for her inability to meet his high standards, making her feel that she was incapable of making decisions on her own, and made her feel she needed to be "instructed" by him as to how she should manage her life.

Hayward clearly believed it was his male privilege to tell Patricia what to do, speaking down to her as though she were a child, forbidding her to eat out and even telling her where to buy her shoes. Patricia complained to her sister and some of her friends about his controlling behavior, but because Hayward's treatment of her had severely eroded her self-confidence, she kept going back to him even as the physical and psychological abuse increased.

Another ploy Bissell used to keep Patty in line was economic abuse, which he practiced by taking the money she received from selling Avon products before she could send it in to the company. According to her friends, he also emptied her bank account of $3,000 during the course of their relationship and even attempted to persuade another woman, a former girlfriend of his, to borrow Patricia's bicycle and then sell it for $50 so he could take the woman to Disney World.

Patricia depended on Hayward for rides to the store, the library, to doctor appointments, and on countless other errands. He took advantage of that dependence by controlling where and when she went places, what she did and how long she stayed once she was there.

As time passed, the physical abuse increased from "swatting" to hitting hard enough to leave bruises . . . and to leave Patty ashamed to admit to some of her acquaintances that she was, indeed, experiencing domestic violence at her boyfriend's hands.

The bruises were signs of physical abuse, but the behavioral signs that Patty was being abused were even more noticeable. In addition to a continuation of her problems with depression, Patty was more withdrawn from her friends and family when she was with Bissell. According to her aunt, he was the first of her boyfriends that she did not bring to meet her family, and even her closest relative, her sister, Charlene, never actually met Bissell in person except on one occasion when he and Patty came through the drive-through window at the restaurant where Charlene worked.

Patricia's self-esteem also decreased greatly when she was with Hayward, and she suffered from frequent headaches and other nagging health problems. These conditions commonly occur among people who are experiencing domestic abuse. Because they also are common among the disabled, they sometimes are attributed to the disability instead of the abuse. Because of her slight mental impairment, Patricia was more vulnerable to abuse and less able to avoid it.

Researchers and service providers are beginning to recognize the abuse of women with disabilities as a problem that is growing to epidemic proportions, and those with mental retardation and other developmental disabilities are even more vulnerable to abuse. Patricia Booher's friends recognized her vulnerability, but despite their desire to help her, they were not able to take effective action toward her protection because she evidently was ashamed and unwilling to admit she was being abused.

In every state, members of the public are allowed to report suspected abuse of adults as well as children. It is not necessary to have proof of the abuse in order to file a report; in most cases, people start by calling the police. This was done by a woman in Patty's apartment building, who reported to the Norwalk Police Department that she suspected a young friend of hers, Patricia, who she said was mentally retarded, was being abused by her boyfriend. The girl, she said, was frightened of the man but was afraid to try to end the relationship for fear that he might retaliate against her.

An officer responded to the call, then went to Hayward Bissell's apartment, where he was assured that there was no problem. The officer reported back that it seemed to be a domestic matter that was now settled.

Hayward then wrote a long note to Patty assuring her that he would never do anything to hurt her and that he only had her best interests at heart. The note was sufficiently sincere to convince Patricia that Hayward really did love her, and she once again resumed the relationship that she had tried several times earlier to end.

In this case, the warning signs of an abusive situation were skillfully masked by Bissell's ability to manipulate. He was able to convince the officer that everything was fine; then he went on to convince Patricia to take him back and accept his engagement ring once again. Both the friend who reported the suspected abuse and the officer who investigated the report did the right things, but if an additional report had been made to adult-protective services, a further investigation might have revealed additional evidence of Patricia's mistreatment.

Women with disabilities often feel they are not attractive, and think they will not be as likely to have successful relationships with men. Once they do become involved romantically, it may be harder for them to leave an unsatisfactory relationship that is not working out. And for many young women with mental retardation, having a boyfriend is very important to their self-esteem. Consequently they may fail to report abusive behavior out of fear of losing the boyfriend.

There is no question that Patricia Booher was as

much a victim of domestic abuse as was Hayward Bissell's first wife, who divorced him after his physical violence against her escalated to the point of assault. Sherry Bissell was the lucky one; she took decisive action to protect herself and her child and left the relationship before suffering permanent physical harm.

Chapter 29

"I don't think things are going to work out for me."

Patricia Booher's mental retardation was so very slight that she was able to attend school, take part in the EHOVE Career Center's program, and successfully graduate from Western Reserve High School. Her adaptive skills, the daily living skills needed to successfully work and live in the community, were excellent, and these helped to balance out her slight intellectual impairment.

At the EHOVE Center, where she was involved in the general-merchandising program, she learned how to work in retail sales and how to display merchandise effectively. Her EHOVE tutors helped her learn employability skills, and were quick to praise her enthusiasm and her desire to please. She was well liked by everyone she came into contact with at EHOVE and in DECA, the Distributive Education Clubs of America, an organization for marketing students.

A majority of mentally retarded adults do not work, but thanks to organizations like EHOVE and The ARC, more and more special-needs students and adults with varying degrees of mental retardation are successfully finding and holding jobs in the communities. Patricia learned through EHOVE that she had many career options and she was encouraged to look forward to graduating from school and going to work. She received training and work experience while she was still in school, took part in an individualized education program, and learned the social skills she needed to enter the workplace.

Unfortunately, Patricia's problems with depression seemed to escalate after she left school, and proved to be an obstacle to achieving many of the goals she had set for herself. She knew how to use the public library and the post office, how to seek medical care and shop for her needs, and how to live on her own, in her own apartment. But transportation was a problem; she desperately wanted to get a driver's license, and wrote in her diary of her frustration at not knowing how to drive.

"I wish I knew someone who had the time to help me with my driving," she wrote. "It's the most important thing to me right now."

Being able to drive would have made Patricia much more independent and self-reliant, and it would have given Hayward Bissell one less way to control her and dictate when and where she was able to travel.

During all her school years, Patricia Booher worked side by side with students who were not mentally disabled. Such integrated settings are credited with helping slightly retarded students develop adaptive skills much faster; in Patricia's case, most of her friends never even realized she was mildly retarded. Her many friendships with fellow church members, other residents in her apartment complex and the people she met at the Friendship Club brought her into contact with a wide range of individuals and helped her develop positive attitudes and self-confidence. But each time Patricia suffered a recurring bout of deep depression, much of her self-esteem and optimism was lost.

At some point in their lives, most people with disabilities experience some form of assault or abuse, and the group at highest risk are those people with some form of intellectual impairment. Patricia's childhood experiences with abuse presented her with a huge obstacle to overcome, but she persevered. She was able to succeed in school and later in independent living, accomplishing as much as she did largely through her own efforts.

Statistics show the rates of depression and other mental illnesses are higher in those with mild retardation as opposed to people with severe retardation. Fortunately, Patricia never hesitated to seek counseling when she felt she needed someone to talk to. Her counselors and friends served as her extended family, providing support and understanding and helping her to cope with her episodes of depression. In Patricia's case, there is no doubt that counseling and therapy were both essential and highly effective in helping her lead an independent life.

Even though Patty had many friends, far more than she ever realized, she suffered many disappointments through the years in her relationships with men. Her diary was filled with accounts of boyfriends who came and went rather quickly, and she had high hopes for each of them to be the one who would offer true love. But that never seemed to be the case.

Patty seemed to realize, after dating Hayward Bissell for several months, that she was never going to be able to have a successful relationship with him because of his increasingly oppressive, controlling behavior and his threats and criticism.

"I don't think things are going to work out for me," she told her sister a few weeks before the murder.

Yet she began seeing Hayward again despite her wish to break up with him permanently. Did she feel she had no other options? Had he worn down her self-esteem to the point that she felt hopelessly trapped in the relationship? It's a shame Patricia couldn't have taken an objective look at her own life and realized what she had been able to accomplish by herself, for herself. Maybe then she would have seen that she did indeed have the strength it would have taken to break away from Hayward Bissell permanently. And scores of her friends and relatives would have been right there by her side, ready to help her in any way they could, if only she would have told them.

Chapter 30

"I'm easy to get along with.
Plus I am a very nice person."

Friendships are a vital part of a healthy emotional life, and to people with mental retardation, having a circle of friends provides a priceless network of support and acceptance. Patricia Booher was very lucky in that respect, for she had many friends throughout her school years and later on, during the time she spent attending the Friendship Club and living independently, but as a part of the community.

Patty's friends ranged from other special-needs students with whom she attended school and met at the EHOVE Career Center, to people without disabilities she met in her church and encountered around town. She was an easy person to like, with her ready smile and eagerness to please, and she always made an effort to get to know the new people who came into the Friendship Club and the Norwalk First Baptist Church.

Patricia was also lucky because throughout her school years, she was a part of the regular school system. Even though she was a shy little girl, she still participated in classroom and school activities and was on an equal footing with her classmates. This likely helped to account for her success in making friends later in life, for authorities stress the importance of relationships between people with and without disabilities. Friends choose one another and support each other emotionally through good times and bad. They provide companionship for community and school activities, share new experiences and enrich each other's lives.

On one occasion, Patricia wrote in her diary about her success in connecting with the people she met during her frequent visits to the Friendship Club.

"I'm like, gee whiz, all these friends I've been accumulating. I'm real impressed with myself," she wrote. "Then again, I'm easy to get along with. Plus I am a very nice person."

At other times, Patricia's problems with depression overcame her confidence and she withdrew, worrying that she was not a good-enough friend to those she attempted to initiate relationships with.

"I've been even more depressed than I was the last time I saw the counselor," she wrote. "The reason for that is, I finally told my new friend how I felt. He said he just wanted to be friends. Everything is okay now that things are out in the open."

Two days later, Patty wrote, "My boyfriend and I decided we should go our separate ways. Things just aren't working out for us. He knows everything now. He wasn't upset like I thought he would be. But I got really depressed. I felt like harming myself. I feel better now."

A couple of weeks later, after writing in her diary that she didn't really think she needed a psychiatrist, since she was already on an antidepressant, Patty began again to worry about her new friend.

"I am scared that whatever I say or do he is not

going to find interesting. I think I should tell him this. I am afraid that would make things worse."

And the following day, "He is a very special friend. Whenever I say or do something, I'm scared I won't be a good enough friend."

Outside of family members, many people with disabilities or with mental or emotional problems have difficulty meeting and getting to know others. They sometimes have fewer freely given and chosen relationships, therefore they greatly value the friendships they make. Patricia was clearly anxious to meet and get to know new people, and occasionally she seemed to try too hard to forge a connection with others. She wrote about a girl she met at the Friendship Club who didn't seem to be very anxious to socialize with her.

"I am trying so hard to become good friends with her, but she just doesn't want to. Part of me still wants to be good friends with her. The other part of me is learning to give up on friendships that aren't meant to be before I end up getting upset or hurt."

When Patricia moved into the Firelands Village apartment and was introduced to Hayward Bissell by a mutual acquaintance, she most likely extended the offer of friendship to him immediately. There is no record of how quickly they became romantically involved after they first got acquainted; her diary entries stopped around a year before the couple met and then resumed at a point when Patricia seemed to clearly realize there was little hope they would be able to have a future together.

"There is a man in my life that I love with all my heart and soul," she wrote. "We are not getting along. I'm depressed because it might come to us splitting up."

Even though Patricia's ability to make friends had served her well for all of her life, her friendship with

Hayward Bissell resulted in her emotional, economic and physical abuse and, ultimately, in her death. Her desire to please made her very easy to take advantage of, and Bissell clearly had a need to dominate and control within his relationships. It is sad that Patricia Booher extended the hand of friendship to Hayward Bissell when they first met, and sadder still that he accepted it.

Chapter 31

"There's a woman killed in the United States every fifteen minutes."

On one occasion while he sat in jail and awaited being charged in Patricia Booher's murder, Hayward Bissell made the nonchalant remark to a jail trusty that killing his girlfriend was not uncommon because there was a woman killed in the United States every fifteen minutes. Where he came up with that figure is unknown, but according to statistics, his estimate was astronomically high. Still, a staggering average of fifteen hundred women are murdered by an intimate partner each year, and women are in more danger of being killed by their current or former husbands or boyfriends than by any other kind of assault.

According to the Silent Witness National Initiative, Patricia Ann Booher was one of 1,247 women murdered by an intimate partner in the year 2000. The U.S. Bureau of Justice reports that in recent years, about a third of all women homicide victims were killed by a husband or boyfriend. And in a twenty-year period, from 1976 to 1996, a shocking total of 31,260 women were murdered by an intimate partner.

The weapon most likely to be used in an intimate

homicide is a firearm, with over two-thirds of victims who were wives and ex-wives being killed with a gun. But ironically, around half the women who were murdered by their boyfriends were killed with knives, like Patricia. And statistically, the group most likely to become victims of intimate homicides are white girlfriends between the ages of sixteen and thirty-four, who are also the group least likely to report domestic assault to the police. Authorities believe only 50 percent of women in that group ever report instances of domestic violence. Poorer women also are more likely to be victims of domestic violence than higher-income women; most women receiving welfare have been abused at some point in their lives. According to these statistics, Patricia Booher fit into a number of high-risk categories for experiencing domestic violence.

Domestic battery is the single major cause of injury to women, and some family violence activists claim that every fifteen seconds a woman is battered in the United States. Hayward Bissell must have struck Patricia on a number of occasions, for she had visible bruises at least once that she attributed to him. And when friends and acquaintances questioned her about his treatment of her, she refused to admit being victimized in some instances, but at other times, she admitted to experiencing economic and verbal abuse at Bissell's hands.

It is impossible to estimate accurately the number of incidents of domestic violence that occur, since abuse is one of the most underreported crimes. But in 1994, *Time* magazine estimated that 2 million women are beaten every year, and other sources claim that figure could conservatively be doubled. Physical violence, they say, is estimated to occur in 4 to 6 million intimate relationships each year in this country.

It is also estimated that over five hundred thousand

women are stalked by an intimate partner each year. Hayward Bissell was reported for stalking on several occasions by at least two young women, and his neighbors in the apartment complex also mentioned to police that they believed he might be a stalker.

That was a distinct possibility, judging by Bissell's behavior as well as his personality. The traits of stalkers include jealousy, insecurity, a poor history of relationships and being emotionally immature. Stalkers make themselves feel more powerful by bullying and intimidating their victims, attempting to control every aspect of their lives, and growing more threatening when their victims leave them or spurn their attentions. Bissell threatened Patricia Booher's safety whenever she attempted to end their relationship, saying that he would take her someplace and beat her up and not let her come back alive. He also threatened the young woman he stalked and confronted at the Greenwich Fireman's Festival in a similar manner, going so far as to make his threats to kill her in the presence of the Greenwich chief of police.

The cost of domestic violence to society is mounting every year, not just in the emotional, psychological and physical toll it takes on its victims and their families. Family violence costs from $5 to $10 billion a year, payable by the American taxpayer. Over half of women who come to emergency rooms, two-thirds of women in need of general medical care, and 20 percent of pregnant women in treatment have experienced domestic violence. There is also the tremendous cost of law enforcement, courts, mental-health care, welfare and more. Businesses lose money when employees are absent or on sick leave, and thirteen thousand acts of violence against women are committed yearly by husbands and boyfriends in the workplace. Schools must bear the expense of dealing with the problems of children who have learning difficulties and behavior problems due to domestic violence in the home. The epidemic of domestic violence reaches out and touches everyone, not just the victims and their batterers.

When Patricia confided in a friend that she was afraid of Bissell and was worried about what he would do because she was trying to break off the relationship, the friend called the police and reported the situation. That was a wise decision, despite the fact that Bissell managed to talk himself out of trouble and no action was taken at that time. Statistics show that women attempting to leave their abusers are among those at the greatest risk for violence.

It is likely that Patricia never considered herself a victim of domestic abuse; she may have grown up believing that such treatment was a normal part of everyday life, and something she would have to endure in silence if she expected to have and keep a boyfriend. Studies show that children exposed to family violence often become insecure, confused and easily discouraged, with low self-esteem. But Patricia's sweet disposition and trusting nature was not hopelessly impaired by whatever experiences may have influenced her during her early years; her ability to succeed in school and to make friends within the community was proof of that.

When Patricia became involved with Bissell, she initially had no reason to believe she would be mistreated. She had a great emotional need to be involved in a relationship, and she was convinced she was "in love" with him. Before long, his behavior became controlling and threatening, and she hoped he would change but seemed to realize it was unlikely. She told her sister she didn't think things were going to work out, and she wrote in her diary that she was afraid it would come to their breaking up. She stayed in the relationship, even though people who knew Bissell told her he was trouble, advising her to get away from him. She was embarrassed to admit he was abusive when friends from church questioned her about his treatment of her, and she felt her options were limited when it came to having and keeping boyfriends. Patricia was in denial when it came to facing the truth about her relationship with Bissell; she longed for romance, but she was getting domination and disrespect instead.

Hayward Bissell must have been very frustrated in his two marriages. Neither of his wives allowed him to dominate them past a certain point. His first wife divorced him because he physically assaulted her. His second wife, from whom he was separated but was still legally married to at the time of Patricia's death, did not report any physical violence, but Bissell's family members suspected that might not have been the case. At any rate, both women eventually refused to be victims and left their relationships with him.

When Patricia came along, physically and mentally unable to defend herself against intimidation, abuse or threats, she must have seemed to Bissell to be an ideal partner for him. He described her as being "Heaven sent" and, to him, she certainly must have been. Here was someone he could control, criticize and put down whenever he wanted to, and all it took to keep her in line were a few occasional sweet words or a kind, considerate note.

After a few months of Bissell's increasing domination, Patricia became afraid of him and began to experience a recurrence of her problems with depression, an increase in physical complaints, nightmares and problems with anger. She was hospitalized with gynecological problems during one of their last breakups, and shortly before her murder, Bissell told Sergeant David Light that Patricia was having muscle spasms, which he attributed to an automobile accident.

Patricia must not have realized she was a victim of domestic violence, which could account for the fact that she apparently didn't seek much help from her friends, family or any of the numbers of social agencies she could have contacted. Several people offered their help, but she was too ashamed, embarrassed and intimidated to reach out to them. She did not know that refusing their help would ultimately cost both her own life and the life of the child she was so pleased to be carrying.

Chapter 32

"I just wish this wouldn't have happened, that's all."

After Patricia Booher's murder, many people expressed regret that they did not take some sort of action to help her break away from the dangerous relationship she had with Hayward Bissell. Those who knew Bissell tried to warn her about him, but others knew nothing of him and his history of unstable behavior and domestic abuse. They did not realize Patricia's life was in jeopardy because she never sought help.

There are several ways that victims of domestic violence can be helped, even those who are in denial about their situation and are reluctant to discuss it. If you suspect someone you know is being abused, the first and most important thing you can do is ask her. Like Patricia, she may initially deny any abuse or refuse to talk about it, but don't let the subject drop if you believe she is being victimized. Ask again later, directly but gently, and let your friend know that you realize the abuse is not her fault. Tell her that any form of mistreatment between intimate partners is not acceptable for any reason, and let her know you will be there to support her when she wants your help.

It is important for victims of domestic violence to

make their own decisions about leaving an abusive relationship. They are the ones who must live with the outcome of those decisions, and most will reconcile with their abusers several times before finally mustering the courage to end the relationship. There is often a continuing emotional attachment to the abuser, as well as the fear she will be harmed if she leaves. A victim who grew up in an atmosphere of family violence may be unfamiliar with what a healthy relationship feels like, and she may lack the confidence or initiative to leave. Those who wish to help a friend must remember that it takes time, plus a lot of emotional strength, to leave an abuser. Be patient, and offer your unconditional support while continuing to encourage your friend to seek help by contacting victim service providers in your area.

After Patricia's death, Hayward Bissell's ex-brother-in-law told the press that he couldn't understand what had gotten into Hayward to make him do such a thing to a tiny, defenseless young woman like Patty.

"I just wish this wouldn't have happened, that's all," he said. He undoubtedly realized more clearly at that time the danger his sister could have been in during her marriage to Bissell, had she been less able to defend herself from his assault. Fortunately for Sherry Bissell, she had the strength and the motivation to take immediate action to protect herself, and she escaped from the relationship without suffering permanent harm.

Teresa Bissell, too, was able to break away from a dangerous situation in which she said she was threatened, but never physically assaulted. Teresa was lucky, separating from Bissell without being harmed, but Patricia's death must have brought the shocking realization that things could have been very different.

If you find yourself in an abusive relationship, there are agencies across the nation that are only a phone call away, ready to help you escape to safety. First and foremost, you can call the National Domestic Violence Hotline at 800-799-SAFE for advice and referrals to agencies in your area. You will receive help that is completely confidential. And don't be afraid to confide in a trusted friend. You won't be judged; you'll be supported and helped. Being the victim of an abuser is *not* your fault, and it's nothing you should be ashamed or embarrassed about. Domestic violence crosses all lines of race, gender and economics, and it is one epidemic that no one is immune to.

But most of all, if you have children, think of them. Growing up in a home where they continually witness abuse and violence will leave them living every day feeling anxious and depressed, and they will suffer from physical and emotional problems throughout their childhood. But worst of all, they will be highly likely to grow up and raise children of their own who will continue the tragic cycle of family violence.

Don't be afraid to do whatever it takes to end the abuse. No one deserves to live in pain. Do it for yourself, do it for your children . . . and do it for Patty.

In 1994, the National Coalition Against Domestic Violence and *Ms.* magazine started a national registry of the names of women who died due to domestic violence. Since then, the coalition has continued to collect information on women who have been killed by an intimate partner. Each year, a poster is produced for Domestic Violence Awareness Month listing the names that have been submitted and documented during that year.

In order to honor her memory, the name of Patricia Ann Booher has been submitted to the registry.

Epilogue

In most instances, the people involved in the three-year nightmare that was the Hayward Bissell case have gradually eased back into the comfortable routines of everyday life they enjoyed before the events of January 23, 2000.

Patricia Booher's family and friends still miss her keenly, and always will. She was a sweet, loving girl who only wanted to be happy and have friends, and she looked forward to raising her baby and showering it with affection. Her childhood had been very rough at times; she was determined that her baby would have a happy life and lots of love and care. It's likely she never realized just how many friends she actually had, but the large turnout at her funeral service was a solid testimony to the number of people who cared for her.

After her death, Patricia continued to touch the hearts of those who became involved in the investigation of her murder. A veteran law enforcement officer, a man who has worked on every conceivable type of murder case and has seen countless horrors inflicted on innocent victims, almost lost his composure on one occasion while talking to me about the case.

In the middle of describing the grisly crime scene very matter-of-factly, he stopped in midsentence and choked up, tears forming in his eyes.

"Her little Mickey Mouse socks," he said, staring down at the floor. "I keep remembering her little Mickey Mouse socks."

Then he turned and walked away without another word.

Sheriff Cecil Reed, Chief Jailer Bill Lands and the rest of the crew at the DeKalb County Sheriff's Department have continued with their routine daily business of combating crime and overseeing punishment, with no other notorious prisoners to deal with; at least, none even remotely like Hayward Bissell. Thankfully, he was one of a kind. There will likely be many other high-profile cases and problematic inmates in days to come, but for now, Reed is looking to the long-range future. The sheriff ran for reelection in 2002 and was kept in office by yet another landslide vote from the county's residents. His plans to retire are being slowed down by the promise of a new, state-of-the-art public-safety complex, which will soon begin construction in DeKalb County. After so many years of dealing with serious jail overcrowding and outdated, dilapidated facilities, the sheriff looks forward to spending a little time in the plush, new complex before he hands over the reins of office to his successor.

"I'd sure like to be in that new building for a little while before I retire," Reed said. "I may run for office for another term; I haven't really made up my mind about it yet. But it would be nice to spend some time in that new facility. It's been a long time coming."

Even though he will greatly enjoy a retirement life of leisure with his wife and family, Cecil Reed will never be out of touch with the officers he worked so closely with for so many years. It's a sure bet that he'll always keep a finger on the pulse of law enforcement in DeKalb County.

District Attorney Mike O'Dell and his staff have remained busy with an ever-increasing number of cases, but they are thankful that none of those have involved multiple, horrendous crimes of murder and assault. O'Dell and his staff are accustomed to handling methamphetamine labs, domestic abuse, burglary and DUI cases on a constant basis, but a high-profile case like Bissell's uses up an incredible amount of time and resources. For over two years, the staff of the DeKalb County District Attorney's Office worked diligently on a case that never came before a jury. Mike O'Dell doesn't regret a minute spent preparing for a trial that never happened, however. He was determined to find a way to keep Hayward Bissell from eventually being back on the streets again, and thanks to the difference in Alabama and Georgia laws, he finally succeeded.

Bissell was by no means O'Dell's first case to gain a great deal of national attention. In 1982, when he was a young assistant DA, he helped convict Judith Ann Neelley for the death of thirteen-year-old Lisa Ann Millican, who was kidnapped, repeatedly raped, injected with drain cleaner, shot in the back and dumped into DeKalb County's Little River Canyon.

A jury found Neelley guilty and recommended that she be sentenced to life in prison without parole, but Judge Randall Cole, the judge who ruled on most of Hayward Bissell's DeKalb County court decisions, overruled the jury's recommendation and gave Neelley the death penalty.

In 1999, during his last workday in office, former Alabama governor Fob James commuted Judith Ann Neelley's death sentence to life in prison. Because of an obscure 1950 statute of which James was not aware, Neelley will be eligible for parole in 2014.

An outraged Mike O'Dell joined with Senate Pro Tem Lowell Barron and scores of other Alabama legislators and district attorneys to form a coalition to support legislation to prevent another uninformed governor from potentially freeing a convicted killer.

"James made no effort to contact the Republican attorney general and ask his opinion to make certain his desired intent would be accomplished," O'Dell said. "Giving James the benefit of the doubt, at best what he did was an incredibly stupid act that will one day allow a vicious criminal to walk our streets again. Had he shown the courtesy of advising us of his intentions, this horrible act might not have been perpetrated on the citizens of Alabama."

Judith Ann Neelley's commutation and the possibility of her eventual parole made Mike O'Dell and his fellow coalition members determined to let no such incidents happen again. Thanks to their efforts, legislation has since been passed to prevent such a situation from ever reoccurring in the state of Alabama.

Buzz Franklin, the Lookout Mountain Judicial Circuit district attorney who prosecuted Hayward Bissell's murder case in Chattooga County, Georgia, has unfortunately not fared as well as Reed and O'Dell. On February 6, 2002, he heard Bissell's guilty plea and sentencing. Only days later, on February 22, one of the biggest and most notorious scandals in Georgia's entire history was dropped squarely, without warning, into Franklin's lap. The horrific case of the Tri-State Crematorium in Noble, Georgia, made continuous national headlines for months when it was discovered that bodies sent there from funeral homes in Georgia, Alabama and Tennessee for cremation had not been cremated at all. Corpses, mostly those of elderly people, had been flung about at random on the floor of sheds and stacked like cordwood inside buildings on the property. Other bodies were discarded in the woods in shallow graves, others lay in caskets above ground, and even more were left lying out in the open to deteriorate in the woods. The scene was a nightmare of incredible proportion that continued for weeks.

"It was just an unbelievable situation," said Investigator Johnny Bass, whose work on the case still continues. "Some of the people working the scene even found the bodies of people they recognized; the deceased parents of friends, things like that. It was just incredibly rough for everybody involved."

Over 331 corpses were eventually recovered, and crematory operator Ray Brent Marsh is charged with so many counts, on so many charges, that District Attorney Franklin's office will be tied up handling cases in connection with the Georgia crematory scandal for years to come. Franklin is still taking files home to work on during weekends and in the evenings, according to Bass.

It will be quite a while before Buzz Franklin and his staff enjoy a return to anything even remotely resembling a normal routine.

Mike James began his law enforcement career in DeKalb County in 1977, working in Valley Head, Geraldine, Fort Payne and the DeKalb County Sheriff's Department. He attended many one- and two-week courses in homicide investigation and trained at the FBI Academy. But as the lead investigator on the Hayward Bissell case, James encountered a situation that was unique in his experience.

Since 1982, James has investigated deaths in DeKalb County. Many people might make the assumption that an investigator would become hardened by dealing with homicides, suicides and accidental deaths on practically a daily basis. James has said that is not the case.

"It's impossible to deal with the horror and sadness that surrounds the tragic and often senseless death of another human being without being affected," he said. "I feel a sense of satisfaction when murder cases are solved to the point that a suspect has been identified and that part of the investigation is over."

But in the death of Patricia Booher, the suspect, Hayward Bissell, was known from the start and was immediately taken into custody. The job of the investigators then became to collect evidence, locate witnesses and take statements in order for the case against Bissell to move forward. James and fellow investigators Danny Smith, Johnny Bass and Eddie Colbert began working together immediately to assemble information in the Bissell case, even as their respective jurisdictions wrangled back and forth to determine whose case it ultimately would be. The men felt there was no time to waste with legal hairsplitting; they had a murder case to work, and they immediately began to do so.

James said that a sense of sadness often surrounds everyone involved in murder cases.

"Not only did the person who died lose their life, but often numerous other lives are changed forever," he said. "Often the murderer's family will suffer just as much as the victim's family. In a murder, there is never a sense of victory, for there are no winners."

In addition to his regular workload following the resolution of the Bissell cases, James remains at work on several unsolved murders in the county, some dating back almost twenty years.

"Unsolved murder cases are never closed," he said, adding that finding the identity of the apparent suicide victim in one 1991 case would always nag at him until, hopefully, someone eventually comes forward with information leading to the dead man's true identity.

James keeps a thick white notebook containing the investigation records into what is known as the Hangman case, a still-unidentified young man who apparently committed suicide by hanging himself in a remote wooded area south of Collinsville in 1991. The skeletal remains were discovered much later by hunters, and James said he still works on the case from time to time.

"It's the case that's been the most personally frustrating to me in my career," he said.

There were countless numbers of clues in the case from the young man's personal items and from other materials found in his abandoned vehicle, but not one of those clues led authorities to the man's identity.

James has several pages of photos showing various stages of forensic reconstruction of a human skull from shots of the skull taken where it was found deep in the woods, to pictures of the finished restoration. In one photo, the clay sculpture of a young man appearing to be in his midtwenties, possibly part Native American, stares with glass eyes at the camera, a forensic scientist's idea of what the dead man might have looked like in life.

James and the majority of other homicide investigators share a common bond when it comes to cases involving children; those, they agree, are the ones that touch everyone the most.

"Anything involving the death of a child, be it by homicide, sudden infant death syndrome, accidents or natural causes, those are the cases that really get next to me," James said. "Second would be cases involving the elderly or others less able to defend themselves."

The murder of Patricia Booher struck a chord with all those who worked the case, for not only was she a tiny, childlike girl, she was also totally unable to defend herself against Hayward Bissell, a giant of a man on a murderous rampage.

It would seem that while Mike James has been working murder cases since 1982, many new developments in technology and technique would cause the business of homicide investigation to undergo sweeping changes. Not true, according to James. In fact, he says, it's just the opposite.

"The basic concepts of homicide investigations have not changed since Cain slew Abel," he said. "Human emotions, fear, greed, jealousy, anger, passion, frustration and pride cause most murders."

James said if homicide investigators can have compassion for everyone, both suspect as well as victim, and deal with the emotional aspects, cases can be successfully investigated.

"Technology has made very few improvements as far as solving cases," he said. "It has made improvements as far as proving the case in a court of law by the use of DNA evidence, improved fingerprint techniques, advanced photography and so forth, but the basic job of a homicide investigator has not changed a great deal. This is a people job; they're the key to success when it comes to murder investigation. You must be able to deal with and understand people in order to be successful."

James closed the thick file on the Hangman case and replaced it on his bookshelf, where it will likely remain active until information surfaces allowing him to identify the victim positively and finally close the case.

"One of these days I'll get the break I need to solve that one," he said.

Investigators Johnny Bass and Eddie Colbert are continuing their day-to-day work in Northwest Georgia, which involves a great number of far more serious crimes than their colleagues in Norwalk, Ohio, are accustomed to handling. During their visits to Ohio,

Bass was amazed at the reaction of both the police and the local press toward Hayward Bissell's case.

"I asked one of the reporters up there why they were so excited about this particular crime," he said, "and she told me they just never had anything like this happening around there. The biggest thing, before the Bissell case, was someone who had gone to sleep on the railroad tracks and was killed. It's an incredibly quiet, low-crime area of the country up there, evidently."

Bass has plenty of excitement to deal with from day to day, and he spends a lot of time working cooperatively with his fellow investigators in other counties of Georgia, Alabama and Tennessee. He and Colbert will be staying busy. But, like Sheriff Reed, they hope they won't have to deal with another Hayward Bissell anytime soon.

Todd Graves served his trafficking sentence and was released from the DeKalb County Jail. When he left the jail, he gave Bissell his small portable television set.

"I felt kind of sorry for the guy," he said. "He never had any visitors or anything. All his family was so far away. That's one thing I learned, when I saw how some of the others in jail never had any visits or mail. I learned just how lucky I was to have the kind of family I've got, to stand by me and be there for me like they were, every single minute. Now that I'm back home again, I'm going to do everything I can to let them know how much I appreciate them."

Graves has been true to his word. He remains closer to his family than ever before, and he has gone to work for the Town of Collinsville's city maintenance department. He handles upkeep of the town's streets, sidewalks and landscaping, and the public parks and playing fields have never looked better. Todd Graves is still doing the right thing.

The 1988 Lincoln Town Car that Bissell talked with Todd Graves about—wondering if he would be able to get the car back—sat in the DeKalb County impound lot until Monday, August 4, 2003. The county commission sold the car at auction on the courthouse steps that day at 11:00 A.M., and only three people showed up.

One of those people was Chief Deputy Dale Orr, the officer who tied Bissell's pants up prior to his first trip to the courtroom, using a piece of cord as a makeshift belt. Orr had ambled across the lawn from the sheriff's department to the courthouse steps to see what was going on, and when no one else placed a bid on Bissell's car, Orr offered $100 for it. He came away the lucky winner, even though he didn't really want the vehicle.

"I'm just going to give it to someone else," he told the press. "I don't know who right now; I don't know if anybody will want it. I only bid on it because nobody else did, and I knew the commission would get the money."

By the following day, Orr had passed the vehicle off to another owner, and other people were inquiring about it.

Sheriff Reed hadn't expected there would be any bids on the car, considering its history.

"It would have been even more surprising if a lot of people had shown up to buy this and there were more bids on the car," he said.

Bill Lands said the car's buyer told him the Lincoln would eventually be auctioned on the Internet.

James and Sue Pumphrey are enjoying a very quiet life in the Appalachian Mountains, staying close to their relatives and enjoying fishing, family activities and outings with the children they are helping to care for. Knowing them as I do, I'm certain these two kind, loving and generous people make outstanding surrogate grandparents. Helping with the children, and lending a hand with other family needs, has helped them to push the awful memories of January 23, 2000, to the back of their thoughts. But I'm afraid Hayward Bissell will continue to inhabit their dreams from time to time.

James Pumphrey has relied on his faith in God to pull him through the worst of his times.

"I know there's a lot of people in this world who just go out and kill people for the fun of it," he told me. "They just walk up and kill another person and think nothing of it. But the Lord God says He wants His people to be different; to love one another. If we can't love one another, how can we expect to please the Lord, our God? We can't. The trouble with the world today, they've got so far away from the Lord God, they don't know right from wrong."

Sue puts her faith in the Lord, but she also gives a lot of credit for their survival to gun ownership.

"If it wasn't for the gun that day, we wouldn't be here. I know there are people in the government who want to take guns away from people, but I'll tell you, it's good to have one when you need it," she said.

"I don't want our guns taken away. People have the right to defend themselves, and if we didn't have the rifle that day, we wouldn't be here. He was coming around to the back to finish us off, but we fooled him.

"It's going to take a long time to get over all this. It's torn our lives up, and it's been really hard. But James has been my backbone through all of this. If it wasn't for James, I never could have made it."

Don and Rhea Pirch are still thrilled by the beauty that surrounds them when they look out their bedroom window at snow-covered peaks and bright blue skies. They are hosts of a nine-room bed-and-breakfast inn, at an elevation of 9,380 feet in the Colorado Rockies. Months after the close of the Bissell case, Don told me about his recurring memories of the assault.

"The Bissell thing has seemed a thing of the past, but has never left us," he said. "Rhea and I are moving just down the street to host a B and B, a great opportunity, but in the packing process I found newspapers relating to the incident. My mind has gone back into a spin. At times, my emotions catch up to me and I get carried away by some thoughts that have been buried, yet remain. However, they don't last.

"Rhea and I invite you to visit us and this overwhelming beauty we live with every day. As I mentioned, we have rooms available, and you are welcome anytime as our guest, so pack your toothbrush!

"Keep on writing. Some day the final page will be written, and it will be time to start another adventure."

I took Don's advice and kept on writing, leaving my job as a reporter to write books about the crimes I've covered. But even though the final page in the saga of Hayward Bissell has now been written, the story and the man himself will never leave my thoughts.

On the day when Hayward Bissell left DeKalb County for the last time, on his way to start serving his sentence in Georgia, I was the only member of the press who was there to see him off. I stood with a few jailers and deputies in the jail's parking lot to get one last photo of the man who had become so familiar to me.

I was shocked at the change in Bissell as he walked, this time without restraints, up the stairs from the jail and out to the waiting patrol car. He seemed weak, pale and slightly fearful, and he looked around uncertainly as though he didn't know what he should do. The hulking giant I had seen for the first time walking down the staircase on the day following his arrest was now gone forever, it seemed. Only a frail husk remained of the man who had done so much harm to so many innocent people.

Bissell walked over to the patrol car and seated himself in the back while the Georgia deputies stood nearby conferring with the jailers for a moment. The car door stood open, and I couldn't resist the opportunity finally to speak to this man I had studied so closely and written about so often. I approached the car, careful to stand on the other side of the open door.

"Mr. Bissell," I said, "I hope things go well for you in Georgia. Is there anything I can do for you, anyone I could call? Your parents, maybe?"

He looked questioningly at me, as though I seemed familiar to him, but he couldn't quite place me in his memory.

"They've already called them," he said.

Those eyes, which had always stared at me so intently as I took countless photos, now held only a blank, puzzled look. I no longer felt uneasy or fearful of Bissell; there didn't seem to be anything left to be afraid of.

"Well, good luck to you in Georgia," I said. "I hope you have a good trip."

As the deputies approached to close the patrol car's door and drive Hayward Bissell away for the last time, he noticed the camera I was carrying. The blank expression swiftly disappeared, replaced by a look of recognition.

"I remember you," he said. "I know who you are."

As the car door closed and the deputies backed the vehicle out of the parking space, Bissell maintained eye contact with me. I was unnerved, but I didn't look away.

The patrol car moved out of the rear parking lot

heading out into the driveway, taking Hayward Bissell away from DeKalb County for good. As he rode away, Bissell turned around in the backseat and kept staring at me from the car's rear window.

Then, just before he rode out of sight, he slowly raised his hand and waved good-bye.

Was Hayward Bissell aware of his crimes at the time he committed them? Was he a psychotic madman who went on a rampage, or was he a highly skilled manipulator who, over the years, learned to tell psychiatrists exactly what they needed to hear in order to give him his "crazy papers"? Did he, as Mike O'Dell believed, use feigned mental illness as his "get out of jail free" card?

The truth is locked away inside Hayward Bissell's mind, in a place no one can reach, and it is a truth we will never know. But all those people who were involved with his case in any way will never forget him. He made an indelible mark on so many lives, leaving behind him a bloody trail that reached from Ohio all the way to a small mountain village in Alabama.

Hayward Bissell is sure to live out the remainder of his life locked away in prison, but his victims and their families will always live with the pain of their injuries and the terror of their encounters with him. They never will be able to escape fully the memory of the crazed killer who drove into their lives one Sunday afternoon during an ice storm, riding along with his girlfriend's mutilated corpse on a highway of blood.